JOHN HENRY NEWMAN
ON TRUTH AND ITS
COUNTERFEITS

SACRA DOCTRINA SERIES

Series Editors

Chad C. Pecknold, *The Catholic University of America*

Thomas Joseph White, OP, *Dominican House of Studies*

JOHN HENRY NEWMAN ON TRUTH & ITS COUNTERFEITS

A GUIDE FOR OUR TIMES

Reinhard Hütter

The Catholic University of America Press
Washington, D.C.

Library of Congress Cataloging-in-Publication Data

Names: Hütter, Reinhard, 1958– author.

Title: John Henry Newman on truth and its counterfeits : a guide for our times /
Reinhard Hütter.

Description: Washington : The Catholic University of America Press, 2020. |
Series: Sacra doctrina | Includes bibliographical references and index.

Identifiers: LCCN 2019048956 | ISBN 9780813232324 (paperback) |
ISBN 9780813232331 (ebook)

Subjects: LCSH: Newman, John Henry, 1801–1890. | Catholic Church—Doctrines.

Classification: LCC BX4705.N5 H78 2020 | DDC 230/.2092—dc23

LC record available at https://lccn.loc.gov/2019048956

In memoriam
Don J. Briel
(1947–2018)

CONTENTS

PREFACE

This book has grown over the course of numerous years and in the context of many conversations with friends and colleagues. I would like to record my thanks especially to Jaime Antúnez Aldunate, Nicanor Austriaco, OP, Christopher O. Blum, Talbot Brewer, Giuseppe Butera, Carlos Casanova Guerra, Fernando María Cavaller, Romanus Cessario, OP, Mark Clark, Paul Connor, OP, John F. Crosby, Joseph E. Davis, David DeLio, Michael Gorman, Paul J. Griffiths, Raymond F. Hain IV, Joseph Henchey, CSS, Judith Heyhoe, Nancy Heitzenrater Hütter, Matthew Levering, Guy Mansini, OSB, Bruce D. Marshall, Andrew Meszaros, Michael Pakaluk, Thomas Pfau, Rodrigo Polanco, R. R. Reno, Philip Rolnick, Michael Root, Richard Schenk, OP, Mary Katherine Tillman, Luca Tuninetti, Candace A. Vogler, and Thomas Joseph White, OP.

It has been a privilege to work with Mary Tonkinson and Paul Higgins in their judicious editing of the text. Special thanks go to David L. Augustine and Meghan Duke for their competent editorial assistance, and to David L. Augustine for preparing and Vincent Birch for completing the indexes. I am indebted to two anonymous peer reviewers for their helpful criticisms, corrections, and suggestions. I thank the editors of *Chicago Studies* and *Nova et Vetera* (English edition) for granting me permission to reprint material that is included here.

Earlier versions of the first three chapters were delivered as Paluch Chair Lectures at the University of Our Lady of the Lake/Mundelein Seminary during my 2015–16 tenure there as the Chester and Margaret Paluch Chair of Theology. I would like to express my gratitude for this intellectually stimulating and spiritually rewarding appointment to the then-rector and now-bishop Robert Barron, who invited me to the university, and to Rector John Kartje and Dean Thomas A. Baima for their warm welcome. My thanks also to the university faculty and staff for their cordial hospitality, to the STL and STD students, as well as Patricia Pintado-Murphy for a stimulating graduate seminar on John Henry Newman's *Oxford University Sermons* and *Grammar of Assent*, and to Matthew and Joy Levering for the gift of their friendship.

I dedicate this book to the memory of Don J. Briel. A noted Newman scholar and passionate Newman disciple, Don Briel founded the Catholic Studies Program at the University of St. Thomas in St. Paul, Minnesota, in 1993, and in 1997 he founded the journal *Logos: A Journal of Catholic Thought and Culture*. From August 2014 until his death in 2018, he held the Blessed John Henry Newman Chair of Liberal Arts at the University of Mary in Bismarck, North Dakota. Don Briel had a keen and ever-growing awareness of John Henry Newman's importance for our own day and age. Nourished spiritually and intellectually by John Henry Newman, Don Briel succeeded at nothing less than creating, despite the formidable cultural challenges of the late twentieth and early twenty-first centuries, the "idea of a university" that animated his great spiritual mentor. Over the course of the past generation, no one in the United States has done more than Don Briel to realize John Henry Newman's theological and pedagogical vision of Catholic higher education.

ACKNOWLEDGMENTS

Earlier versions of chapter 1 were presented in 2012 at Providence College as the Randall Chair Lecture, at New York University, and at a *First Things* seminar; in 2014 at the Lumen Christi Institute at the University of Chicago and at Blackfriars, Oxford University; in 2015 as the Paluch Chair Lecture for the University of Our Lady of the Lake/Mundelein Seminary at the Chicago University Club and at the Universidad de los Andes, Santiago, Chile; in 2017 at the Oratorian Community of St. Philip Neri in Washington, D.C., and at the Franciscan University of Steubenville, Ohio; and in 2018 at George Mason University in Fairfax, Virginia. An extended version was published in *Nova et Vetera* (English edition) 12, no. 3 (2014): 701–67; and a briefer version appeared in *Chicago Studies* 55, no. 2 (2016): 43–66.

An earlier version of chapter 2 was delivered in 2015 as the Paluch Chair Lecture at the University of Our Lady of the Lake/Mundelein Seminary; as a Lumen Christi Institute Lecture at the University of Chicago; and at the Pontificia Universidad Católica de Chile, Santiago, Chile. It was published in *Chicago Studies* 55, no. 2 (2016): 9–42.

An earlier version of chapter 3 was presented in 2016 as the Paluch Chair Lecture at the University of Our Lady of the Lake/Mundelein Seminary and at the University of Virginia. It was published in *Chicago Studies* 55, no. 3 (2016): 80–107.

Earlier versions of chapter 4 were presented as lectures in 2013 at New York University; in 2015 at the Pontificia Universidad Católica de Chile, Santiago, Chile; in 2017 at Harvard University; and in 2018 at the University of Virginia and again at New York University. An extended version was published in *Nova et Vetera* (English edition) 11, no. 4 (2013): 1017–56. A briefer version appeared in English in *Acta Philosophica: Rivista internationale di filosofia* 22, no. 2 (2013): 235–56; and in Spanish in *Humanitas: Revista de Antropología y Cultura Cristianas* 72 (Spring 2013): 752–75.

The epilogue draws on my article "Relinquishing the Principle of Private Judgment in Matters of Divine Truth: A Protestant Theologian's Journey into the Catholic Church," *Nova et Vetera* (English edition) 9, no. 4 (2011): 865–81.

ABBREVIATIONS

Works by John Henry Newman

Abbreviations for the works of John Henry Newman follow the conventions established in Joseph Rickaby, SJ, *Index to the Works of John Henry Cardinal Newman* (London: Longmans, Green, and Co., 1914). Quotations from Newman's works here follow the Longmans Uniform Edition, the text of which is available online in the Newman Reader (newmanreader.org/works/index.html) maintained by the National Institute for Newman Studies (NINS).

Diff. (i–ii)	*Certain Difficulties Felt by Anglicans in Catholic Teaching*
Dev.	*An Essay on the Development of Christian Doctrine*
G.A.	*An Essay in Aid of a Grammar of Assent*
Idea	*The Idea of a University*
L.D.	*The Letters and Diaries of John Henry Newman*
Mix.	*Discourses to Mixed Congregations*

Works by Other Authors

PL	Patrologiae Cursus Completus: Series Latina (ed. J.-P. Migne)
Sent.	Thomas Aquinas, *Scriptum super libros Sententiarum magistri Petri Lombardi episcopi Parisiensis*
ST	Thomas Aquinas, *Summa theologiae*

JOHN HENRY NEWMAN
ON TRUTH AND ITS
COUNTERFEITS

PROLOGUE

Newman and Us

John Henry Newman, England's greatest theologian of the nineteenth century, was an assiduous student and exemplary translator of the Church Fathers, East and West; an exquisite preacher; a brilliant rhetorician and controversialist; an astute logician; and an exceptional composer of prayers, hymns, and meditations. Yet most relevant to our present purposes, this imperial intellect was a connoisseur and astute theological critic of a profoundly problematic predicament common to both his day and our own. It is for this reason, first and foremost, that Newman can speak to us as if he were our contemporary.

Newman uses three related terms to characterize various aspects of this shared predicament: the spirit of liberalism in religion, the usurpation of religion and faith by rationalism, and the unfettered rule of the principle of private judgment in religion. Newman expected that this predicament would eventually usher in an age of unbelief ruled by the spirit of infidelity. In 1873, at the opening of the St. Bernard's Seminary in the diocese of Birmingham, he made the following prophetic remarks in a homily entitled "The Infidelity of the Future":

I am speaking of evils, which in their intensity and breadth are peculiar to these times. But I have not yet spoken of the root of all these falsehoods—the root as it ever has been, but hidden; but in this age exposed to view and unblushingly avowed—I mean, that spirit of infidelity itself which I began by referring to as the great evil of our times.... The elementary proposition of this new philosophy which is now so threatening is this—that in all things we must go by reason, in nothing by faith, that things are known and are to be received so far as they can be proved. Its advocates say, all other knowledge has proof—why should religion be an exception?... Why should not that method which has done so much in physics, avail also as regards that higher knowledge which the world has believed it had gained through revelation? There is no revelation from above. There is no exercise of faith. Seeing and proving is the only ground for believing. They go on to say, that since proof admits of degrees, a demonstration can hardly be had except in mathematics; we never can have simple knowledge; truths are only probably such. So that faith is a mistake in two ways. First, because it usurps the place of reason, and secondly because it implies an absolute assent to doctrines, and is dogmatic, which absolute assent is irrational. Accordingly you will find, certainly in the future, nay more, *even now, even now*, that the writers and thinkers of the day do not even believe there is a God.[1]

In order to realize that Newman is describing the age we live in, one need not read Feuerbach's *Essence of Christianity*, Dostoevsky's *Demons*, Nietzsche's *The Antichrist* and *Ecce Homo*, or Sartre's *Being and Nothingness*—let alone works by the recent "new atheists" Dawkins, Dennett, Hitchens, and Harris.[2]

1. John Henry Newman, Sermon 9, "The Infidelity of the Future: Opening of St. Bernard's Seminary, October 2, 1873," in John Henry Newman, *Faith and Prejudice and Other Sermons*, ed. Birmingham Oratory (New York: Sheed and Ward, 1956), 123–24.

2. Ludwig Feuerbach, *The Essence of Christianity*, trans. George Eliot (Mineola, N.Y.: Dover, 2008); Fyodor Dostoevsky, *Demons*, trans. Robert A. Maguire (New York: Penguin Classics, 2008); Friedrich Nietzsche, *The Anti-Christ, Ecce Homo, Twilight of the Idols and Other Writings*, ed. Aaron Ridley and Judith Norman, trans. Judith Norman (Cambridge: Cambridge University Press, 2005); Jean-Paul Sartre, *Being and Nothingness: An Essay on Phenomenological Ontology*, trans. Hazel Barnes (New York: Philosophical Library, 1956); Richard Dawkins, *The God Delusion* (Boston: Houghton Mifflin, 2006); Daniel Dennett, *Breaking the Spell: Religion as a Natural Phenomenon* (New York: Penguin, 2006); Christopher Hitchens, *God is Not Great: How Religion Poisons Everything* (New York: Twelve, 2007); Sam Harris, *The End of Faith: Religion, Terror, and the Future of Reason* (New York: Norton, 2004). The most comprehensive and profound philosophical analysis of atheism is still Cornelio Fabro, *God in Exile: Modern Atheism from Its Roots in the Cartesian Cogito to the Present Day*, ed. and trans. Arthur Gibson (Westminster, Md.: Newman Press, 1968). For a clear and incisive philosophical critique of the arguments made by Dawkins, Dennett, Hitchins, and Harris, see Edward Feser, *The Last Superstition: A Refutation of the New Atheism* (South Bend, Ind.: St. Augustine's Press, 2008).

More than a century later, in the final homily he gave in 2005 before becoming Pope Benedict XVI, Cardinal Joseph Ratzinger famously characterized this predicament as the "dictatorship of relativism that does not recognize anything as definitive and whose ultimate goal consists solely of one's own ego and desires."[3] It is this—the emergence, establishment, and exaltation of the sovereign subject—that Newman saw commencing and our age sees completed. In his *Confessions*, St. Augustine might very well have used the following words to praise God: "In the beginning is you, in the middle is you, and in the end is you." Yet nowadays a tea company celebrates with these very words the consumer as the sovereign subject, as the center of a sovereignly constructed world of meaning with as many parallel worlds of meaning as there are sovereign subjects. What the tea-company logo expresses in three brief phrases, Supreme Court Justice Anthony Kennedy felt moved to render in misplaced metaphysical terms in *Planned Parenthood vs. Casey*: "At the heart of liberty is the right to define one's own concept of existence, of meaning, of the universe, and of the mystery of human life." The liberty endorsed in these words is nothing but the unfettered autonomy of the sovereign subject, the ruling self-image of the present age.

The theological program that the spirit of liberalism in religion sets in motion consists in the infusion of the Christian faith with the era's prevailing self-image and the consequent reconstruction of the Christian faith's content in light of this new self-image. In his famous "Biglietto Speech," delivered in 1879 in Rome on the occasion of his appointment as cardinal, Newman stated that the unifying theme of his career had been his consistent opposition to "the spirit of liberalism in religion." Because the matter Newman addresses has now become a predominant reality, this crucial passage from the "Biglietto Speech" is worth citing in full:

I rejoice to say, to one great mischief I have from the first opposed myself. For thirty, forty, fifty years I have resisted to the best of my powers the spirit of Liberalism in religion. Never did Holy Church need champions against it more sorely than now, when, alas! it is an error overspreading, as a snare, the whole earth;

3. Cardinal Joseph Ratzinger, "Pro Eligendo Romano Pontifice," Vatican Basilica, April 18, 2005; available at www.vatican.va.

and on this great occasion, when it is natural for one who is in my place to look out upon the world, and upon Holy Church as in it, and upon her future, it will not, I hope, be considered out of place, if I renew the protest against it which I have made so often. Liberalism in religion is the doctrine that there is no positive truth in religion, but that one creed is as good as another, and this is the teaching which is gaining substance and force daily. It is inconsistent with any recognition of any religion, as *true*. It teaches that all are to be tolerated, for all are matters of opinion. Revealed religion is not a truth, but a sentiment and a taste; not an objective fact, not miraculous; and it is the right of each individual to make it say just what strikes his fancy. Devotion is not necessarily founded on faith. Men may go to Protestant Churches and to Catholic, may get good from both and belong to neither. They may fraternise together in spiritual thoughts and feelings, without having any views at all of doctrines in common, or seeing the need of them. Since, then, religion is so personal a peculiarity and so private a possession, we must of necessity ignore it in the intercourse of man with man. If a man puts on a new religion every morning, what is that to you? It is as impertinent to think about a man's religion as about his sources of income or his management of his family.[4]

One characteristic of most if not all versions of theological liberalism since the eighteenth century is the "neo-logist" tendency to reconstruct and repurpose central Christian notions by associating new meanings with traditional words. On the lexical level, the result sounds very much like the received Christian faith; but on the semantic level, the change is dramatic. Differently put, the reconstruction closely resembles the familiar currency, but it is actually a counterfeit meant to accommodate the Christian faith to the normative tenets of Enlightenment modernity and its imperious truth-claims. Keenly identifying counterfeits and replacing them again with the true currency of the Christian faith is one of Newman's enduring theological contributions.

Yet one of the most subtle strategies for advancing theological liberalism has been to co-opt Newman in such a way that he seems to support—indeed, to legitimize—the very counterfeits produced by the spirit of liberalism in religion that he unmasks and refutes. Not long after New-

---

4. Quoted from Wilfrid Ward, *The Life of John Henry Cardinal Newman Based on His Private Journals and Correspondence* (London: Longmans, Green, and Co., 1912), 2:459–62, here 2:460.

man's death, liberal Catholic theologians undertook the recurring effort to turn Newman into his own counterfeit by making him support what he actually rejects. What makes Newman vulnerable to being co-opted in such a way is not only his deep awareness of historical existence, which can be easily mistaken for an embrace of modern historicism, but especially his profound personalism, which can be easily misrepresented as an endorsement of modern individualism.[5] Yet it is precisely his focus on the concrete reality of the human person, intellectual and existential, that keeps Newman from becoming a mere reactionary to modern times and problems and enables him to identify the counterfeit of the human person, that is, the self-image of the sovereign subject that haunts the modern period.

Newman's Sojourn "from Shadows and Images into Truth"

John Henry Newman's life spanned almost the whole of the nineteenth century. He was born on February 21, 1801, and died on August 11, 1890. His reception into the full communion of the Catholic church fell right in the middle of his life, dividing it into Anglican and Catholic periods of about equal length.[6] Newman, the eldest of six children, was born in London into a moderately wealthy family. His father was a fairly successful banker until 1814, when his business began to decline so that eventually the elder Newman had to declare bankruptcy. His family belonged to

5. For an astute and lucid discussion of Newman's personalism, see John F. Crosby, *The Personalism of John Henry Newman* (Washington, D.C.: The Catholic University of America Press, 2014).

6. The reader interested in Newman's biography can do no better than to turn to his own *Apologia pro Vita Sua* (London: Longmans, 1864) for a compellingly rendered and beautifully written account of this most remarkable spiritual and theological sojourn from shadows and images into the truth. For an excellent account, written from the scholarly perspective of the historian, see Ian Ker's *John Henry Newman: A Biography* (Oxford: Oxford University Press, 1988) and for a fuller account of the Catholic period of Newman's life, see Ward, *Life of Newman.* For the best introduction to Newman's theology, see Avery Cardinal Dulles, SJ, *John Henry Newman* (London: Continuum, 2002). Dulles also provides a commendably concise account of Newman's life. In the following summary, which is indebted to Dulles's presentation, I will limit myself to the bare outline of Newman's life and will highlight only those events that have a special bearing on his journey into Catholicism and the central concerns of this book.

the Church of England, regularly attending services on Sunday and saying prayers at meals. But, as Newman would later recollect, he had no formal religious convictions until he was fifteen. In 1808, the seven-year-old John Henry was sent to Ealing, a boarding school near London, where Latin, literature, and mathematics formed the core of the curriculum. As an adolescent, he began to read the works of Enlightenment authors—Thomas Paine, David Hume, and Voltaire—and subsequently began to entertain religious doubts. After a serious illness Newman underwent a profound conversion to the Christian faith. It was so definite an experience that even decades later he was still able to recollect that it began on August 1 and ended on December 21, 1816. The human instrument of his conversion was Rev. Walter Mayers, a clergyman and master at Ealing. Under his influence Newman's initial religious outlook took the form of a pronounced evangelicalism of a Calvinist bent.

In June 1817, at the age of sixteen, Newman went up to Trinity College, Oxford, where he read the Greek and Latin classics and advanced considerably in higher mathematics. He became an enthusiastic reader of Walter Scott's novels and began to immerse himself in the works of the philosophers Francis Bacon and John Locke and the historian Edward Gibbon. Newman was a brilliant student, and in December 1820 everyone who knew him at Oxford expected that he would pass his exams with high honors. Newman, however, suffered a nervous breakdown during the exams, managing to pass them but without distinction. Nevertheless, he continued to study intensively and, in April 1822, won a prestigious and extremely competitive fellowship at Oriel College—at that time the most respected and intellectually rigorous college at Oxford.

During his first years as a fellow, Newman was affiliated with a group of remarkable intellectuals known as the "Oriel Noetics." Their leader, Richard Whately, who was among other things an accomplished logician, trained Newman in Aristotelian logic and began to draw him away from the evangelical Calvinism of his initial conversion toward what Newman would retrospectively characterize as a spirit of intellectualism and liberalism in religion. After just a few years, Newman distanced himself from what he came to regard as the theologically dangerous and spiritually detrimental attitudes endorsed and encouraged by the Oriel Noetics. Yet he had been part of their inner circle long enough to understand theological intellectualism and liberalism from the inside and was for this very reason later able to diagnose and critique it with the acuity and precision that only intimate familiarity affords.

In 1824, Newman was ordained a deacon, and in 1825 a priest of the Church of England. During the early years of his Anglican ministry, while he served in the parish of St. Clement, Newman came under the influence of Edward Hawkins, another fellow at Oriel College, who introduced Newman to the importance of tradition and of working within the visible church. In 1826, when Newman was appointed a tutor at Oriel College, he also became vicar of the University Church of St. Mary the Virgin. As a tutor at Oriel College and especially as a preacher at St. Mary's, Newman began to exert a powerful influence over the student body at Oxford.

From the late 1820s onward, Newman was also part of a circle of intellectually brilliant, literarily productive, and ecclesially active High Church Anglicans that included John Keble, Edward Pusey, and Richard Hurrell Froude. Keble obtained for Newman from Germany a scholarly Greek and Latin edition of the Church Fathers, and beginning in 1827, Newman immersed himself in a systematic study of their writings that issued in his first monograph, published in 1833, *The Arians of the Fourth Century*.

In 1832, after submitting the manuscript to the publisher, Newman undertook what turned out to be a critically important voyage to the Mediterranean with his close friend Richard Hurrell Froude and Froude's father. They visited Malta, Greece, Corfu, Naples, and Rome. When the time came to return to England, Newman decided to stay behind and explore the island of Sicily on his own. At the very heart of Sicily, he caught what appeared to be typhoid fever and almost died. The weeks of struggling with the deadly fever and of slow recovery were a spiritually intense and crucial time in Newman's life. While awaiting a ship in Palermo, he had unexpectedly positive experiences in Catholic churches and began to be drawn to Catholicism. Two things are important to keep in mind when one considers Newman's inaugural encounter with Italian Catholicism: first, Englishmen of the nineteenth century by and large detested what they considered the superstition and squalor of Italian Catholicism;

second, Anglicanism itself—whether in its Low Church or High Church instantiation—was intensely anti-Catholic. So was the young John Henry Newman. During his time in Sicily and especially in Palermo, Newman overcame the first impediment; and in the years between 1833 and 1845, the year of his conversion, he overcame the second.

Newman returned to Oxford in the summer of 1833 just in time to join what eventually came to be known as the Oxford Movement. Initially, Keble, Pusey, Froude, and Newman fought two principal enemies: theological liberalism—that is, the intrusion of Enlightenment rationalism into the Christian faith—and the Erastianism characteristic of the Anglican establishment—that is, the complete political dependence of the Church of England on the civil government. Yet after only a brief period, they undertook a much wider agenda, namely, to reclaim the Catholic roots of the Church of England and to rid the latter of its Protestant traits. The Oxford Movement depicted Anglicanism as the *via media* between Continental Protestantism and Roman Catholicism. Newman gave the *via media* its theological justification in his 1836 *Lectures on the Prophetical Office of the Church*.

As a result of his extraordinary success as a preacher, in the course of the late 1830s, Newman acquired an extensive and ebullient following among Oxford students, who congregated in ever-growing numbers in the University Church of St. Mary the Virgin to hear his sermons, which would later be published in the best-selling *Parochial and Plain Sermons*. Through them and his writings, primarily his contributions to the *Tracts of the Times*, Newman became a nationally recognized figure, celebrated by some, notorious to others. A series of widely distributed pamphlets, launched in 1833 and written chiefly by Newman, Keble, and Pusey, the *Tracts of the Times* were the principal weapon of struggle for the Oxford Movement. Because the *Tracts* were its main literary output, the movement was also called "Tractarianism." Several of Newman's tracts gave Low Church as well as High Church opponents of the Oxford Movement a welcome opportunity to publicly accuse Newman, and with him the whole movement, of gravitating toward Roman Catholicism. The opponents of Tractarianism rested their case mainly on Tract 75, which focused on the Latin Breviary; Tract 85, which focused on scripture in relation to the Catholic creed; and especially Tract 90. In Tract 90, published in February 1841, Newman attempted to prove that the *Thirty-nine Articles of Religion*—the theologically normative articles of faith in the Church of England, an uneven amalgam of Lutheran and Reformed theology—admitted of a Catholic interpretation. Although Newman continued to differ in Tract 90 with the Catholic stance on issues such as transubstantiation, the veneration of the Virgin Mary, the invocation of the saints, and the teaching on Purgatory, he did defend the teachings of the Council of Trent on the Mass and on the Eucharistic sacrifice.

Tract 90 unleashed a storm of opposition and censure from the bishops of the Church of England and from the heads of Oxford colleges. Overnight, Newman turned from a national celebrity into a universal *persona non grata*. Newman suspended the *Tracts* and withdrew to the village of Littlemore, right outside Oxford. There he lived with a few like-minded friends, observing a strict monastic life of prayer, study, and work. In the seclusion of Littlemore, Newman continued his studies of the Church Fathers, and in 1842 he published *Select Treatises of St. Athanasius* in two volumes. Over the course of his immersion in the Church Fathers, he gradually came to the realization that the *via media* had been all along a mere mental construct of his own, a nonexistent "paper church." In September 1843, suspecting that Catholicism might be the one true faith after all, Newman resigned from his post as vicar of St. Mary's Church.

Newman preached the last of his *Oxford University Sermons* in February 1843. Its topic was the development of doctrine. The longest and most elaborate of his university sermons, this sermon displays Newman's incipient realization that doctrine does in fact develop as the church's understanding of all aspects of the truth, implicit in the apostolic deposit, continually grows under the guidance of the Holy Spirit. Newman felt that now only one important issue was left for him to find clarity on. The Church of England acknowledged the early ecumenical councils that produced the Nicene Creed and the Christological dogma of Chalcedon. These were legitimate and authentic instances of what was implicit in the New Testament being made explicit in the Trinitarian and Christological dogmas. But what about later developments in the Catholic church—were they corruptions, as the Church of England claimed, or were they, too, legitimate and authentic developments of doctrine, as Catholicism maintained? Newman searched for a criterion that would permit him to discern true developments from false ones. For Newman this became a decisive question, the answer to which was essential for discerning his future path.

Newman confronted this question in his famous *Essay on the Development of Christian Doctrine*, which he composed in 1844–45. While writing this book, he came to the realization that Catholic doctrines, such as papal primacy and Purgatory, as well as Catholic pious practices, such as the veneration of the Virgin Mary and the invocation of the saints, had developed from the tradition of the early church in an organic and logical way. Tridentine Catholicism—the Catholicism of the sixteenth-century Catholic Reform—was indeed the true successor to the doctrinal faith of the Church Fathers. As soon as he arrives at this critical insight, Newman brings his manuscript to a rather abrupt close with an appeal directly addressed to the reader:

Such were the thoughts concerning the "Blessed Vision of Peace," of one whose long-continued petition had been that the Most Merciful would not despise the work of His own Hands, nor leave him to himself;—while yet his eyes were dim, and his breast laden, and he could but employ Reason in the things of Faith. And now, dear Reader, time is short, eternity is long. Put not from you what you have here found; regard it not as mere matter of present controversy; set not out resolved to refute it, and looking about for the best way of doing so; seduce not yourself with the imagination that it comes of disappointment, or disgust, or restlessness, or wounded feeling, or undue sensibility, or other weakness. Wrap not yourself round in the associations of years past, nor determine that to be truth which you wish to be so, nor make an idol of cherished anticipations. Time is short, eternity is long.

NUNC DIMITTIS SERVUM TUUM, DOMINE,

SECUNDUM VERBUM TUUM IN PACE:

QUIA VIDERUNT OCULI MEI SALUTARE TUUM.

THE END.[7]

---

7. John Henry Newman, *An Essay on the Development of Christian Doctrine* [1845], ed. Stanley L. Jaki (Pinckney, Mich.: Real View Books, 2003), 431.

Without further delay, Newman reached out to the Italian Passionist priest, Dominic Barberi, who at the time was doing missionary work in Oxfordshire; after a first general confession that took two days, Newman entered into full communion with the Catholic church on October 9, 1845.

With this momentous step, the narrative dynamic of Newman's life has reached a decisive climax: he used his own private judgment in religion in order "ultimately to supersede it," "as a man out of doors uses a lamp in a dark night and puts it out when he gets home."[8] His act of assent to the Catholic faith and, with it, to the church's authority entailed the simultaneous renunciation of the principle of private judgment in matters of divine truth. Having found his way from shadows and images back to the light the truth of the Catholic faith afforded, Newman saw that the light of his own private judgment had become superfluous, indeed, counterproductive.

In September 1846, Newman went to Rome to study at the College of the Propaganda (now the Pontifical Urban University) in preparation for the priesthood in the Catholic church. During his time in Rome Newman drew up plans for establishing an English Oratory in the spirit of St. Philip Neri, who in the sixteenth century had founded the Congregation of the Oratory in Rome and who, due to his extraordinary impact as a preacher, confessor, and spiritual director, has been called the "third apostle of Rome" after the apostles Peter and Paul. Following Newman's return to England in December 1847, he was appointed superior of the new oratory, which he moved in 1849 from Maryvale to Birmingham and finally, in 1852, to the Birmingham suburb of Edgebaston.

Not long after the Oratorians had arrived in Birmingham, in September 1850, Pope Pius IX restored the Catholic hierarchy in England. This event triggered a rather violent outbreak across England of "no-Popery," which Newman regarded as his duty publicly to denounce. In the summer of 1851, he produced and delivered at the Oratory his most fiercely polemical work, a set of *Lectures on the Present Position of Catholics in England*, in which he relentlessly exposed and definitively debunked the

8. Ian Ker, *John Henry Newman: A Biography* (Oxford: Oxford University Press, 1988), 335.

most notorious contemporary prejudices against as well as stereotypes about the Catholic church.

In April 1851, Newman's famous "Catholic University" episode began and, because of it, his association with Dublin, Ireland. It was then that Archbishop Paul Cullen of Armagh invited Newman to establish a Catholic University of Ireland. To make a long story short: due to insurmountable conflicts among the Irish bishops, ongoing difficulties in finding professors, and the persistent lack of an appropriate student body in Ireland, the endeavor failed to meet the initial rather high expectations of the archbishop and other members of the Irish Catholic hierarchy. After at last being installed officially as rector in June 1854, Newman resigned in February 1858. While this episode was definitely taxing for Newman, it provided the occasion for one of his most famous works, *The Idea of a University*. The book contains nine of the ten lectures that Newman originally composed—only five of which he publicly delivered in Dublin in 1852. The ten lectures were published in early 1853 under the title *Discourses on the Scope and Nature of University Education*. In 1859, Newman published a related work, *Lectures and Essays on University Subjects*. Eventually, in 1873, omitting the original fifth discourse, he published edited versions of the remaining nine lectures together with the *Lectures and Essays* in one volume under the title *The Idea of a University*. In this version, the book has become the single most important and still-unsurpassed work penned about the university in the modern period, a brilliant presentation of the classical vision of a liberal education, complemented and completed by the light that divine revelation affords.

The span of years from 1855 to 1865 were probably the most difficult of Newman's life as a Catholic. Things came to a head in the early 1860s, when the rumor spread that Newman, disappointed by his experiences in the Catholic church, was ready to return to the Church of England. A particularly insidious attack offered him the opportunity to demonstrate his unequivocal allegiance to the Roman Catholic church. In January 1864, the Protestant novelist Charles Kingsley published an article in which he claimed that Newman—and with him most other Catholic priests—had little if any regard for truth. Newman demanded a public retraction from Kingsley. As a public apology was not forthcoming, Newman composed in rapid succession a weekly series of seven pamphlets that were published between April 21 and June 2, 1864, and received wide acclaim. In the following year Newman decided to republish these pamphlets as a history of his religious opinions. He omitted two explicitly controversial and directly polemical pamphlets and issued the remaining five under the title *Apologia pro Vita Sua*. Together with Augustine's *Confessions* and Thérèse of Lisieux's *Story of a Soul*, the *Apologia* ranks among the most important Catholic spiritual autobiographies. After the publication of the *Apologia* in 1865, Newman became again a national celebrity, highly esteemed by Anglicans as well as Catholics.

In the summer of 1866, Newman went on a well-deserved vacation to Switzerland. During this journey he conceived the central idea and the rough outline of his *Essay in Aid of a Grammar of Assent*, which was eventually published in 1870. This book is Newman's most developed and exacting presentation of his epistemology and psychology of belief in general and of faith in particular. In this conceptually demanding work, Newman brings to surpassing fruition the examination of faith and reason begun in his *Oxford University Sermons*.

Just as Newman was finishing the *Essay in Aid of a Grammar of Assent*, the First Vatican Council convened and the dogma of papal infallibility was promulgated. In 1874, England's former prime minister William E. Gladstone published an attack on the conciliar decrees. Urged on by many friends, Newman defended Pius IX and the Vatican Council against Gladstone's attack. In his *Letter to the Duke of Norfolk*, Newman articulated his mature view of conscience and advanced a balanced, sober, and consistently minimalist interpretation of the First Vatican Council's dogma of papal infallibility.

At this late point in his life, Newman began to receive numerous tributes. In 1878 he was created an honorary fellow of Trinity College, Oxford, the first person ever to receive this honor. On May 12, 1879, Newman was created a cardinal by Pope Leo XIII. The last years of Newman's life were marked by the afflictions characteristic of old age and failing health, counterbalanced by his undiminished serenity of spirit and deep personal faith. Newman died in the Birmingham Oratory on August 11, 1890. His tombstone carries the inscription *Ex umbris et imaginibus in veritatem* (Out of shadows and images into the truth).

Structure, Scope, and Objective

The book is structured around the concept of the *counterfeit*. A counterfeit of some reality is a false or deformed version of it that is nonetheless similar enough to that reality—for example, in terms of what it is called and how it is talked about—for people to mistake one for the other. Separate chapters discuss four significant aspects of Christianity, each of which not only is contested or rejected by secular unbelief but also has one or several counterfeits for which, sadly, not only Protestants but also Catholics have fallen. The counterfeit of conscience feigns conscience, the primordial source of the moral constitution of the human person. This counterfeit is the "conscience" of the sovereign subject (chapter 1). The second counterfeit substitutes for faith, the primordial source of Christian existence. The counterfeit of faith is the "faith" of one who does not submit to the living authority through which God communicates (chapter 2). The third counterfeit reframes doctrine, the primordial source of Christian truth. The counterfeit of doctrinal development is actually twofold: (1) paying lip service to development while only selectively accepting its consequences on the grounds of a specious antiquarianism; and (2) invoking development theory to justify all sorts of contemporary changes according to the present *Zeitgeist* (chapter 3). Finally, the fourth counterfeit mimics and simultaneously repurposes in a most intensive and expansive way the principal institutional instrument of educating and thereby perfecting the human mind—the university. The counterfeit of the university are all those "universities" designed not to educate and thereby perfect the intellect but rather to feed more efficiently the empire of desire that is informed by today's techno-consumerism (chapter 4). The scarlet thread through each chapter is Newman's battle against the principle of private judgment and the concomitant "sovereign subject," a principle that, in one way or another, is involved in all of the counterfeits. The book concludes with an epilogue in which I briefly narrate my own Newmanian theological journey "out of shadows and images into the truth" (*ex umbris et imagi-*

bus in veritatem), in the course of which I learned to distinguish between faith and its counterfeit and thus became able to relinquish the principle of private judgment in matters of divine truth.

One of the peculiarly disconcerting characteristics of our age is the way that these four counterfeits have found not only entrance into but also broad acceptance in European and American Catholicism. Moreover—and more alarmingly—these counterfeits have fueled a dismayingly rapid self-secularization of Catholicism across Europe, with the exception of Poland and places where Catholics are a marginal minority, such as Sweden and Norway. Nineteenth-century Anglicanism ignored Newman at its own peril by failing to embrace his arguments and to follow him on his spiritual and theological sojourn. Contemporary Catholicism ignores Newman at its own peril by recklessly endorsing the "joys and the hopes [*gaudium et spes*] of the men of this age" and simultaneously dismissing Newman's repeated warnings about the rising spirit of infidelity—even in the very midst of the church herself. In this small book I wish to illustrate a simple proposition: in order to expose and eliminate from contemporary Catholicism the counterfeits that mimic conscience, faith, the authentic development of doctrine, and the principal institutional instrument of educating and thereby perfecting the human mind, we can hardly find a more resourceful modern guide than John Henry Newman.

Some readers may find it surprising that in three of this book's four chapters Thomas Aquinas emerges as a main interlocutor. I do not mean to establish any historical connection between Aquinas's and Newman's thought; nor do I intend to claim Newman as a crypto-Thomist or anything else along those lines. The reason for Aquinas's conspicuous presence is simple: in the case of conscience, Newman himself draws upon Thomas Aquinas; in the case of faith, Thomas Aquinas offers what I think is the best theorctical explication of the view Newman expresses in a rather abbreviated way in two important homilies from his early Catholic period; and in the case of the university, finally, Newman's vision converges in remarkable ways with Aquinas's thoughts about a university and a university education and with how some contemporary Thomists have articulated Aquinas's vision—often by drawing at least implicitly on Newman's thought.

I am simply following Newman's own lead into the thought of Thomas Aquinas, where he incorporates it either explicitly or implicitly into the substance of his own thought and line of argumentation. Responding in 1878 to an anxious letter from his friend Robert Whitty, SJ, about Newman's *Grammar of Assent* in light of Leo XIII's encyclical *Aeterni Patris*—urging a return to St. Thomas's thought—Newman calmly and with his characteristic deference to Catholic theology declares: "If anyone is obliged to say 'speak under correction' it is I; for I am no theologian and am too old, and ever have been, to become one. All I can say is I have no suspicion, and do not anticipate, that I shall be found in substance to disagree with St. Thomas."[9] This interesting epistolary remark is not to be taken lightly, as a facile aside to a friend. Rather, it is a remark best understood in light of Edward Sillem's record that

Newman possessed even at Oriel the complete set of the 28 volumes of St. Thomas's Works in the *Editio Altera Veneta* (1781). He has marked the whole of Questions XVI and XVII of the *De Veritate* on conscience; some of the First Book of the *Contra Gentes*; some parts of the treatises on Faith in the *Secunda-Secundae*, on God and the Trinity in the *Prima Pars*. He seems to have read chapters I and LXI of the *Compendium Theologiae*, and the best part of Dist. XIX–XXXIV from the First Book of the *Commentary on the Sentences*, i.e. pp. 227–393 of Tome IX of the Venice edition. He had also a copy of the *Summa Theologica* with Cajetan's Commentary printed in Lyons in 1558 "apud Hugonem a Porta." The Irish Jesuit Fathers gave him a presentation copy of the *Contra Gentes* in 2 volumes which is now in his room. The First Book is marked and annotated here and there, parts of the Third (ch. XXXIX–XLI), and the chapters on the Trinity in the Fourth Book. The chances are that Newman had read more of St. Thomas than we can prove.[10]

Newman's familiarity with Thomas's philosophical and theological thought, especially on conscience and faith, must then be regarded as considerable. This remarkable fact should be kept in mind for the remainder of the present study.

9. *L.D.*, 28:431.
10. "General Introduction to the Study of Newman's Philosophy," in *The Philosophical Notebook of John Henry Newman*, ed. Edward Sillem and Adrian J. Boekraad (Louvain: Nauwelaerts Publishing House, 1969–70), 1:235–36n187.

During his year in Rome, Newman had hoped to receive a serious and competent introduction to the philosophy of Thomas Aquinas—something that contemporary students of the common doctor can easily avail themselves of by way of many excellent works on Aquinas's philosophy published in the course of the twentieth and early twenty-first centuries. Yet for Newman the year in Rome turned out to be a severe disappointment in this regard. In a letter to one of his Oratorian brethren back in England, Newman reports:

A talk we had yesterday with one of the Jesuit fathers here shows we shall find little philosophy. It arose from our talking of the Greek studies of the Propaganda and asking whether the youths learned Aristotle. "O no—he said—Aristotle is in no favour here—no, not in Rome:—not St. Thomas. I have read Aristotle and St. Thos [*sic*], and owe a great deal to them, but they are out of favour here and throughout Italy. St. Thomas was a great saint—people don't dare to speak against him, but put him aside." I asked what philosophy they did adopt. He said *none.* "Odds and ends—whatever seems to them best—like St. Clement's Stromata. They have no philosophy. *Facts* are the great things, and nothing else. Exegesis, not doctrine." He went on to say that many privately were sorry for this, many Jesuits, he said; but no one dared oppose the fashion.[11]

The first who did dare to oppose the Roman fashion dominant around the middle of the nineteenth century and, together with a few others, helped to prepare the way for Pope Leo XIII's 1879 encyclical letter *Aeterni Patris*, was the German Jesuit theologian Joseph Kleutgen. Between 1853 and 1870, Kleutgen produced the four-volume work *Die Theologie der Vorzeit* (*Theology of the Pre-Modern Age*), and between 1860 and 1863 the two-volume work *Die Philosophie der Vorzeit* (*Philosophy of the Pre-Modern Age*).[12] Newman owned the French translation of the latter (*La Philosophie Scholastique* in four volumes), and he seems to have studied at least the first volume, in which Kleutgen not only defends Scholastic and especially Thomist epistemology against Cartesian, Lockean, and

11. *L.D.*, 11:279.
12. Joseph Kleutgen, *Die Theologie der Vorzeit*, 4 vols. (Münster: Theissigsche Buchhandlung, 1853–70; 2nd ed., 1867–74); *Die Philosophie der Vorzeit*, 2 vols. (Münster: Theissigsche Buchhandlung, 1860–63; 2nd ed., Innsbruck: Felician Rauch, 1878). See now the recent English translation of the first volume of *Die Philosophie der Vorzeit*: Josef Kleutgen, SJ, *Pre-Modern Philosophy Defended*, trans. William H. Marshner (South Bend, Ind.: St. Augustine's Press, 2019).

Kantian epistemology but also demonstrates the theoretical superiority of Scholastic epistemology over its modern rivals.

Hence, when it comes to the question of which intellectual context is best suited to Newman's thought, I follow the lead of the German Jesuit Erich Przywara in the still-untranslated introduction to his study of Newman,[13] about which the noted English scholar Henry Tristram wrote: "It is accounted to [Przywara's] praise, that he has grasped the principle, that, whether Newman knew much or little of scholasticism, having some acquaintance with Aristotelianism, and being widely read in patristic literature, his work must be interpreted with the traditional philosophy and theology of the Church as its essential background."[14] Irrespective of the fact that Newman anticipated important *philosophical* insights that are developed more fully in the contemporary analytic epistemology of testimonial knowledge that sits at the heart of recent social and virtue epistemology, as well as certain insights unfolded more deeply in twentieth-century personalism—insights that I regard as important— I nevertheless take Przywara's and Tristram's position to be correct overall.[15] Reading Newman in conjunction with Thomas Aquinas casts central aspects of Newman's *theological* insights—aspects of considerable contemporary relevance—into greater relief and thus affords a deeper understanding of how they are rooted in and arise from the church's theological-philosophical patrimony.[16]

13. Erich Przywara, SJ, *Einführung im Newmans Wesen und Werk* (Freiburg im Breisgau: Herder, 1922).

14. Henry Tristram, "Introduction," in Philip Flanagan, *Newman, Faith and the Believer* (London: Sands and Co., 1946), xi–xii.

15. For a lucid account of the analytic epistemology of testimonial knowledge, see John McDowell, "Knowledge by Hearsay," in *Meaning, Knowledge, and Reality* (Cambridge, Mass.: Harvard University Press, 1998), 414–44; and for a pertinent application of it to theology, see Mats Wahlberg, *Revelation as Testimony: A Philosophical-Theological Study* (Grand Rapids, Mich.: Eerdmans, 2014). For a clear and comprehensive account of virtue epistemology, see Linda Zagzebski, *Epistemic Authority: A Theory of Trust, Authority, and Autonomy in Belief* (Oxford: Oxford University Press, 2012); and for reading Newman in dialogue with social and virtue epistemology, see Frederick D. Aquino, *Communities of Informed Judgment: Newman's Illative Sense and Accounts of Rationality* (Washington, D.C.: The Catholic University of America Press, 2004), and *An Integrative Habit of Mind: John Henry Newman on the Path to Wisdom* (DeKalb: Northern Illinois University Press, 2012). For Newman's anticipation of central personalist insights and positions, see Crosby, *The Personalism of John Henry Newman*.

16. The church's theological and philosophical patrimony and its implicit mandate to contemporary Catholic philosophers and theologians has been articulated in an authoritative way most

In the following chapters I will demonstrate how Newman opens up with his keen psychological, phenomenological (*avant la lettre*), and logical analyses, and with his high awareness of the suppositions that his interlocutors and opponents would hold, what I will call the theological *context of discovery*. Newman's genius was that of a psychologist, phenomenologist, and controversialist—defending the truth of the Catholic faith in critical engagement with its detractors and recovering its full personal and existential import, not just its notions but its reality. Newman had neither the patience nor the proper formal training—and he was the first to admit it—in Catholic theology. Yet the Catholic Newman always genuinely respected the careful doctrinal and speculative labor of Catholic theology, even if he did not endorse it in each instantiation. I therefore regard it as neither artificial nor forced to supplement the theological context of discovery that Newman provides with a corresponding theological *context of justification*. What is initially brought to light, described, and tentatively explained in the context of discovery receives in the context of justification a fuller and deeper warrant.[17] The context of discovery and the context of justification stand in a relationship of asymmetrical reciprocity to each other. Each context informs the other yet precisely in their respective specificity. I regard Thomas Aquinas to be the theologian who best serves in the context of justification, not only because the church has for so long regarded him as *doctor communis*, as the one in whom the church's philosophical and theological patrimony finds a uniquely luminous expression, but also because of the central philosophical point of reference Aquinas shares with Newman. Aristotle was, after all, the philosophical master of both.[18]

---

recently by Pope St. John Paul II in his *Fides et Ratio, On the Relationship Between Faith and Reason*, Encyclical Letter, September 14, 1998 (available at www.vatican.va), in which Newman is explicitly mentioned (par. 74).

17. The philosopher of science Hans Reichenbach (1891–1953) first formulated the distinction between the context of discovery and the context of justification with regard to mathematics in *Experience and Prediction: An Analysis of the Foundations and the Structure of Knowledge* (Chicago: University of Chicago Press, 1938). The German Protestant theologian Gerhard Sauter later applied this distinction to the field of systematic theology; see Gerhard Sauter et al., *Wissenschaftstheoretische Kritik der Theologie: Die Theologie und die neuere wissenschaftstheoretische Diskussion* (Munich: Kaiser, 1973). I rely on Sauter's use of this distinction.

18. For an instructive work that brings together Newman and Duns Scotus in order to explore commonalities, see *The Newman-Scotus Reader: Contexts and Commonalities*, ed. Edward J.

My objective with this book is not to contribute to the ongoing exegesis of Newman but rather to introduce the salient aspects of Newman's thought into considerations of today's most pressing issues from a Catholic perspective. In other words, the book does not so much contribute to that field of Newman scholarship that pursues an ever-more minute reconstruction of Newman's thought in its own historical context. Instead, I hope this book will contribute to that portion of Newman studies which seeks to bring to bear Newman's thought upon the wider contemporary theological and philosophical discourse. It is for this very reason that I am intentionally selective in the choice of works I draw on in order best to advance the argument at hand—the ongoing relevance of Newman's thought.

Ondrako, OFM Conv. (New Bedford, Mass.: Academy of the Immaculate, 2015). While the approaches in this collaborative effort are quite varied, the volume's overall approach is methodologically reflective of my own systematic distinction between the contexts of discovery and justification. For those wishing to explore Newman's indirect rootedness in and indebtedness to central tenets of medieval philosophy and theology (and their organic extensions into Baroque Scholasticism), this reader will be a useful complement. It becomes quite patent that there is more to gain from reading Newman in relation to medieval philosophy and theology and its extension through the eighteenth century than much Newman scholarship since the late 1960s has been ready and willing to assume.

CHAPTER 1

CONSCIENCE AND ITS COUNTERFEIT

On December 27, 1874, John Henry Cardinal Newman published an open letter addressed to the duke of Norfolk, a fellow Catholic and a graduate of Newman's oratory school in Birmingham. This now-famous letter was penned in response to an intensely polemical pamphlet, *The Vatican Decrees in Their Bearing on Civil Allegiance*, by the liberal politician and former prime minister of England William Gladstone. In this diatribe, Gladstone took the promulgation of the dogma of papal infallibility at the First Vatican Council in 1870 as occasion to argue that Catholic subjects of the queen who were committed to papal infallibility could no longer "be trusted to participate loyally and thoughtfully in the nation's civic life."[1]

---

1. James Gaffney, "Introduction," in John Henry Newman, *Conscience, Consensus, and the Development of Doctrine*, ed. Gaffney (New York: Doubleday, 1992), 432. Gaffney summarizes Gladstone's assertion in his brief introduction to the excerpt of Newman's *Letter* included in this useful volume.

In *A Letter Addressed to His Grace the Duke of Norfolk*, Newman brilliantly refuted this and other related allegations advanced by Gladstone. More importantly, however, the *Letter* offered Newman a welcome opportunity to present a condensed account of his understanding of conscience—what it is and how to distinguish it from its counterfeit. The treatment of conscience in the *Letter* represents the Catholic Newman's mature thought. A lifetime of intense engagement as a preacher, polemicist, philosopher, and theologian with this fundamental factor in the life of human persons comes to fruition in this extraordinary piece of Catholic apologetics. Should Newman ever be declared a doctor of the church, he might most appropriately be given the title Doctor of Conscience.[2] The central place of conscience in Newman's thought is perhaps best attested to by his famous toast in the section of the *Letter* titled "Conscience": "If I am obliged to bring religion into after-dinner toasts ... I shall drink—to the Pope, if you please,—still, to Conscience first, and to the Pope afterwards."[3]

Yet what exactly is Newman trying to convey in his toast to conscience? Taken in isolation from the rest of Newman's *Letter*, this pithy statement has all too frequently been misinterpreted in ways that blatantly contradict the thrust of Newman's argument in the *Letter*.[4] The common error of these widespread misinterpretations is the confusion of conscience with its counterfeit. The argument for this counterfeit goes something like this: *Major premise*, freedom of conscience signifies the sovereign act of my autonomous will, to which all external instruction and guidance, whether divine or human, are secondary. *Minor premise*, papal teaching is external instruction and guidance. *Conclusion*: freedom of conscience trumps papal teaching. Conscience (so-called) comes first, the pope second—if at all.

The problem with this interpretation of Newman's after-dinner toast

2. J. H. Walgrave, OP, *Newman the Theologian: The Nature of Belief and Doctrine as Exemplified in His Life and Works*, trans. A. V. Littledale (New York: Sheed and Ward, 1960): "In Newman's thought, the primary factor is always conscience" (25).

3. John Henry Cardinal Newman, *Certain Difficulties Felt by Anglicans in Catholic Teaching* (London: Longmans, Green, and Co., 1900) [hereafter "*Diff.*"], ii., 261.

4. In the Longmans Uniform Edition of Newman's works, the *Letter to the Duke of Norfolk* fills 203 pages.

is twofold. The syllogism on which it relies rests, first, on a major premise that is built upon a false notion of conscience—the counterfeit of conscience—and, second, on an underdeveloped and hence misleading minor premise. In order to capture the true meaning of the toast and the precise meaning of freedom of conscience it entails, one must both understand the notion of conscience from which Newman operates and fully appreciate the role of the papal magisterium in relation to conscience in its true sense.

But before entering into such discussions, let us examine two hypothetical cases adduced by Newman to test Gladstone's assertion that Catholics' loyalties were inherently divided between allegiance to their nation and obedience to their pope. Newman begins by defining the conditions for this alleged conflict, declaring that "the circumferences of State jurisdiction and of Papal are for the most part quite apart from each other; there are just some few degrees out of the 360 in which they intersect."[5] So such a conflict, we should expect, will be rare. But what if one should occur within the few degrees where state and papal jurisdiction do indeed converge?

Newman considers two cases:

Were I ... a soldier or sailor in her Majesty's service, and sent to take part in a war which I could not in my conscience see to be unjust, and should the Pope suddenly bid all Catholic soldiers and sailors to retire from the service ... taking the advice of others, as best I could, I should not obey him.[6]

Suppose, for instance, an Act was passed in Parliament, bidding Catholics to attend Protestant service every week, and the Pope distinctly told us not to do so, for it was to violate our duty to our faith—I should obey the Pope and not the Law.[7]

What are some of the underlying assumptions of Newman's two cases? First, popes are not infallible in particular political and practical judgments that a properly informed conscience might direct a person to judge differently. Second, while the state has a legitimate claim upon the loyalty of all citizens and upon their due respect for its laws, the state has

5. *Diff.*, ii., 240.
6. *Diff.*, ii., 241–42.
7. *Diff.*, ii., 240.

no legitimate authority over the substance of faith and morals or over matters that fall under the universal papal jurisdiction—that is, over matters that pertain specifically to the organization of the life of faith, divine worship, the appointment of bishops, etc. Third, each of Newman's cases presupposes both the existence of conscience and its proper formation and operation. Conscience, we begin to see from Newman's examples, is an interior forum (*forum internum*) of moral truth and moral duty, where legitimate claims upon one's allegiance are distinguishable from illegitimate claims; moral truth and hence moral duty are perceived; and, consequently, a more or less clear command is given for a certain course of moral action. Moreover, each case displays Newman's understanding of the freedom of conscience as positive in nature, a freedom not *from* something but rather *for* something—that is, the freedom to perform one's moral duty and to realize the moral good through one's moral agency. In sum, we might initially observe that conscience for Newman comprises two essential elements, the sense of moral truth and the sense of duty. Newman's understanding of the freedom of conscience might best be characterized as freedom in the truth.

But what, precisely, is conscience? And what does freedom of conscience as positive freedom in the truth mean, precisely? And, finally, what is the counterfeit of conscience? Because Newman draws explicitly upon Thomas Aquinas as an important point of reference and warrant for his own account in *A Letter to the Duke of Norfolk*, I shall use Aquinas's teaching to nuance and deepen Newman's Catholic doctrine of conscience.

John Henry Newman on Conscience and Its Counterfeit

Newman is crystal clear that any proper understanding of conscience must first and foremost articulate the *theonomic nature of conscience*, that is, its grounding in the divine law.[8] Conscience is not simply a human fac-

---

8. For accessible introductions to Newman's treatment of conscience across his *oeuvre*, see Charles Morerod, OP, "Conscience according to John Henry Newman," *Nova et Vetera* (English edition) 11, no. 4 (2013): 1057–79, and Gerard J. Hughes, "Conscience," in *The Cambridge Companion*

ulty. It is constituted by the eternal law, the divine wisdom communicated to the human intellect. It is exclusively upon the intellect's theonomic nature that the prerogatives and the supreme authority of conscience are founded. Newman states:

The Supreme Being is of a certain character, which, expressed in human language, we call ethical. He has the attributes of justice, truth, wisdom, sanctity, benevolence and mercy, as eternal characteristics in His nature, the very Law of His being, identical with Himself; and next, when He became Creator, He implanted this Law, which is Himself, in the intelligence of all His rational creatures. The Divine Law, then, is the rule of ethical truth, the standard of right and wrong, a sovereign, irreversible, absolute authority in the presence of men and Angels.[9]

Newman's conception of conscience as essentially theonomic stands in stark contrast to the widespread idea that the voice of conscience is an interior voice that indulges our whims and wishes, the actual voice of sovereign self-determination. Newman impresses on his readers the rather startling fact that "conscience … is a messenger from Him, who, both in nature and in grace, speaks to us behind a veil, and teaches and rules us

---

to John Henry Newman, ed. Ian Ker and Terrence Merrigan (Cambridge: Cambridge University Press, 2009), 189–220. For the historical and biographical context, see Ker, John Henry Newman: A Biography, 651–93. For an informative account of the complex intellectual history of the concept of conscience from ancient to contemporary philosophy, see H. Reiner, "Gewissen," in Historisches Wörterbuch der Philosophie, ed. Joachim Ritter, K. Gründer, and G. Gabriel, 13 vols. (Stuttgart: Schwabe and Co., 1971–2007), 3:574–92. For a comprehensive treatment of conscience, see Eberhard Schockenhoff, Wie gewiss ist das Gewissen? Eine ethische Orientierung (Freiburg: Herder, 2003). Schockenhoff offers clear and nuanced treatments of the biblical accounts of conscience; analyzes Augustine's, Aquinas's, and Newman's teachings on conscience; and discusses the dignity of conscience according to Vatican II. The book culminates in a dense reflection on freedom and the truth—freedom for the sake of truth. I have learned much from Schockenhoff's study, although I see a significantly greater compatibility and, indeed, complementarity between Aquinas's and Newman's accounts of conscience than Schockenhoff seems to perceive. The one substantive reservation, however, that I have to register regarding Schockenhoff's account of the moral act is the subtle but quite discernible absorption of the object of the moral act (objectum actus) by the intention of the act such that the object of the act is ultimately legitimated by the (presumably good) intention of the act. It is this move that makes Schockenhoff's account of the moral act and ultimately also his account of conscience vulnerable to the strategies of the counterfeit of conscience, for quite obviously a whole range of objects of the act that a dominant spirit of the age proposes or imposes as legitimate or even normative may under his construal be legitimately embraced by a subjectively good intention. Aquinas's account of the moral act does not permit such a conceptual move and John Paul II's 1993 encyclical Veritatis Splendor quite explicitly forestalls it.

9. Diff., ii., 246.

by His representatives."[10] Conscience, "truly so called," denotes the divine standard of moral truth received into the human intellect.[11] It is theonomic all the way down.

Newman's stern definition might provoke objections from those who accept moral relativism and perspectivalism: "The Divine Law"—which is God himself—is "a sovereign, irreversible, absolute authority in the presence of men and Angels."[12] Is Newman here invoking some dark and by now hopefully obsolete image of a tyrannical deity produced by the medieval mind, or is he possibly indulging his own personal obsession with a dictatorial, Old Testament-style *Über*-father, a picture that, as the story goes, was finally abolished at the Second Vatican Council? Far from it. In fact, the magisterial reception and explication of Vatican II suggests that Newman's understanding of conscience as essentially theonomic aligns closely with the theology affirmed by the Council. The 1992 *Catechism of the Catholic Church*, for example, in explaining the teaching of Vatican II on conscience, cites Newman's description of conscience as a messenger of God, culminating in Newman's beautiful and memorable phrase: "Conscience is the aboriginal Vicar of Christ."[13] The *Catechism* suggests that Newman simply teaches the common Christian understanding of conscience.

Newman himself, in his *Letter to the Duke of Norfolk*, points to the broad consensus between Catholics and most Protestant groups in nineteenth-century Great Britain regarding the theonomic nature of conscience:

10. *Diff.*, ii., 248. See Newman's concise parallel statement in the later Catholic version of *An Essay on the Development of Doctrine* (London: Longman, Green, and Co., 1909): "It must be borne in mind that, as the essence of all religion is authority and obedience, so the distinction between natural religion and revealed lies in this, that the one has a subjective authority, and the other an objective. Revelation consists in the manifestation of the Invisible Divine Power, or in the substitution of the voice of a Lawgiver for the voice of conscience. The supremacy of conscience is the essence of natural religion; the supremacy of Apostle, or Pope, or Church, or Bishop, is the essence of revealed; and when such external authority is taken away, the mind falls back again of necessity upon that inward guide which it possessed even before Revelation was vouchsafed. Thus, what conscience is in the system of nature, such is the voice of Scripture, or of the Church, or of the Holy See, as we may determine it, in the system of Revelation. It may be objected, in deed, that conscience is not infallible; it is true, but still it is ever to be obeyed" (86).

11. *Diff.*, ii., 257.

12. *Diff.*, ii., 246.

13. *Catechism of the Catholic Church: Second Edition Revised in Accordance with the Official Latin Text Promulgated by Pope John Paul II* (Vatican City: Libreria Editrice Vaticana, 1997), no. 1778.

When Anglicans, Wesleyans, the various Presbyterian sects in Scotland, and other denominations among us, speak of conscience, they mean what we mean, the voice of God in the nature and heart of man, as distinct from the voice of Revelation. They speak of a principle planted within us, before we have had any training, although training and experience are necessary for its strength, growth, and due formation.... They consider it, as Catholics consider it, to be the internal witness of both the existence and the law of God.[14]

Newman also recognized, however, the rise of a false notion of conscience among British elites influenced by the post-Enlightenment ascendancy of the natural sciences in modern thought. Newman observes that "it is fashionable on all hands now to consider [conscience] in one way or another a creation of man."[15] Conscience so-called, as Newman aptly put it, is regarded as at best "a desire to be consistent with oneself," a consistency constructed among the discrete dictates of the sovereign self-determination.[16] Today this false notion of conscience has become conventional wisdom among politicians, journalists, and the so-called person on the street, and even among American mainstream Protestants. For those who have drunk from the wells of a neuroscientifically informed, neo-Darwinian sociobiology, conscience is nothing but a noble word for "a long-sighted selfishness" resulting from a particular configuration of genes that has determined one particular species—*homo sapiens*.[17] In short, a conscience is merely selfishness produced by forces beyond human control, forces, to use Nietzsche's famous expression, "beyond good and evil."[18]

14. *Diff.*, ii., 247–48. For Luther and Calvin on Conscience, see appendix 2 of this chapter.
15. *Diff.*, ii., 247.
16. *Diff.*, ii., 248. For an account that differentiates well between the shallow self-consistency of sovereign self-determination and a proper human authenticity, which cannot come about without following conscience, truly so-called, see Charles Taylor, *The Ethics of Authenticity* (Cambridge, Mass.: Harvard University Press, 1991).
17. *Diff.*, ii., 248. For a recent neo-Darwinian account of sociobiology with ethical aspirations that is as consistent as it is comprehensive in scope, see Richard Dawkins, *The Selfish Gene* (Oxford: Oxford University Press, 2006).
18. See Friedrich Nietzsche, "'Guilt,' 'Bad Conscience,' and the Like," in *On the Genealogy of Morals*, trans. Walter Kaufmann and R. J. Hollingdale, and *Ecce Homo*, ed. and trans. Walter Kaufmann (New York: Vintage Books, 1989). In section 16 of "'Guilt,' 'Bad Conscience,' and the Like," Nietzsche displays the full import of embracing the counterfeit of conscience with complete awareness of the logical consequences: "Hostility, cruelty, joy in persecuting, in attacking, in change, in destruction—all this turned against the possessors of such instincts: *that* is the origin of the 'bad conscience'" (85). And in section 17 he states openly: "This *instinct for freedom* forcibly

Newman felt the early waves of this dramatic denial of theonomic conscience implanted in the human intellect throughout most of his adult life. "All through my day," he observed:

There has been a resolute warfare, I had almost said conspiracy, against the rights of conscience.... We are told that conscience is but a twist in primitive and untutored man; that its dictate is an imagination; that the very notion of guiltiness, which that dictate enforces, is simply irrational, for how can there possibly be freedom of will, how can there be consequent responsibility, in that infinite eternal network of cause and effect, in which we helplessly lie? And what retribution have we to fear, when we have had no real choice to do good or evil?[19]

Newman was also prescient in anticipating how appeals to this counterfeit of conscience would be made. It might at first seem surprising that appeals to conscience would survive the denial of theonomic conscience. If God does not exist and human beings are causally determined in their acts—whether by Darwinian genetic competition, Marxist socioeconomic forces and social systems, the Freudian "id" or subconscious, or by some combination of all these factors—then why appeal to conscience at all?[20] It being presumably pointless, one would expect that in an increasingly secular culture the appeal to conscience would be moot. But this has not been the case, as any observer of public and political life in late-modern secularist democracies is well aware. The appeal to conscience has not disappeared but has been completely transformed. As Newman observes:

---

made latent ... this instinct for freedom pushed back and repressed, incarcerated within and finally able to discharge and vent itself only on itself: that, and that alone, is what the *bad conscience* is in its beginnings" (87). The instinct for freedom is nothing but the "will to power" (87), or as he puts it in section 3, sovereign self-affirmation and self-determination "to possess ... the right *to affirm oneself*" (60). This is the counterfeit of conscience pursued with consistency. As the best form of defense is attack, it is a given that Nietzsche should identify the residual evidence of theonomic conscience as bad conscience and should attempt to discard it by way of a naturalist genealogy. No recent neo-Darwinian "new atheist" and despiser of Christianity has been able to match Nietzsche's radical consistency "beyond good and evil." Compared to him, the new atheists remain residually bourgeois, beholden to beliefs about scientific enlightenment and historical progress toward an ever-brighter transhuman future. In the mid-twentieth century, Nietzsche's concept of the "bad conscience" was popularized by Simone de Beauvoir and Jean-Paul Sartre as the "mauvaise foi" and later found its way into literature, movies, and music. In this widespread and culturally embedded existentialist "creed," inauthenticity is the *only* sin.

19. *Diff.*, ii., 249.

20. For a nuanced engagement of conscience in the discussion of contemporary psychology, see Schockenhoff, *Wie gewiss ist das Gewissen?*, 142–51.

When men advocate the rights of conscience, they in no sense mean the rights of the Creator, nor the duty to Him, in thought and deed, of the creature; but the right of thinking, speaking, writing, and acting, according to their judgment or their humour, without any thought of God at all ... Conscience has rights because it has duties; but in this age, with a large portion of the public, it is the very right and freedom of conscience to dispense with conscience, to ignore a Lawgiver and Judge, to be independent of unseen obligations. It becomes a license to take up any or no religion, to take up this or that and let it go again.... It is the right of self-will.[21]

Unmoored from its theonomic anchorage, the word *conscience* has come to stand for its counterfeit, denoting not the divine law impressed upon the human intellect but the decisions of the individual's sovereign self-determination. The realm of sovereign self-determination encompasses first and foremost one's body, which is now regarded as one's property. As a result, it extends to the choices that lie open to a person as the owner of his or her body—for example, choices related to gender identity or sexual activity, including the kind and number of intimate partners one elects to have. Sovereign self-determination extends as well to questions of whether to conceive children in the womb, how many children to have, and control over their genetic characteristics. Finally, it includes choices about when and how one's life will end.[22] Sovereign freedom's only limitation is linked to the liberal principle of harm: all choices are permissible so long as they do not restrict the freedom of indifference of everyone else.[23]

No one gave a clearer account of this negative freedom than Newman's contemporary John Stuart Mill, who stated in *On Liberty* "that the

21. *Diff.*, ii., 250.

22. According to Locke, the body is the principal object over which to exercise freedom of indifference. On the erroneous modern idea of self-proprietorship and its philosophical roots in the thought of Descartes, Hobbes, and Locke, see Bernd Wannenwetsch, "Owning Our Bodies? The Politics of Self-Possession and the Body of Christ (Hobbes, Locke and Paul)," *Studies in Christian Ethics* 26, no. 1 (2013): 50–65.

23. The Achilles' heel of this principle, of course, is the definition of "everyone else." The useless, the unwanted, the unexpectedly self-imposing, the unproductive, and the inconveniently needy might not fall within the scope of "everyone else." Without a robust metaphysical concept of human nature, the beginning of human life, the human soul, and a corresponding understanding of the dignity of the human person, secularist liberal democratic regimes stand in danger of reducing the liberal principle of harm to a community of the self-elected, with everyone else becoming discardable—abortable, euthanizable, or institutionalizable.

only freedom which deserves the name" consists in "pursuing our own good in our own way."[24] The ideological breeding ground of the negative freedom of sovereign self-determination is a misguided liberalism, falsely conceived as "neutralism." In a striking engagement with David A. J. Richards's *Tolerance and the Constitution*, political philosopher Ronald Beiner advances a scathing indictment of Richards's strategy for legitimizing sovereign self-determination by appealing to the freedom of conscience:

The spuriousness of this recurrent appeal to the sacredness of conscience is very clearly displayed in the discussion of pornography. How can this possibly be a matter of *conscience*? What is at issue here, surely, is the sacredness of consumer preferences. The individual's sovereign prerogative to purchase magazines like *Penthouse* and *Hustler* has little to do with free *speech* (let alone rights of conscience); the only liberty at stake is that of unhindered consumption.... Or again consider the following passage: "The right to drug use, if it is a right, is a right associated with the control of consciousness and thus with the right of conscience itself" ([Chief Justice] Roberts, 281). By this contorted reasoning, the decision to snort cocaine constitutes an act of conscience.[25]

Beiner is articulating with exemplary clarity in this still-pertinent critique the inner consistency of the counterfeit of conscience as it continues to unfold the full consequences of sovereign self-determination.

In his manifesto *The Closing of the American Mind*, Allan Bloom has characterized the concrete forms taken by this negative freedom of sovereign self-determination since the 1970s, as ever-growing numbers of the educated professional elites in Europe and the United States embraced and deeply internalized it:

They can be anything they want to be, but they have no particular reason to be anything in particular. Not only are they free to decide their place, but they are also free to decide whether they will believe in God or be atheists, or leave their options open by being agnostic; whether they will be straight or gay, or, again, keep their options open; whether they will marry and whether they will stay mar-

24. John Stuart Mill, *On Liberty and Other Essays*, ed. Jonathan Gray (Oxford: Oxford University Press, 1991), 17.

25. Ronald Beiner, *Philosophy in a Time of Lost Spirit* (Toronto: University of Toronto Press, 1997), 29–30, commenting on David A. J. Richards, *Tolerance and the Constitution* (New York: Oxford University Press, 1986).

ried; whether they will have children—and so on endlessly. There is no necessity, no morality, no social pressure, no sacrifice to be made that militates going in or turning away from any of these directions, and there are desires pointing toward each, with mutually contradictory arguments to buttress them.[26]

As has become increasingly clear in more recent years, Bloom's all-too-accurate description captures only a particular moment of a deeper fall. Now the modern subject—a precondition for sovereign self-determination—is undergoing its postmodern disintegration. In light of allegedly ground-breaking insights in neurobiology, a journalistic evolutionary scientism with a missionary impulse urges humanity in the Western Hemisphere to embrace a life "after the subject"—the life of an advanced primate, a hom-inid, equipped with consciousness and desires but devoid of conscience, truly so-called.[27] By internalizing the false premises of this subscientific and aphilosophical biologism, to employ the philosopher Robert Spae-mann's striking statement, "the human being itself becomes an anthropo-morphism to itself."[28] Enlightened by the deliveries of scientism, humans are induced to think that they know—scientifically—that they are but primates, determined by their instincts and desires, while in their every-day lives they must nevertheless continue to pretend to be persons, hold-ing others accountable for their actions and being held accountable for their own actions. The result is a profound estrangement from our own

26. Allan Bloom, *The Closing of the American Mind* (New York: Simon and Schuster, 1987), 87.

27. For two popularizing accounts of this reductive materialist scientism, see Dawkins, *The God Delusion*, and Dennett, *Breaking the Spell*. Consider the construal of memes as units of imitation that have a distinct survival value: "Just as genes propagate themselves in the gene pool by leaping from body to body via sperms or eggs, so memes propagate themselves in the meme pool by leap-ing from brain to brain via a process which, in the broad sense, can be called imitation.... When you plant a fertile meme in my mind, you literally parasitize my brain, turning it into a vehicle of the meme's propagation in just the way that a virus may parasitize the genetic mechanism of a host cell.... The meme for, say, 'belief in life after death' is actually realized physically, millions of times over, a structure in the nervous systems of individual men the world over" (Dawkins, *The Selfish Gene*, 192). The meme serves as a functionalist replacement of complex human thought, insight, be-lief, and, most fundamentally, the intuition of first principles and of intentionality. Without the intuition of first principles and intentionality, however, human agency collapses into behavior, a properly amoral, descriptive category of biology that reductive scientism now propagates as the true causal account of what appears to the scientifically unenlightened as moral truth and moral agency, a presumptive account that should henceforth inform the self-understanding of human beings.

28. Robert Spaemann, "Ende der Modernität?," in *Philosophische Essays*, 2nd ed. (Stuttgart: Reclam, 1994), 232–60: "So wird der Mensch selbst sich zum Anthropomorphismus" (240).

immediate and irreducibly experience of ourselves and others as moral agents.

Given the dramatic change during Newman's own lifetime in the understanding of conscience, it is of special significance that he did not deem it necessary to advance some philosophical demonstration that would prove the existence of a theonomic conscience. For those who have faith, divine revelation and the church's consistent teachings on conscience authoritatively establish the existence and theonomic nature of conscience. Moreover, Newman assumes that those who have faith will also experience the theonomic reality of conscience with a clarity that a philosophical demonstration could hardly improve upon. For those without faith and for those whose notion of conscience is warped by erroneous opinions, Newman seems to assume that the inescapable experience of the interior forum of conscience will eventually produce the kind of evidence for the theonomic nature of conscience that no philosophical demonstration could hope to achieve. Theonomic conscience, in Newman's eyes, is an aboriginal and universal datum of the human mind conveying the first principles of moral truth. The principles of conscience are known self-evidently, much like the principle of noncontradiction. Just as the principle of noncontradiction cannot be demonstrated but serves as the basis for proving other truths, so the first principles of the theonomic conscience cannot be demonstrated by a proof. Rather, their self-evidence serves as the grounds for proving other truths—for Newman, the existence of God.[29]

Faced with the counterfeit of conscience, Newman simply trusts that the ontological truth of theonomic conscience, its objective reality, and its eventual operation will again and again break through the layers of self-deception and thereby establish the only persuasive evidence of its existence. And therefore, in the very presence of the counterfeit of conscience, Newman continues to use "the word 'conscience' in the high sense ... as a dutiful obedience to what claims to be a divine voice, speaking within us; and that this is the view properly to be taken of it, I shall not attempt to prove here, but I shall assume it as a first principle."[30]

29. See appendix 1 to this chapter for a summary of Newman's argument from conscience to the existence of God.
30. *Diff.*, ii., 255.

Drawing upon the rich and nuanced tradition of Catholic teaching on conscience in his *Letter*, Newman understands conscience to have two distinct functions. First and foremost is what he calls the echo of the divine voice within us, this echo being nothing but the presence in the intellect of the first principles of moral truth. Second, there are the practical dictates about what here and now is to be pursued as good or avoided as evil. Conscience, Newman says, "bears immediately on conduct, on something to be done or not done."[31] It is at this very point that Newman refers to Aquinas's doctrine of conscience.[32]

Aquinas on *Synderesis* and *Conscientia*

Newman points to the deep congruity between Augustine's and Aquinas's teachings on the theonomic nature of conscience: "'The eternal law,' says St. Augustine, 'is the Divine Reason or Will of God, commanding the observance, forbidding the disturbance, of the natural order of things.'"[33] But how are the eternal law and conscience connected? In order to answer this question, Newman turns from Augustine to Aquinas:

"The natural law," says St. Thomas, "is an impression of the Divine Light in us, a participation of the eternal law in the rational creature." … This law, as apprehended in the minds of individual [human beings], is called "conscience"; and though it may suffer refraction in passing into the intellectual medium of each, it is not therefore so affected as to lose its character of being the Divine Law, but still has, as such, the prerogative of commanding obedience.[34]

Newman draws on a crucial distinction at the very center of Aquinas's doctrine of conscience, between, on the one hand, the existence of an in-

---

31. *Diff.*, ii., 256.

32. For Aquinas's understanding of *synderesis*, see Dennis J. Billy, CSSR, "Aquinas on the Content of Synderesis," *Studia Moralia* 29 (1991): 61–83; Vernon J. Bourke, "The Background of Aquinas's Synderesis Principle," in *Graceful Reason: Essays in Ancient and Medieval Philosophy Presented to Joseph Owens, C.Ss.R.*, ed. Lloyd P. Gerson (Toronto: Pontifical Institute of Mediaeval Studies, 1983), 345–60; Michael Bertram Crowe, "Synderesis and the Notion of Law in Saint Thomas," in *L'homme et son destin d'après les penseurs du Moyen Âge: Actes du Premier Congrès International de Philosophie Médiévale, Louvain-Bruxelles, 28 août–4 septembre 1958* (Louvain: Éditions Nauwelaerts, 1960), 601–9; and Odon D. Lottin, "Syndérèse et conscience aux xiie et xiiie siècles," *Problèmes de morale* (Louvain: Abbaye de Mont César, 1948), 2.1:101–349.

33. *Diff.*, ii., 246–47.

34. *Diff.*, ii., 247.

nate first principle and the first precept—Aquinas calls this *synderesis*—and, on the other hand, the intuitive bearing of the first principle and first precept upon a particular case, a judgment of practical reason that Aquinas calls *con-scientia*, the "knowing together" of the first principle and precept with a concrete case, prospectively or retrospectively, in a specific interior judgment.

To name the ontological level of conscience, Aquinas uses a technical term provided by tradition and employed by the theologians of his day: *synderesis*. In his treatment of *synderesis*, Aquinas appropriates and refines the thought of his principal teacher, the Dominican St. Albert the Great, and of his elder theological contemporary and colleague at the University of Paris, the Franciscan St. Bonaventure.[35] He also integrates the patristic tradition, especially the works of Jerome and Augustine, and the classical Greek traditions, especially those of Aristotle and the Stoics. The Dominican Servais Pinckaers, doyen of post-Vatican II moral theologians, helpfully observes how Aquinas

went to the trouble of explaining St. Jerome's comparison [of *synderesis* with the "spark of conscience"] and made the distinction between the spark, the purest part of fire, which shoots out above the flame, and the fire itself, which is mixed with alien matter that alters its purity. The spark is *synderesis*, the pure light of truth; the fire is conscience, which can err accidentally by attaching itself to a particular object that is inferior to reason. *Synderesis* is, strictly speaking, the spark of conscience, the origin of the light that illuminates it.[36]

35. On the biblical, patristic, and medieval background of the *synderesis* principle, see Vernon J. Bourke, "The Background of Aquinas's Synderesis Principle"; on the arguments that Aquinas adduces for its existence, see Michael Bertram Crowe, "Synderesis and the Notion of Law in Saint Thomas"; and for a lucid summary of Aquinas's debts to and differences from Albert and Bonaventure, see Daniel Westberg, *Right Practical Reason: Aristotle, Action, and Prudence in Aquinas* (Oxford: Clarendon Press, 1994), 100–105. An important study by Oskar Renz, *Die Synteresis nach dem Hl. Thomas von Aquin* (Münster: Aschendorff, 1911), remains the only comprehensive monograph on the function of *synderesis* in Aquinas's moral theology.

36. Servais Pinckaers, OP, "Conscience, Truth, and Prudence," in *Crisis of Conscience: Philosophers and Theologians Analyze Our Growing Inability to Discern Right from Wrong*, ed. John M. Haas (New York: Crossroad, 1996), 79–92, at 88. See Aquinas, *De veritate*, q. 17, a. 2, ad 3; English-language quotations of this work here follow Thomas Aquinas, *Truth*, trans. Robert W. Mulligan, James V. McGlynn, SJ, and Robert W. Schmidt (Indianapolis, Ind.: Hackett, 1994), 2:325. In his commentary on Ezekiel, in the context of Ezekiel's vision of the four creatures in human form (Ezek 1:4–12), Jerome makes reference to the term συντήρησις as the Greek equivalent of the Latin *scintilla conscientiae*, the spark of conscience. See his *Commentarius in Ezechielem*, I, 1, in the

For Aquinas, *synderesis* is "a natural [*habitus*] of first principles of action, which are the universal principles of the natural law."[37] Unlike an acquired *habitus*, which denotes the state of a trained disposition to act in a certain way when encountering specific objects or situations, a natural *habitus* is an innate disposition of a human capacity. In this case, it is the disposition of practical reason, the general human capacity for resolving, through reasoning, the question of what action one is to take. *Synderesis* is practical reason "perfected by a completely determined [*habitus*]."[38] As Pinckaers aptly puts it, *synderesis* "offers a solid base for the recognition of the universal and permanent character of moral laws coming from within us in the form of a light that illuminates our intellect. The strength of moral law derived from this light does not come to [human beings] from a merely exterior will; it has its root in [our] intellect and is at the origin of [our] freedom."[39]

The natural determination of practical reason thus consists in "a primordial perception of the good proper to [the human being]."[40] It is, however, important not to misunderstand this fundamental point. The content of *synderesis* is not realized through divine illumination or some innate apprehension. Rather, the intellect in its theoretical and in its practical aspects intuits self-evident principles before rational deliberation but after learning the terms of these principles through basic sensory experience.[41]

Patrologiae Cursus Completus: Series Latina, ed. J.-P. Migne (Paris: Garnier Frères, 1958–) [hereafter "PL"], 25:22. John Mahoney rightly points out that this Greek word is not the result of a copyist's error for συνείδησις (*conscientia*), as was wrongly held in the latter part of the twentieth century, but rather reflects the use of the verb συντηρέω in late antique Greek. See John Mahoney, SJ, *The Making of Moral Theology: A Study of the Roman Catholic Tradition* (Oxford: Oxford University Press, 1987), 187nn41–42.

37. Aquinas, *De veritate*, q. 16, a. 1, co. (*Truth*, 2:304). See also his *Scriptum super libros Sententiarum magistri Petri Lombardi episcopi Parisiensis* [hereafter "*In Sent.*"] II, d. 24, q. 2, a. 3; and *Summa theologiae* I, q. 79, a. 12. Quotations of the *Summa theologiae* [hereafter "*ST*"] here follow the Fathers of the English Dominican Province edition, *The Summa Theologica* (New York: Benziger Bros., 1947–48). Emendations are indicated by brackets. Unless otherwise noted, all translations of passages from other works by Aquinas are my own.

38. Aquinas, *De veritate*, q. 16, a. 2, ad 4 (*Truth*, 2:310).

39. Pinckaers, "Truth," 88. For a discussion of then cardinal Joseph Ratzinger's proposal to replace *synderesis* with *anamnesis*, see appendix 6 to this chapter.

40. Servais Pinckaers, OP, *The Sources of Christian Ethics*, trans. Sr. Mary Thomas Noble, OP (Washington, D.C.: The Catholic University of America Press, 1995), 384.

41. Aquinas succinctly explains this matter when discussing whether any *habitus* is natural,

Let us now consider the operative level of conscience.[42] *Conscientia*, "knowing together," refers to two phenomena: first, the actualization of the natural *habitus* of the first principles of moral truth in the form of a concrete judgment and, second, the application of this knowledge to action, a kind of dictate or command of reason.[43] Newman understands this second aspect of conscience to be a particular directive with an immediate bearing on what is to be done: "'Conscience,' says St. Thomas, 'is the practical judgment or dictate of reason, by which we judge what *hic et nunc* is to be done as being good, or to be avoided as evil.'"[44] Aquinas spells out the dynamic of this judgment of conscience in instructive detail:

Conscience is said to witness, to bind, or incite, and also to accuse, torment, or rebuke. And all these follow the application of knowledge or science to what we do: which application is made in three ways. One way in so far as we recognize that we have done or not done something; *Your conscience knows that you have often spoken evil of others* (Eccles. vii, 23), and according to this, conscience is said to witness. In another way, so far as through the conscience we judge that something should be done or not done; and in this sense, conscience is said to incite or to bind. In the third way so far as by conscience we judge that something done is well done or ill done, and in this sense conscience is said to excuse, accuse, or torment. Now, it is clear that all these things follow the actual application of knowledge to what we do. Wherefore, properly speaking, conscience denominates an act.[45]

---

that is, innate: "The understanding of first principles is called a natural habit. For it is owing to the very nature of the intellectual soul that [a human being], having once grasped what is a whole and what is a part, should at once perceive that every whole is larger than its part: and in like manner with regard to other such principles. Yet what is a whole, and what is a part—this he cannot know except through the intelligible species which he has received from phantasms: and for this reason, the Philosopher at the end of the *Posterior Analytics* shows that knowledge of principles comes to us from the senses" (*ST* I-II, q. 51, a. 1, co.).

42. The Greek term for this actualization is συνείδησις and its literal Latin translation is *conscientia*. By the time the Apostle Paul wrote his epistles, both terms were commonplace in everyday Greek and Latin usage. Paul uses συνείδησις frequently: Rom 2:15; 1 Cor 8:7, 8:10, 8:12, and 10:28–29; 2 Cor 1:12–13; 1 Tm 1:19; and Ti 1:15.

43. *ST* I, q. 79, a. 13, co.; and *ST* I-II, q. 19, a. 5, co. See also Aquinas, *De veritate*, q. 17, a. 1; and *In II Sent.*, d. 24, q. 2, a. 4.

44. *Diff.*, ii., 256. The late Thomist philosopher Ralph McInerny put it thus: "Conscience ... is a particular judgment as to what is to be done in the light of a common principle. The term means the *act* of application, but *conscience* can also mean the judgment made, as when someone tells us *what* his conscience tells him." "Conscience and the Object of the Moral Act," in *Crisis of Conscience* (ed. Haas), 93–110, at 97.

45. *ST* I, q. 79, a. 13, co.

Aquinas's account of how the judgment of conscience occurs is not only remarkably comprehensive but also empirically accurate. The judgment of *conscientia* may occur prospectively, before the execution of a specific action; but it may also occur retrospectively, after the execution or the omission of this specific action. In sum, according to Aquinas, the judgment of conscience prospectively bears witness, exhorts, commands, forbids, or permits and retrospectively evaluates either positively or negatively.

Like Aquinas, Newman regards the natural *habitus* of *synderesis* as universal, incorruptible, and infallible, although the concrete exercise of *conscientia* is vulnerable to personal defects (ignorance, imprudence, or habituation to vice) and, over longer historical periods, to collective sociocultural corruption. Hence, as noted above, Newman can forego any attempt to prove the existence of conscience to its detractors. While those who embrace the sovereign rule of self-will can deny, suppress, and flee from the interior forum, they can never escape the eventual interior manifestation of theonomic conscience.[46]

Three aspects of Aquinas's doctrine of conscience are of crucial importance to understanding its contrary, the counterfeit of conscience: first, the innate *habitus* of *synderesis*; second, the important relationship between conscience and the virtue of prudence; and, third, the complex phenomenon of the erroneous conscience.

Synderesis

Synderesis is the natural *habitus* of the intellect that contains the first principle ("good is that which all things seek after") and the first precept of practical reason ("good is to be done and pursued, and evil is to be avoided").[47] Aquinas understands the natural law fundamentally as the rational creature's participation in the eternal law, which "is nothing else than the type of Divine Wisdom, as directing all actions and movements."[48]

46. For Immanuel Kant's instructive but problematic account of the interior forum, see appendix 3 to this chapter.

47. *ST* I-II, q. 94, a. 2, co.; see also a. 4, co. I am here bracketing discussion of various theories on how the first precept relates to the first principle. Some commentators make a simple distinction, others derive the precept from the principle, and still others identify the precept with the principle. For the relevant literature, see Billy, "Aquinas on the Content of Synderesis," 65n11.

48. *ST* I-II, q. 93, a. 1, co. For an instructive treatment of this crucial aspect of Aquinas's

Humans are thus "partakers of a share of providence, by being both provident for [themselves] and for others."[49] This participation occurs by way of the natural inclination of practical reason to the proper act and end of the rational creature. As Aquinas explains, "On the part of practical reason, [the human being] has a natural participation of the eternal law, according to certain general principles."[50] Aquinas indicates quite clearly the theonomic character of *synderesis*, called here "the light of natural reason" (*lumen rationis naturalis*), yielding the first principle and the first precept of the natural law:

The Psalmist after saying (Ps 4:6): *Offer up the sacrifice of justice*, as though someone asked what the works of justice are, adds: *Many say, Who showeth us good things?* In answer to which question he says: *The light of Thy countenance, O Lord, is signed upon us*: thus implying that the light of natural reason, whereby we discern what is good and what is evil, which is the function of the natural law, is nothing else than an imprint on us of the Divine light [*impressio divini luminis in nobis*]. It is therefore evident that the natural law is nothing else than the rational creature's participation of the eternal law.[51]

And the eternal law is nothing other than an encompassing teleology for the whole of creation. God is the first cause and the final end of the universe, and the divine wisdom directs all acts and movements to the common good of the universe, which is God. In order for the human to participate as a rational being in the eternal law, the apprehensive and appetitive faculties that all animals display are insufficient. Voluntary agency presupposes not only the perception of an end or good but also the perception of its character (*ratio finis*) and the agent's relationship to it. This more perfect kind of cognition allows the rational being to move, by way of deliberation, toward the end or not to move toward it. Furthermore, genuine human participation in the eternal law requires the mutual influence of intellect and will such that both faculties include one another in

sapiential moral theology, see John Rziha, *Perfecting Human Actions: St. Thomas Aquinas on Human Participation in Eternal Law* (Washington, D.C.: The Catholic University of America Press, 2009), esp. 199–230.

49. *ST* I-II, q. 91, a. 2, co.
50. *ST* I-II, q. 91, a. 3, ad 1.
51. *ST* I-II, q. 91, a. 2, co.

their acts: "The intellect understands that the will wills and the will wills the intellect to understand. In the same way good is contained in truth, inasmuch as it is an understood truth, and truth in good, inasmuch as it is a desired good."[52] We desire to know truth because it is a specific good (knowledge perfects the intellect), and only the good that is understood as good attracts the will.[53] Hence, due to the profound interaction of intellect and will in practical reason, there must be a first principle and a first precept of *synderesis*. With respect to the intellect, *synderesis* has the character of first principle, the formality of the understood good (*bonum apprehensum*). With respect to the will (which desires the understood good), *synderesis* has the character of first precept:

"Good" is the first thing that falls under the apprehension of the practical reason, which is directed to action: since every agent acts for an end under the aspect of good. Consequently, the first principle in the practical reason is founded on the notion of good, viz. that "good is that which all things seek after." Hence this is the first precept of law, that "good is to be done and pursued, and evil is to be avoided."[54]

The first precept of the natural law, it is important to note, is not to be confused with Kant's categorical imperative, which expresses a purely formal duty of practical reason. By contrast, the first precept expresses the inherent attraction of the good understood as good. As Servais Pinckaers helpfully explains: "[This first precept] does not primarily signify an obligation to do the good. Rather, it expresses the attraction of the good.... It is this urgency of the truth within the good, within the very attraction of the good, that is at the heart of the intimate awareness of duty and

---

52. *ST* I, q. 82, a. 4, ad 1 (emphasis added); see also *ST* I, q. 16, a. 4, ad 1; *ST* I-II, q. 9, a. 1, co. Truth is the specific good toward which the will moves the intellect as an efficient cause; and the intellect moves the will as formal cause by providing the formality or character of good. Improperly speaking, by thus providing the understood good, the intellect moves the will *per modum finis*; properly speaking, however, what is perceived by the intellect under the character of good (*bonum apprehensum*) moves the will as a formal cause.

53. "The will moves the intellect as to the exercise of its act; since even the true itself which is the perfection of the intellect, is included in the universal good, as a particular good. But as to the determination of the act, which the act derives from the object, the intellect moves the will; since the good itself is apprehended under a special aspect as contained in the universal true" (*ST* I-II, q. 9, a. 1, ad 3).

54. *ST* I-II, q. 94, a. 2, co.

obligation."[55] The natural *habitus* of first principle and first precept enables the rational creature not only to move toward some perceived good but to realize the *ratio finis*, the character of the good. Because good is the perfection that every created being desires and to which every created being moves as its final end, *synderesis* enables the rational creature to realize this teleology of the good as *rational* creature by participating in the eternal law through the natural law.[56]

In his excellent book, *Perfecting Human Actions,* John Rziha rightly points out how genuine human freedom arises precisely from participation in the eternal law:

> For Thomas, freedom does not come from a blind movement of the will or sense appetites but comes from the will and sense appetites being determined by human reason to intend and choose acts in accord with the ultimate end of humanity.... Hence, freedom is bound up in rationality, which derives its light and intellectual forms from the eternal law.... Authentic human freedom is first and foremost caused by the eternal law and only caused by the human through the soul's participation in the eternal law.[57]

It is for this reason that conscience truly so called is indispensable for achieving the perfection of human freedom, that is, positive freedom, freedom in the truth.

The fundamental teleological order of the universe that is reflected in the innate *habitus* of *synderesis* obviates the so-called naturalistic fallacy, according to which it is impossible to transition from a statement of fact—an is—to a moral precept—an ought.[58] As creatures of the ordered universe, humans—like all other beings—are teleologically constituted

55. Servais Pinckaers, OP, *Morality: The Catholic View*, trans. Michael Sherwin, OP (South Bend, Ind.: St. Augustine's Press, 2001), 99–100.

56. *ST* I, q. 5, aa. 1 and 4.

57. Rziha, *Perfecting Human Actions*, 265.

58. The supposed problem of the naturalistic fallacy was first raised by David Hume in his anonymously published 1739/40 *Treatise of Human Nature Being an Attempt to Introduce the Experimental Method of Reasoning into Moral Subjects*, 3.1.1. The term was coined by analytic philosopher G. E. Moore in his 1903 *Principia Ethica* (chap. 2). One can, of course, argue that *synderesis* does not exist. But human history provides overwhelming empirical evidence to the contrary. For a modern discussion of the problem raised by Hume, see *The Is-Ought Question*, ed. William Donald Hudson (London: Macmillan, 1969); and for a substantive treatment of this problematic, see Piotr Lichacz, "Did St. Thomas Aquinas Justify the Transition from 'Is' to 'Ought'?" (STD diss., University of Fribourg, 2008).

by way of fundamental natural inclinations. As rational creatures, they are endowed with *synderesis*, "an habitual light [*lumen habituale*]," by virtue of which they understand the character of good; so as soon as something is apprehended in some respect as good, their rational appetite, the will, is attracted by it.[59] Hence, *synderesis* is not only a formal but a teleological principle inherent in practical reason itself. As a tendency to its proper end or good, the ought is embedded in the is of every being and especially in those beings who realize their perfection through the exercise of practical reason.

There is one further implication of practical reason's interior teleological constitution. Because *synderesis* is a habitual light, the dictates of conscience cannot be heteronomous—that is, imposed by some external authority. For the dictates of conscience truly so-called are nothing but the concrete application, by way of judgment, of those principles and precepts that constitute the teleological order of practical reason itself. For this reason, a teleological ethics centered on *synderesis* and the natural inclinations escapes the interminable conflict between heteronomy and autonomy that haunts most modern moral philosophy.[60]

Because humans are rational beings created in the image of God, the innate first principles of understanding and acting are specific properties of human nature. Rejecting *synderesis*—and with it the teleological order of reality—and embracing instead the negative freedom of sovereign self-determination, the counterfeit of conscience is condemned to a neverending vigilance against the constant threat of a hostile takeover by the will of an "Other," whether human or divine. Sovereignty of self-will neutralizes the first threat, while atheism eliminates the second threat—and, voilà, we are left with the characteristic features of modern nihilism's will to power.[61]

59. On the "habitual light" of *synderesis*, see *De veritate*, q. 16, a. 3 (*Truth*, 2:312). On fundamental natural inclinations, see *ST* I-II, q. 94, a. 2, co.

60. See J. B. Schneewind, *The Invention of Autonomy: A History of Modern Moral Philosophy* (Cambridge: Cambridge University Press, 1998). *Synderesis* is nothing but a participatory theonomy that transcends the paralyzing opposition of heteronomy and autonomy in which the late-modern counterfeit of conscience is fatefully caught. See John Paul II, *Veritatis Splendor*, Encyclical Letter, August 6, 1993, par. 41; available at www.vatican.va.

61. On the emergence of modern nihilism from late-medieval voluntarism through its flowering in early modern sovereign self-determination to its late-modern celebration of the will to

Conscience and Prudence

In order to gain a deeper understanding of conscience truly so-called and its counterfeit, we must consider briefly how conscience relates to the principal cardinal virtue, prudence, which Aquinas defines as "right practical reason." *Synderesis* is a natural, innate *habitus*, while a virtue is, by contrast, an operative *habitus*—that is, a *habitus* acquired through acts of virtue or infused by grace and productive of good actions. Virtues make both those who possess them and their actions good. Prudence is the virtue that resides in practical reason—reason ordered to action—and applies right reason to action. The prudent person not only makes sound judgments but also chooses and executes right courses of action in specific situations.

Aquinas views conscience and prudence not as identical but as profoundly related.[62] Pinckaers emphasizes the difference between conscience and prudence when he observes that conscience, "although it judges the moral quality of our behavior, is not a virtue; it is the application of *synderesis* in the appraisal of acts we have carried out or will carry out."[63] In an analysis of the relationship between conscience and prudence as Aquinas defines it, Ralph McInerny cuts to the core of the matter: "To have cognitive knowledge of what I ought to do here and now is not a function of, is not dependent upon, being related to the good known as good. A bad [person] can have a correct conscience. The correctness of conscience does not of itself guarantee that action and choice will be in accord with it."[64]

The morally weak person, the incontinent person "knows what he ought to do, his conscience is all right, but his knowledge of the good is not complemented by an effective appetitive disposition to the good as good. That is why in the crunch, in choosing (which is a meld of mind and appetite), he goes wrong."[65] In short, the antecedent judgment of

---

power, see Michael Allen Gillespie, *Nihilism before Nietzsche* (Chicago: University of Chicago Press, 1994).

62. "*Synderesis* moves prudence, just as the understanding of principles moves science" (*ST* II-II, q. 47, a. 6, ad 3).

63. Pinckaers, "Truth," 89.

64. Ralph McInerny, "Prudence and Conscience," *The Thomist* 38 (1974): 291–305, at 303.

65. Ibid.

conscientia testifies to the right course of action and commands that it be taken; it is not, however, in and of itself efficacious in choosing and doing the good. Among the three acts related to the virtue of prudence—to take counsel (*consiliari*), to judge (*iudicare*), and to command (*praecipere*)—*conscientia* comprises the second act when this judgment is right and certain, that is, when it is indeed properly formed by the acquired or infused *habitus* of prudence.[66] But efficaciously choosing and doing the good requires the two other acts of prudence—taking counsel[67] and command—as well as the other three cardinal virtues: justice, fortitude, and temperance. Rightly formed conscience convicts the adulterer of the act of adultery, but it cannot on its own prevent an act of adultery. Nor can conscience truly so-called prevent on its own the adulterer's habituation to this vice, let alone free the habitual adulterer from the vice. *Conscientia* lacks the power of execution.[68] A successful prevention of the adulterer's habituation to this vice would require acts of prudence, justice, chastity, and courage, acts displaying the four cardinal virtues.

In the case of Christians in a state of grace, such acts of virtue, now themselves infused by grace, would be commanded by the theological virtues of faith, hope, and charity. Judgments of *conscientia* are, nevertheless,

---

66. *ST* II-II, q. 47, a. 8.

67. For Aquinas, the ideal act of taking counsel comprises five steps: "*Memory* [*memoria*] of the past, *intelligence* [*intelligentia*] of the present, *shrewdness* [*solertia*] in considering the future outcome, *reasoning* [*ratiocinatio*] which compares one thing with another, *docility* [*docilitas*] in accepting the opinions of others. He that takes counsel descends by these steps in due order" (*ST* II-II, q. 53, a. 3, co.). These five steps are not solitary events in the agent's soul but, on the contrary, reflect distinct aspects of the deliberative process: "Counsel properly implies a conference held between several; the very word [*consilium*] denotes this, for it means a sitting together [*considium*], from the fact that many sit together in order to confer with one another" (*ST* I-II, q. 14, a. 3, co.). I am indebted to Raymond F. Hain IV for helping me to understand counsel as a primarily social activity. See the section entitled "Is Consilium a Social Activity?" in Hain's dissertation, "Practical Virtues: Instrumental Practical Reason and the Virtues" (PhD diss., University of Notre Dame, 2009), 177–82.

68. Command (*imperium*) is an act of the intellect moved by the will (*ST* I-II, q. 17, a. 1). When *imperium* is an act integral to the virtue of prudence (instead of being the result of precipitation or thoughtlessness), Aquinas calls it *praecipium*, command as informed by right judgment. Indeed, he regards the act of command (*praecipere*) as the principal act of prudence. Practical reason is directed to action. Therefore, after counsel or deliberation and judgment, the third act of prudence is "to command[,] which act consists in applying to action the things counselled and judged. And since this act approaches nearer to the end of the practical reason, it follows that it is the chief act of the practical reason, and consequently of prudence" (*ST* II-II, q. 47, a. 8, co.).

absolutely indispensable for moral goodness and, indeed, holiness of life (1 Jn 3:3). Yet the antecedent judgments of *conscientia* remain powerless unless they are carried forward into the realization of morally good acts by the four cardinal virtues under the primacy of prudence. More importantly, in light of the supernatural end of the human life—the beatific vision, the surpassing and everlasting beatitude of the union of intellect and will with God, the first truth and the supreme good—the judgment of conscience must be complemented by the infused moral virtues and the gifts of the Holy Spirit and realized in meritorious acts informed by the theological virtue of charity. What propels the judgments of conscience into right action is the virtue of prudence in unity with the other cardinal virtues. What perfects them is "the sympathy and connaturality for Divine things" that "is the result of charity, which unites us to God."[69] Bereft of the virtues, moral and theological, and the gifts of the Holy Spirit, such judgments are at best true judgments of a morally incontinent or, worse, a vicious person with a properly formed and therefore bad conscience consisting entirely of accusatory consequent judgments.[70]

When right and certain, the antecedent judgment of *conscientia* is

69. "Now this sympathy or connaturality for Divine things is the result of charity, which unites us to God" (*ST* II-II, q. 45, a. 2, co.). Aquinas makes this statement in the context of considering the gift of wisdom, a gift that has its cause in the will but its essence in the intellect, "a gift of the Holy Spirit to judge aright about [divine things] on account of connaturality with them" (ibid.). *Nota bene:* the judgment of wisdom is the supernatural analogue of the judgment of *conscientia*. The judgment of *conscientia* applies the principles of *synderesis*; the judgment of wisdom applies, *via* connaturality, what pertains to the eternal law: "Wisdom denotes a certain rectitude of judgment according to the Eternal Law" (ibid.).

70. The relationship between conscience and prudence bestows an important lesson. While *synderesis* and *conscientia* are indispensable, the exercise of the virtue of prudence, acquired as well as infused, is of a surpassingly greater significance for the moral life and especially for the *viator* on the pilgrimage to the supernatural final end—communion with the Trinity in the beatific vision. (Of equal importance are the gifts of the Holy Spirit, in our context especially the gift of counsel; see *ST* II-II, q. 52.) Hence it is to be expected that, in Thomist moral theology, the acquired and the infused virtues together with the gifts of the Holy Spirit take center stage, while *synderesis/conscientia* hold a subordinate, though indispensable, position. When post-Tridentine Catholic moral theology, especially from the eighteenth century onward, shifted the emphasis from grace, the gifts of the Holy Spirit, and the beatitudes to conscience and law, many of the best insights of Thomist sapiential moral theology fell by the wayside. For an instructive analysis of the problem, see Pinckaers, *Sources of Christian Ethics*, 254–79; for a lucid discussion of the role played by the gifts of the Holy Spirit in the Christian moral life, see Steven A. Long, "The Gifts of the Holy Spirit and Their Indispensability for the Christian Moral Life: Grace as *Motus*," *Nova et Vetera* (English edition) 11, no. 2 (2013): 357–73.

an integral component of the virtue of prudence. But once the *habitus* of prudence has been diminished or completely lost due to contrary acts of imprudence, and the act of counsel prevented by precipitation or by thoughtlessness,[71] the flight from the synderistic indicator of moral truth and from the interior forum prepares for the indulgence in the counterfeit of conscience. Regarding its own decisions as intrinsically infallible expressions of a sovereign self-determination, the counterfeit forgoes counsel, the interior as well as exterior source leading to a rightly formed judgment of *conscientia*. The decisions that the counterfeit posits create the semblance of a true and therefore good conscience precisely because the counterfeit's decisions are held to be infallible. The sovereignty of self-determination guarantees consistency with oneself, which is to replace the synderistic truth-indicator. Eschewing the internal forum and embracing the attitude of sovereign self-determination, the counterfeit of conscience now blocks access to the synderistic root of right judgment.

The Erroneous Conscience

The phenomenon of the counterfeit of conscience producing a simulacrum of the true and therefore good conscience raises the complex issue of the erroneous conscience. First, a brief word on Aquinas's distinct approach. Aquinas is engaged in an objective analysis of the principles and judgments of conscience with respect to truth and goodness. He therefore distinguishes the subjective position of the moral agent from the objective position of *sacra doctrina*—the science of divine realties proceeding from divine revelation—which comprises the first principles and the correct inferences of more remote principles. An integral component of *sacra doctrina* is sapiential moral theology. It is only from the objective perspective of this theology that the distinction between a conscience that is subjectively good (a judgment based on a good intention) but objectively erroneous can be meaningfully introduced and defended. The objective perspective is, in its perfection, identical with divine knowledge itself and becomes accessible to sapiential moral theology in an imperfect

71. *ST* II-II, q. 53, aa. 3 and 4.

but reliable form only through participation in the eternal law as affirmed and perfected by the revealed principles of the divine knowledge. Reason participates in the eternal law by way of the natural law. The objective perspective is to some degree also accessible to philosophical wisdom that is able to infer correctly secondary principles and precepts from the first principle and precept of *synderesis*.

Aquinas stresses that the antecedent judgment of *conscientia*, the application of the universal principles of *synderesis* to a particular case, is not infallible. When properly informed by prudence—that is, when conformed to right intention according to the principles and precepts of *synderesis* and when subjectively certain—the judgment of *conscientia* is practically true and right. But the agent may suffer from ignorance and thus be objectively burdened by an erroneous conscience. Hence the characteristic deficiency of an erroneous conscience is ignorance, which can be voluntary or involuntary, vincible or invincible.[72]

As the dictate of conscience binds and must be obeyed, a dictate issuing from an objectively erroneous conscience must nevertheless be obeyed subjectively. If the objective perspective were completely available this side of the beatific vision, then the only relevant perspective would be that of the moral agent. And from the agent's perspective, the only way to sin would be to act against one's conscience, to act according to a consciously bad intention. This was famously Peter Abelard's position, to which Aquinas implicitly responds.[73] Consider how Aquinas distinguishes between the objective and the subjective perspectives:

72. *ST* I-II, q. 76.

73. The thesis to which Aquinas responds here can be found in Abelard's *Ethica seu liber dictus scito te ipsum*: "Peccatum non est nisi contra conscientiam [There is no sin except that against conscience]." This text can be found in the Patrologiae Cursus Completus: Series Latina, ed. J.-P. Migne (Paris: Garnier Frères, 1958), 178:653C. Abelard elevates subjective conscience to the highest moral authority and thereby contributes to the eventual invention of the counterfeit of conscience. This is not a matter of purely antiquarian interest, for Abelard's approach to conscience found a sophisticated modern advocate in the voice of Karl Rahner, who penned an influential essay published originally under the title "Vom irrenden Gewissen" in *Orientierung* 48 (1983): 246B–250A. See appendix 5 for further discussion of Rahner's construal of conscience. For a lucid treatment of this difficult issue and an incisive interrogation of Rahner's construal, see Théo G. Belmans, O. Praem., "Le paradoxe de la conscience erronée d'Abélard à Karl Rahner," *Revue Thomiste* 90 (1990): 570–86.

Conscience is said to bind in so far as one sins if he does not follow his conscience, but not in the sense that he acts correctly if he does follow it.... Conscience is not said to bind in the sense that what one does according to such a conscience will be good, but in the sense that in not following it he will sin.... A correct conscience and a false conscience bind in different ways. The correct conscience binds absolutely and for an intrinsic reason; the false binds in a qualified way and for an extrinsic reason.[74]

The erroneous conscience does indeed bind, not because it is correct but because the judgment of *conscientia* is all a person can go by in a decisive moment. Nevertheless, the erroneous conscience will eventually be identified as such because it depends upon the logical priority of the correct conscience, which applies the principles of *synderesis* rightly. From the agent's perspective it is possible to discover whether or not one has acted from an erroneous conscience through instruction, counsel, or self-examination by way of a subsequent judgment of *conscientia*, either in the form of a moral self-critique that elicits regret and remorse in the case of a formerly erroneous conscience or in the form of a simple retrospective affirmation that one's true and therefore good conscience has indeed also been right. Because the *habitus* of *synderesis* is innate, the first moral principles are ever-present; therefore the concrete possibility of self-correction always obtains. Thus while the erroneous conscience indeed binds, it does not automatically excuse. Aquinas explains:

If ... reason or conscience should err voluntarily, either directly or because of negligence, being in error about something one is held to know, then such error does not prevent the will which is in accord with erring reason or conscience from being evil.... Similarly, supposing error of reason or conscience which proceeds from a non-excusing ignorance, evil in the will necessarily follows. However, such a man is not *perplexus*, because he can correct his error, since his ignorance is both vincible and voluntary.[75]

---

74. Aquinas, *De veritate*, q. 17, a. 4, co. (*Truth*, 2:331–32); see also *ST* I-II, q. 19, a. 5, co. Aquinas holds that the correct conscience binds absolutely and for an intrinsic reason: because a judgment of *conscientia* that is practically true is necessarily also right.

75. *ST* I-II, q. 19, a. 6, co. and ad 3 (McInerny's translation; McInerny, "Object," 99–100). To be *perplexus* is to suffer from the contingent deficiency of circumstantial inculpable ignorance. See the following section, entitled "Invincible Ignorance," in this chapter.

Culpable erroneous conscience is caused either by negligence (lack of due solicitude),[76] which makes it indirectly voluntary, or by willful ignorance, which makes it directly voluntary.[77] In his *Commentary on the Sentences*, the young Aquinas offers a pithy summary of this complex matter: to follow one's erring conscience means to be unable to avoid sinning (*peccatum non evaditur*), but to act against one's conscience means to incur sin directly (*peccatum incurritur*).[78] The person who acts against the antecedent judgment of conscience always sins, because the only way the *synderistic* truth-indicator can be applied is by way of a judgment of antecedent conscience. A person is therefore always culpable for turning intentionally against such a judgment, because doing so means that one cuts oneself off from the very possibility of following moral truth. To follow one's erring conscience means to do what seems subjectively right but is objectively wrong. McInerny aptly summarizes: "An erroneous conscience is an instance of ignorance, of not knowing the correct assessment of a proposed course of action. If the ignorance in which one acts is voluntary, then it does not excuse.... It may be indirectly voluntary if it is a matter of negligence, of one not putting his mind to know what he is held to know."[79] Hence, in order to achieve moral rectitude, simply following one's subjective conscience does not suffice. Rather, moral rectitude requires that one strive to have a right conscience, which entails study, seeking counsel, acceptance of proper authority, and the regular examination of conscience (that is, permitting, seeking, and encouraging the subsequent judgments of *conscientia*).

In light of humans' supernatural destiny, these prerequisites and their goal, moral rectitude, while indispensable, are radically insufficient.[80] The faithful in a state of grace will rely heavily on the infused virtue of prudence—especially on the related infused virtue of *eubulia* (εὐβουλία),[81] which disposes a person to seek good counsel in human conduct and to accept the counsel when given, and on the infused gift of counsel that will

76. See *ST* II-II, q. 54.

77. See *ST* I-II, qq. 54 and 76.

78. Aquinas, *In II Sent.*, d. 39, q. 3, a. 3. See also his later *Quaestiones quodlibetales*, ed. Raymund M. Spiazzi, OP (Rome: Marietti, 1949), III, q. 12, a. 2, ad 2 (66).

79. McInerny, "Object," 99.

80. *ST* I-II, q. 1, a. 8, and q. 3, a. 8.

81. *ST* II-II, q. 51, aa. 1 and 2.

allow them to immerse themselves more deeply in the church's teaching on faith and morals and to be directed as though counseled by God.[82] Aquinas reminds his readers that to be "counseled by God as to what [one] ought to do in matters necessary for salvation is common to all holy persons."[83]

Invincible Ignorance

Finally, a brief word is apposite on the borderline case of a conscience afflicted by invincible ignorance. Vatican II's *Gaudium et Spes* states that "conscience frequently errs from invincible ignorance without losing its dignity."[84] This is, of course, true: even a conscience that errs due to invincible ignorance carries the dignity of conscience. Yet in order to understand correctly the teaching of *Gaudium et Spes*, it is crucial to keep in mind that this document emphasizes explicitly that the dignity of conscience consists in the very obedience to the law written by God in the human heart. Drawing upon this principle in his 1993 encyclical letter, *Veritatis Splendor*, John Paul II concludes: "It is always from the truth that the dignity of conscience derives."[85] Hence the erroneous conscience, due to invincible ignorance, derives its dignity from its infallible theonomic root, from the first principle and precept of *synderesis*, and ulti-

---

82. *ST* II-II, q. 52.

83. *ST* II-II, q. 52, a. 1, ad 2.

84. "In the depths of his conscience, man detects a law which he does not impose upon himself, but which holds him to obedience. Always summoning him to love good and avoid evil, the voice of conscience when necessary speaks to his heart: do this, shun that. For man has in his heart a law written by God; to obey it is the very dignity of man; according to it he will be judged. (Cf. *Rom.* 2:15–16.) Conscience is the most secret core and sanctuary of a man. There he is alone with God, Whose voice echoes in his depths. (Cf. Pius XII, *Radio address on the correct formation of a Christian conscience in the young*, March 23, 1952: *AAS* [1952], p. 271.) In a wonderful manner conscience reveals that law which is fulfilled by love of God and neighbor. (Cf. *Matt.* 22:37–40; *Gal.* 5:14.) In fidelity to conscience, Christians are joined with the rest of men in the search for truth, and for the genuine solution to the numerous problems which arise in the life of individuals from social relationships. Hence the more right conscience holds sway, the more persons and groups turn aside from blind choice and strive to be guided by the objective norms of morality. Conscience frequently errs from invincible ignorance without losing its dignity. *The same cannot be said for a man who cares but little for truth and goodness, or for a conscience which by degrees grows practically sightless as a result of habitual sin.*" Vatican Council II, *Gaudium et Spes*, December 7, 1965, no. 16 (emphasis added); available at www.vatican.va.

85. John Paul II, *Veritatis Splendor*, par. 63.

mately from the divine origin of the infallible and incorruptible habitual light that makes possible the judgments of *conscientia*. The dignity of conscience cannot be grounded in the judgments of *conscientia* themselves, whether correct or erroneous.[86] Nor is the dignity of conscience derived from some alleged transcendental experience of freedom and responsibility that would surpass and possibly even replace *synderesis*.[87]

Furthermore, invincible ignorance cannot be a state of ongoing moral existence but rather denotes an extraordinary temporary phenomenon (though one that can last for a considerable amount of time) arising from a unique constellation of subjective obstacles, none of which, however, are in principle insurmountable. In other words, invincible ignorance can never be a proper attribute of theonomic conscience in itself; it can be only an accidental attribute denoting a contingent deficiency that one might call circumstantial ignorance or perplexity (*perplexitas*).[88] The state of moral perplexity—seeing sin on both sides, that of commission and that of omission—can never be unconditional. Rather, it always pertains to the unavoidability of sin under certain conditions and denotes "an instance of ignorance, of not knowing the correct assessment of a proposed course of action."[89]

86. This dignity is absent from the counterfeit of conscience to which *Gaudium et Spes* obliquely refers at the very end of the passage cited just above in note 84 (no. 16).

87. See appendix 5 of this chapter for a brief discussion of Rahner's influential construal of such a position.

88. Invincible ignorance in its maximum state occurs, according to Aquinas, only in those who, due to profound mental or psychological impediments, are not responsible for their actions (*Quodlibet* III, q. 12, a. 2, ad 2). McInerny rightly concludes that "an act performed in invincible ignorance—an ignorance for which one can in no way be held accountable—would fail to qualify as a human act" (McInerny, "Object," 100). McInerny's point is not evaluative (as if a person "acting" in such a way would offer a "subhuman" performance). Rather, his point is conceptual. A genuinely human act is essentially intelligible and voluntary and therefore always entails at least minimal accountability. Absolute ignorance would entail the absence of all intelligibility, in which case such an act would not qualify as a human act. Aquinas puts the matter tersely in *ST* I-II, q. 1, a. 1, co.: "Those acts alone are properly called human [*actiones humanae*] which are of his own deliberate willing [*ex voluntate deliberata*]. Others that may be attributed to him may be called 'acts of man' [*hominis actiones*], but not 'human acts' [*actiones humanae*], since they are not his precisely as a human being [*non sint hominis inquantum est homo*]" (trans. Thomas Gilby, OP). On the intelligible act as the most basic unit of human action, see the instructive essay by Alasdair MacIntyre, "The Intelligibility of Action," in *Rationality, Relativism, and Human Sciences*, ed. J. Margolis, M. Krausz, and R. M. Burian (Dordrecht: Nijhoff, 1986), 63–80.

89. McInerny, "Object," 99. For a discussion that is as learned as it is lucid on conditional

The Erroneous Conscience and the Counterfeit of Conscience

How does it differ from the counterfeit of conscience? First, from the objective perspective afforded by *sacra doctrina* and the moral science proceeding from it, the reality of an erroneous conscience presupposes an objective moral order and reliable knowledge of it. If we assume a consistent moral subjectivism and a concomitant rule of self-will, an erroneous conscience would be an utterly meaningless notion. The subjectivist counterfeit of conscience, by contrast, posits its own dictates of self-will; it is, by definition, infallible. Because it constitutes the law of its own dictates, there is nothing in light of which the counterfeit of conscience can possibly err. Johann Gottlieb Fichte's subjective idealism offers probably the most consistent but also most problematic account of the inherently infallible conscience.[90]

In *Veritatis Splendor*, John Paul II penned one of the most astute recent descriptions of the subjectivist nature of the counterfeit of conscience:

The individual conscience is accorded the status of a supreme tribunal of moral judgment which hands down categorical and infallible decisions about good and evil. To the affirmation that one has a duty to follow one's conscience is unduly added the affirmation that one's moral judgment is true merely by the fact that it has its origin in the conscience. But in this way the inescapable claims of truth disappear, yielding their place to a criterion of sincerity, authenticity and "being at peace with oneself," so much so that some have come to adopt a radically subjectivistic conception of moral judgment.[91]

Usage of the phrase "primacy of conscience" by ethicists and moral theologians in recent years has been a strong indication that the point of reference may not be conscience truly so-called—which would call for the primacy of the "rule of ethical truth"[92] implemented by the virtue of pru-

---

perplexity, see Richard Schenk, OP, "*Perplexus supposito quodam*: Notizen zu einem vergessenen Schlüsselbegriff thomanischer Gewissenslehre," *Recherches de théologie ancienne et médiévale* 57 (1990): 62–95.

90. See appendix 4 of this chapter for a brief discussion of Fichte's view of conscience.

91. John Paul II, *Veritatis Splendor*, par. 32.

92. *Diff.*, ii., 246.

dence—but may instead be the counterfeit of conscience, sovereign self-determination authenticated by emotive self-affirmation.

Second, from the moral agent's perspective, the very possibility of an erroneous conscience entails an antecedent and a consequent personal duty. The antecedent duty is to avoid ignorance and imprudence. Formulated positively, the antecedent duty is always to seek counsel, to have one's conscience formed by those one regards as wiser and better informed than oneself, and, above all, to avail oneself of instruction by and guidance from those whose specific vocation it is to offer instruction regarding the natural and the revealed law. The consequent duty is to avoid negligence and indifference by means of a regular examination of conscience, a sincere review of past judgments, and repentance for acts based on an erroneous conscience. For the Catholic faithful, the primary guide of conscience must be the church's moral instruction undertaken by those appointed to teach authoritatively about faith and morals, namely, the bishops in communion with the pope in respective dioceses and the pope through his ordinary magisterium with respect to the universal church.

Third, in light of Aquinas's doctrine of conscience, it is clear that the counterfeit of conscience is a result of willful ignorance, or at least of negligence and thoughtlessness. In the worst case, the counterfeit is an intentional, self-conscious flight from conscience truly so-called when a person acts in direct opposition to the judgments of a correct conscience by positing decisions of the self-will as authoritative. This does not mean that the counterfeit of conscience is able to extinguish *synderesis* entirely. As Aquinas explains in *De veritate*, *synderesis* cannot be extinguished in its root, as an innate *habitus*, "for this light belongs to the nature of the soul, since by reason of this the soul is intellectual."[93] Yet in regard to actualizing the *habitus*, *synderesis* can be interfered with completely and can, indeed, be deflected toward the contrary. *Synderesis* is interfered with completely "in those who do not have the use of free choice or of reason because of an impediment due to an injury to the bodily organs from which our reason needs help."[94] It is deflected by the counterfeit of conscience: "The act of synderesis is deflected toward the contrary of

93. Aquinas, *De veritate*, q. 16, a. 3, co. (*Truth*, 2:312).
94. Ibid. A famous case that illustrates Aquinas's point is that of Phineas Gage. During a work

synderesis. It is impossible for the universal judgment of synderesis to be destroyed in this way, but in a particular activity it is destroyed whenever one sins in choice. For the force of concupiscence, or of another passion, so absorbs reason that in choice the universal judgment of synderesis is not applied to the particular act."[95]

It is here that Aquinas points to what we might call the dark secret of the counterfeit of conscience. What looks to the person fleeing theonomic conscience like the sovereign decisions of self-determination is rather the product of a profound self-deception. The flight from theonomic conscience and thereby from the "habitual light" of *synderesis* that informs reason actually makes the moral agent subject to the power of the passions and the variegated desires of the will to which they give rise. The postmodern experience of the self as a conscious bundle of passions and desires fits with Aquinas's analysis of sin. Because *synderesis* cannot be destroyed, but only fled from or suppressed, the counterfeit of conscience remains inherently unstable, a self-deception that must be willfully maintained, directly or—more frequently—indirectly. For all the decisions that the counterfeit sovereignly posits remain exposed to the "habitual light" that the first principle and the first precept of *synderesis* shed on the agent's reason. The counterfeit is therefore inherently unable to afford the peace that is characteristic of a conscience, truly so-called, that is both subjectively true and therefore good and objectively correct.[96]

Aquinas and Newman—Complementary Accounts of Conscience?

It will by now have become clear that, according to the argument of this opening chapter, Newman's and Aquinas's accounts of conscience complement each other in such a way that Newman had good reasons to turn in his *Letter* to the *doctor communis*. It also seems quite obvious that New-

---

accident, this nineteenth-century workman had a tamping iron driven through his head. Gage survived the accident, but his personality was altered for the worse.

95. Ibid.

96. But even for a conscience truly so called such a peace remains a fragile reality unless it is one of the fruits of the Spirit (*ST* I-II, q. 70) arising from the gifts of wisdom and counsel (*ST* II-II, qq. 45 and 52).

man's reasons for drawing upon the Thomist doctrine of conscience were of a substantive theological and conceptual nature. They did not reflect, as some might suppose, a merely tactical show of ecclesiastical *obsequium* to a papal act of Catholic philosophical renewal, retrospectively called neo-Scholasticism. Newman's *Letter* appeared five years before Leo XIII promulgated his famous encyclical letter *Aeterni Patris* (August 4, 1879), in which he called all Catholic teachers of philosophy and theology to return to the sound philosophical principles of Thomas Aquinas. But was Newman's turn to Aquinas a defensible move? Are Newman and Aquinas's respective philosophical approaches to the theological task even compatible?

Two differences between Newman and Aquinas must be briefly addressed. The first is only an apparent difference, the second a surmountable difference. First, the seeming difference of incompatible approaches: throughout his long life as preacher and writer, Newman advanced an astute phenomenological (*avant la lettre*) account of conscience from the experiential perspective of one whose own conscience was exceedingly acute, well-formed, and undergirded by the Christian faith. In short, Newman analyzed conscience primarily from the agent's first-person perspective. Aquinas, by contrast, undertook his analysis of the principles and operation of conscience from the third-person perspective characteristic of an inquiry into causes and principles. In his excellent *Introduction to Phenomenology*, Robert Sokolowski has suggested that phenomenology does not contradict but rather complements Thomism.[97] While Newman was, of course, no phenomenologist in the proper sense of the term, his arguably proto-phenomenological approach to conscience and Aquinas's theory of conscience, developed within the framework of a sapiential moral theology, enhance rather than undermine each other. Hence, in the *Letter*, where Newman pursues an objective exposition and defense of the Catholic doctrine of conscience, he turns to Aquinas's doctrine for good reason.

Second, there is a real but surmountable difference between Newman and Aquinas's precise accounts of the theonomic root of conscience. A

---

97. Robert Sokolowski, *Introduction to Phenomenology* (Cambridge: Cambridge University Press, 2000), 207.

certain tension, if not conflict, exists between their respective concepts. In some passages Newman seems to understand the theonomic root of conscience to be a divine address or illumination, one that is direct and interior. Aquinas teaches that it is an innate *habitus* of the first principle and precept of practical reason. This tension can be resolved if one understands Newman's characterization of conscience as the "aboriginal Vicar of Christ"[98] as a *theological* identification of the root of conscience, and his characterization of conscience as "the echo of a voice"[99] as a phenomenological description of how this root of conscience is present in human reason. The metaphor of the "echo" reflects accurately the empirical evidence of conscience's theonomic root and comports with the notion of *synderesis* as an innate *habitus*. An echo suggests an indirect elocution. In order to understand clearly what an echo conveys, one must listen attentively. Likewise, one must intentionally realize the "voice" of conscience in one's mind through judgments in order to understand how it pertains to what is to be done here and now. In Aquinas's terms, the natural *habitus* of *synderesis* is partially an act insofar as it is a distinct determination of a potency. Yet only when the *habitus* is fully reduced to a particular judgment about what is to be done here and now is *conscientia* realized. The "echo" and *synderesis* refer to the selfsame reality—the rational creature's participation in the eternal law. And for both Aquinas and Newman, this participation pertains primarily to the intellect. Law—eternal, natural, revealed—is for neither of them an external authority because it informs reason, which is the rule and measure of human acts. Newman turns to Aquinas precisely in order to affirm this fundamental point: God, Newman says, "implanted this Law, which is Himself, in the intelligence of all His rational creatures."[100]

Last but not least, Aquinas and Newman share a philosophical point of reference, namely, Aristotle and, more specifically, his analysis of the virtue of prudence (*phronēsis*) in *Nicomachean Ethics* VI.[101] While both

---

98. *Diff.*, ii., 248.

99. Newman, *An Essay in Aid of a Grammar of Assent* (London: Longmans, Green, and Co., 1903) [hereafter "*G.A.*"], 107.

100. *Diff.*, ii., 246. See *ST* I-II, q. 90, aa. 1–4.

101. Both Aquinas and Newman had a deep familiarity with the *Nicomachean Ethics*. Aquinas, of course, wrote an extensive commentary on it, and Newman taught Aristotle's ethics at Oriel

Aquinas and Newman correlate conscience with the virtue of prudence, the ways in which they relate various aspects of the operation of conscience to prudence reflect their different but complementary approaches. Taking the objective approach of sapiential moral theology, Aquinas stresses the function of the first principles of practical reason in human action: "*Synderesis* is said to be the law of our mind [*lex intellectus nostri*], because it is a [*habitus*] containing the precepts of the natural law, which are the first principles of human actions."[102] In the practical order,

College, Oxford, where he was a fellow from 1822 to 1845. For his classes Newman used the Greek/ Latin edition, *Aristotelis Ethicorum Nicomacheorum libri decem*, ed. William Wilkinson, 4th ed. (Oxford: Clarendon, 1818). Newman's personal copy of this edition is housed in the archives at the Birmingham Oratory. Late in his life, during the Fairbairn Controversy (see note 105 below), Newman consulted the translation by Drummond Percy Chase (1820–1902), who mentions Newman in the foreword to his *The Nicomachean Ethics of Aristotle: A New Translation, Mainly from the Text of Bekker. With Explanatory Notes* (Oxford: William Graham, 1847). Newman's encounter with the thought of Aristotle was, however, not limited to the *Nicomachean Ethics*. As an undergraduate he studied closely Aristotle's *Rhetoric* and *Poetics*, and a letter of December 13, 1820, written to his aunt suggests that he also studied Aristotle's *Metaphysics* on his own. His Aristotelian studies came to fruition in an article for *The Christian Observer* of March 6, 1821, "On the Analogous Nature of the Difficulties in Mathematics and those of Religion." For a detailed account, see Franz Michel Willam, "Die philosophischen Grundpositionen Newmans," *Newman-Studien: Dritte Folge*, ed. Heinrich Fries and Werner Becker (Nürnberg: Glock und Lutz, 1957), 111–56, esp. 135–48, and A. Dwight Culler, *The Imperial Intellect: A Study of Cardinal Newman's Educational Ideal* (New Haven, Conn.: Yale University Press, 1955), 1–22. During the early years of his Oriel College fellowship, Newman's intellectual mentor was Richard Whately (1787–1863), another Oriel fellow who drew Newman into his project of reviving Aristotelian logic (*Elements of Logic*, 1826) and Aristotelian reasoning in practical and public matters (*Elements of Rhetoric*, 1828). In 1828, Newman published in the *London Review* a substantive essay entitled "Poetry with Reference to Aristotle's Poetics," a publication he judged sufficiently worthy to warrant inclusion in the first volume of his *Essays Critical and Historical*. Many years later, in his *The Idea of a University Defined and Illustrated* (London: Longmans, Green, and Co., 1907) [hereafter "*Idea*"], he states: "Do not suppose, that in thus appealing to the ancients, I am throwing back the world two thousand years, and fettering Philosophy with the reasonings of paganism. While the world lasts, will Aristotle's doctrine on these matters last, for he is the oracle of nature and of truth. While we are men, we cannot help, to a great extent, being Aristotelians, for the great Master does but analyze the thoughts, feelings, views, and opinions of human kind. He has told us the meaning of our own words and ideas, before we were born. In many subject-matters, to think correctly, is to think like Aristotle; and we are his disciples whether we will or no, though we may not know it" (109–10). For an instructive study of Whately's work in Aristotelian logic, rhetoric, and metaphysics; of Newman's involvement in preparing Whately's publications; and of Whately's impact on Newman's thought, see Franz Michel Willam, *Aristotelische Erkenntnislehre bei Whately und Newman und ihre Bezüge zur Gegenwart* (Freiburg: Herder, 1960).

102. *ST* I-II, q. 94, a. 1, ad 2. The phrase *lex intellectus nostri* is an oblique reference to John of Damascus, *De fide orthodoxa* IV.22, to which Aquinas makes an explicit reference in *ST* I, q. 79, a. 13, co.

the first principle, *synderesis*, appoints the end to moral virtues to which they consequently tend. The virtue of prudence determines the means to the end and is itself moved to the end by *synderesis* as a final cause.[103] Consistent with the comprehensive theological view of sapiential moral theology, the principal cardinal virtue of prudence and the practical order to which it relates are embedded in an encompassing teleological order established by the eternal law. As stated above, *synderesis* is the root of the rational creature's participation in this encompassing teleological order. As an innate *habitus*, *synderesis* appoints the end; and prudence, moved by *synderesis*, determines the means by which to reach the end. In this way Aquinas integrates Aristotle's profound inquiry into *phronēsis* into the much wider and elevated horizon of sapiential moral theology without diminishing the integrity of Aristotle's acute analysis.

Consider Aquinas's use of *Nicomachean Ethics* VI in answering the question of whether prudence appoints the end to the moral virtues: "The Philosopher says (*Ethics* vi, 12) that 'moral virtue ensures the rectitude of the intention of the end, while prudence ensures the rectitude of the means.' Therefore it does not belong to prudence to appoint the end to moral virtues, but only to regulate the means."[104] Implied in Aquinas's answer are two points: first, that *synderesis* enables the rectitude of the intention of the end. Precisely because *synderesis* is a natural *habitus* and not an innate illumination of the intellect with certain ideas, and because the intellect provides the will with the formality or character of goodness (*bonum apprehensum*), the first principle and the first precept pertain primordially to the intellect as well as to the will. Second, he implies that this *habitus* of *synderesis* must be actualized in the judgment of *conscientia* to enable prudence to regulate and command the means to that end.

Newman, on the other hand, taking an experiential and phenomenological approach, emphasizes a faculty that he calls "moral sense," which has "truth for its direct object." Newman understands this to be one spe-

---

103. "Natural reason known by the name of *synderesis* appoints the end to moral virtues.... The end concerns the moral virtues, not as though they appointed the end, but because they tend to the end which is appointed by natural reason. In this they are helped by prudence, which prepares the way for them, by disposing the means.... Yet *synderesis* moves prudence, just as the understanding of principles moves science" (*ST* II-II, q. 47, a. 6, ad 1 and 3).

104. *ST* II-II, q. 47, a. 6, s.c.

cific aspect of the faculty that Aristotle calls *noûs*.[105] For Aristotle, *noûs* (in Latin, *intellectus*) comprises the basic capacity for immediate perception of particular cases as well as the virtue of the intellect that apprehends indemonstrable first principles by process of induction.[106] In order to account for the *de facto* operation of the judgment of conscience, Newman's exclusive concern is the former aspect of *noûs*, the immediate perception of the particular and the relevant minor premise of the practical syllogism.[107] (Lest his quite specific line of argumentation be burdened

105. Newman, *Stray Essays on Controversial Points, Variously Illustrated by Cardinal Newman* (privately printed, 1890), 97–98; see also *The Theological Papers of John Henry Newman on Faith and Certainty*, ed. Hugo M. de Achaval and J. Derek Holmes (Oxford: Clarendon Press, 1976), 152–53. For an instructive discussion of Newman's take on *noûs* in his response to the Congregationalist minister and academic Andrew Martin Fairbairn's accusation of philosophical skepticism—the topic of Newman's essay "Revelation in Its Relation to Faith"—and for an interpretation of Newman on *noûs* that corroborates my own, see Andrew Meszaros, "Newman and First Principles: The Noetic Dimension of the Illative Sense," *Heythrop Journal* 59 (2018): 770–82. At the center of Newman's response to Fairbairn's charge stands his appeal to Aristotle's understanding of *noûs* and of the noetic faculty: "There is a faculty in the mind which acts as a complement to reasoning, and as having truth for its direct object thereby secures its use for rightful purposes. This faculty, viewed in its relation to religion, is, as I have before said, the moral sense; but it has a wider subject-matter than religion, and a more comprehensive office and scope, as being 'the apprehension of first principles,' and Aristotle has taught me to call it *noûs*, or the *noetic* faculty" (*Theological Papers*, 152–53). Newman seems to have in mind the passage from Aristotle, *Nicomachean Ethics*, trans. H. Rackham (London: W. Heinemann, 1926), VI.10–11 (1143a35–b5): "Intelligence [*noûs*] apprehends the ultimates in both aspects—since ultimates as well as primary definitions are grasped by Intelligence [*noûs*] and not reached by reasoning: in demonstrations, Intelligence [*noûs*] apprehends the immutable and primary definitions; in practical inferences, it apprehends the ultimate and contingent fact, and the minor premise, since these are the first principles from which the end is inferred, as general rules are based on particular cases; hence we must have perception of particulars, and this immediate perception is Intelligence [*noûs*]. This is why it is thought that these qualities are a natural gift, and that a man is considerate, understanding and intelligent by nature, though no one is a wise man by nature." For Aquinas's discussion of the relevant passages in *Nicomachean Ethics* VI, see his *Sententia Libri Ethicorum* VI, lect. IX (Marietti, nos. 1247–49), in the translation by C. J. Litzinger, OP: *Commentary on Artistotle's Nicomachean Ethics* (South Bend, Ind.: Dumb Ox Books, 1993), 393–94.

106. Aristotle, *Nicomachean Ethics* VI.6 (1141a5–8). For Aquinas's discussion of the relevant passages of the *Nicomachean Ethics*, see his *Sententia Libri Ethicorum* VI, lect. V (Marietti, nos. 1175–83) and VII (Marietti, nos. 1214–16), 373–75 and 384–85.

107. To clarify what I mean by *particular* and *minor premise*, I simplify and update Aristotle's example of a practical syllogism from his *De motu animalium* VII (701a17–20). Major premise: I need covering (covering satisfies a need). Minor premise: a raincoat is a covering. The conclusion of the practical syllogism is an action: I have to buy a raincoat. This specific practical syllogism is triggered by the "particular," the raincoat that I perceive and immediately recognize while hurrying by a shop window as rain begins to pour down.

with unnecessary theoretical baggage, Newman brackets the second aspect of *noûs*.) This intuitive element of prudence, that is, the immediate apprehension of the contingent particular, together with the relevant minor premise of the practical syllogism, is indispensable for the judgment of *conscientia*. We must have some immediate apprehension of the contingent particular act in order meaningfully to apply the first principle ("good is that which all things seek after") and the first precept ("good is to be done and pursued, and evil is to be avoided") of *synderesis*.

For the concrete judgment of *conscientia*, both aspects of *noûs* are absolutely indispensable; but only in the context of consideration, counsel, and the examination of one's conscience do the secondary precepts of *synderesis* become explicit in the agent's perspective. And to avoid ignorance of "secondary and more detailed precepts," the formation of conscience is necessary, that is, the expansion of the pool of secondary, more detailed precepts that are held by the innate *habitus* of *synderesis*.[108] This *habitus* can be expanded and strengthened by an increasing number of specifications of the first precept that we acquire by way of instruction, counsel, and reflection.

Conscience and the Magisterium

The proper operation of conscience requires regular attention to two essentially vincible imperfections and their necessary repair: ignorance (*ignorantia*) and thoughtlessness (*inconsideratio*). We avoid or correct ignorance through the ongoing formation of conscience, and we prevent or curb thoughtlessness through the regular examination of conscience. Yet formation and examination require concrete social contexts of accountability, distinct practices of formation and examination, and a proper authority equipped to teach and guide the examination of conscience—in short, magisterial competency and authority. In the absence of these three conditions, the formation of conscience stands in danger of an unintended acculturation into the counterfeit of conscience, and the examination of conscience risks becoming a mere exercise in self-affirmation and self-exculpation.

108. *ST* I-II, q. 94, a. 6, co.

To many a contemporary Catholic, in Europe as well as in North America, any strong notion of magisterial competency—let alone authority and, especially, infallibility—in matters of faith and morals is very hard, if not impossible, to accept.[109] For such a notion seems to contradict the very dignity and freedom of conscience. Newman is keenly aware of the danger that Catholics living under the present conditions of modern subjectivity will capitulate to the counterfeit of conscience. This danger of capitulating to, or willingly embracing, the counterfeit of conscience only increases when Catholics find themselves in a democratic regime where the "nation" regards itself as "church" and where "democracy" becomes a hegemonic program of immanent salvation advanced by an ideology of sovereign secularism, a program in which the optimum degree of progress coincides with the maximization of "democracy" culminating in a secularist global "democratization." In such a political environment, the counterfeit of conscience quickly evolves into a publicly accepted prejudice, supported and advanced by the government and legally codified and enforced. Eventually, the willing embrace of the collective prejudice by every citizen will be regarded as an indispensable entailment of loyal citizenship and as the proper expression of national identity. When Catholics instead insist on following the judgments of a well-formed theonomic conscience, the political and ideological acolytes of a secularist democratic regime will predictably conclude—to use Gladstone's words—that these Catholics can no longer "be trusted to participate loyally and thoughtfully in the nation's civic life."[110]

To the acolytes of such a regime—not to mention those Catholics thoroughly acculturated to the seductive material comforts and consolations these usually affluent societies afford—Newman's remarks on how a well-formed conscience (truly so called) should regard papal instruction must sound alarming and indeed extravagant. Even in those matters that fall under the pope's ordinary magisterium and to which the infallibility of the pope's extraordinary magisterium does not pertain, Newman presses upon his Catholic audience an uncomfortable but crucial point:

109. For an astute treatment of this urgent topic, see Kevin E. O'Reilly, OP, "The Church as the Defender of Conscience in Our Age," *Nova et Vetera* (English edition) 12, no. 1 (2014): 193–215.
110. Newman, *Conscience, Consensus, and the Development of Doctrine*, 432.

When [conscience truly so called] has the right of opposing the supreme, though not infallible Authority of the Pope, it must be something more than that miserable counterfeit which, as I have said above, now goes by the name. If in a particular case it is to be taken as a sacred and sovereign monitor, its dictate, in order to prevail against the voice of the Pope, must follow upon serious thought, prayer, and all available means of arriving at a right judgment on the matter in question. And further, obedience to the Pope is what is called "in possession"; that is, the *onus probandi* of establishing a case against him lies, as in all cases of exception, on the side of conscience. Unless a man is able to say to himself, as in the Presence of God, that he must not, and dare not, act upon the Papal injunction, he is bound to obey it, and would commit a great sin in disobeying it. *Primā facie* it is his bounden duty, even from a sentiment of loyalty, to believe the Pope right and to act accordingly. He must vanquish that mean, ungenerous, selfish, vulgar spirit of his nature, which, at the very first rumour of a command, places itself in opposition to the Superior who gives it, asks itself whether he is not exceeding his right, and rejoices, in a moral and practical matter, to commence with skepticism.[111]

What then—according to Newman now rightly understood—is the proper relationship between theonomic conscience and the magisterium of the Catholic church? It is by now sufficiently obvious that Newman recognizes two very different vicars of the one Christ who is the eternal Word of God through which the world was created, who became incarnate, who was "handed over to death for our sins, and raised to life for our justification" (Rom 4:25).

The first vicar of Christ is the spark of conscience, *synderesis*, the origin of the light that illumines reason by providing the natural *habitus* of the first principles of moral truth. Aquinas rather tersely describes the function of *synderesis* as "inciting to good and murmuring at evil."[112] Newman points to the same reality when he says, with characteristic rhetorical force, that "Conscience is the aboriginal Vicar of Christ, a prophet in its informations, a monarch in its peremptoriness, a priest in its blessings and anathemas."[113] As discussed above, Newman offers here a theological identification of the theonomic root of conscience. Indeed, there

111. *Diff.*, ii., 257–58.
112. *ST* I, q. 79, a. 12, co.
113. *Diff.*, ii., 248–49.

is an explicit Christological allusion to the threefold office of Christ as prophet, king, and priest in Newman's account. This theological identification (i.e., aboriginal vicar) should not, however, be confused with the phenomenological description of the theonomic root of conscience as it is evinced in human reason (i.e., the echo of a voice).

The second vicar of Christ is, obviously, the historical vicar, the pope. Either directly through his ordinary magisterium or indirectly through the universal magisterium of the bishops in union with him, the pope informs, educates, instructs, and sharpens conscience. Newman rightly emphasizes an obvious but seldom acknowledged truth. The pope's instruction presupposes the reality of conscience, without which the pope's instruction could not be properly received. Newman drives the point home:

Did the Pope speak against Conscience in the true sense of the word, he would commit a suicidal act. He would be cutting the ground from under his feet. His very mission is to proclaim the moral law, and to protect and strengthen that "Light which enlighteneth every man that cometh into the world." On the law of conscience and its sacredness are founded both his authority in theory and his power in fact.... It is by the *universal sense of right and wrong*, the consciousness of transgression, the pangs of guilt, and the dread of retribution, as *first principles* deeply lodged in the hearts of men, it is thus and only thus, that [the Pope] has gained his footing in the world and achieved his success.[114]

At the same time, conscience stands in need of papal authority to protect it from being muted or repressed by its counterfeit, the sovereign rule of self-will. Newman states:

It is [the pope's] claim to come from the Divine Lawgiver, in order to elicit, protect, and enforce those truths which the Lawgiver has sown in our very nature, it is this and this only that is the explanation of his length of life more than antediluvian. The championship of the Moral Law and of conscience is [the pope's] *raison d'être*. The fact of his mission is the answer to the complaints of those who feel the insufficiency of the natural light; and the insufficiency of that light is the justification of his mission.[115]

---

114. *Diff.*, ii., 252–53 (emphasis added).
115. *Diff.*, ii., 253.

While recognizing that *synderesis* will ultimately adduce the irrefutable interior evidence of its existence, Newman is keenly aware of how easily this echo of the divine voice can be ignored, muted, or distorted such that conscience begins to err in its judgments:

The sense of right and wrong, which is the first element in religion, is so delicate, so fitful, so easily puzzled, obscured, perverted, so subtle in its argumentative methods, so impressible by education, so biased by pride and passion, so unsteady in its course that, in the struggle for existence amid the various exercises and triumphs of the human intellect, this sense is at once the highest of all teachers, yet the least luminous; and the Church, the Pope, the Hierarchy are, in the Divine purpose, the supply of an urgent demand.[116]

Newman's view is consonant with Aquinas's teaching. If the secondary precepts of the natural law are "blotted out from the human heart," the sense of right and wrong can be seriously obscured or perverted. In the *Summa theologiae*, Aquinas explicitly addresses the question "Whether the Law of Nature Can Be Abolished from the Heart of Man?" His response is unequivocal:

There belong to the natural law, first, certain most general precepts, that are known to all; and secondly, certain secondary and more detailed precepts, which are, as it were, conclusions following closely from first principles. As to those general principles, the natural law, in the abstract, can nowise be blotted out from [human] hearts. But it is blotted out in the case of a particular action, in so far as reason is hindered from applying the general principle to a particular point of practice, on account of concupiscence or some other passion, as stated above [*ST* I-II, q. 77, a. 2]. But as to the other, i.e., the secondary precepts, the natural law can be blotted out from the human heart, either by evil persuasions, just as in speculative matters errors occur in respect of necessary conclusions; or by vicious customs and corrupt habits, as among some men, theft, and even unnatural vices, as the Apostle states [Rom 1], were not esteemed sinful.[117]

The church's mission through the universal magisterium of the bishops and especially through the ordinary magisterium of the pope is, first, to support and strengthen the divine spark of conscience, *synderesis*, by

116. *Diff.*, ii., 253–54.
117. *ST* I-II, q. 94, a. 6, co.

explicitly reaffirming the first principles of moral action; and, second, to form the conscience not only by making explicit the precepts of the natural law—the general as well as the more detailed secondary principles—but also by confirming and extending those precepts through catechesis of the divine law.[118]

And so it is indeed the case, as McInerny states, that "St. Thomas would ... agree with the order of precedence in Newman's toasts: first to conscience, then to the pope, since this means, God first, then the pope."[119] For Newman's sequence presupposes the theonomic constitution of conscience and not, as all too many have wrongly assumed, its counterfeit, the sovereign rule of self-will. Consider once more Newman's formulation, but remember that for Newman the notion of religion *per se* is virtually identical with the notion of theonomy, for religion is all about the knowledge of and obedience to the holy will of God: "If I am obliged to bring religion into after-dinner toasts ... I shall drink,—to the Pope, if you please,—still, to Conscience first, and to the Pope afterwards."[120]

---

118. Regarding the church's competence to interpret and apply the natural law, and thereby to instruct the theonomic conscience not only of Catholics but of all persons of good will, Pius XII declared, "The power of the Church is not bound by the limits of 'matters strictly religious,' as they say, but the whole matter of the natural law, its foundation, its interpretation, its application, so far as their moral aspects extend, are within the Church's power. For the keeping of the natural law, by God's appointment, has reference to the road by which man has to approach his supernatural end. But, on this road, the Church is man's guide and guardian in what concerns his supreme end." In *Acta Apostolicae Sedis* 46 (1954): 671–72, trans. J. R. Lerch and included as "Teaching Authority of the Church" in *New Catholic Encyclopedia* 13 (1967): 964.

119. McInerny, "Object," 106.

120. *Diff.*, ii., 261. On Newman's understanding of religion, consider his poignant statement in the second of his *Oxford University Sermons*, "The Influence of Natural and Revealed Religion Respectively": "It is obvious that Conscience is the essential principle and sanction of Religion in the mind. Conscience implies a relation between the soul and a something exterior, and that, moreover, superior to itself; a relation to an excellence which it does not possess, and to a tribunal over which it has no power. And since the more closely this inward monitor is respected and followed, the clearer, the more exalted, and the more varied its dictates become, and the standard of excellence is ever outstripping, while it guides, our obedience, a moral conviction is thus at length obtained of the unapproachable nature as well as the supreme authority of That, whatever it is, which is the object of the mind's contemplation. Here, then, at once, we have the elements of a religious system; for what is Religion but the system of relations existing between us and a Supreme Power, claiming our habitual obedience: 'the blessed and only Potentate, who only hath immortality, dwelling in light unapproachable, whom no man hath seen or can see'?" *Fifteen Sermons Preached before the University of Oxford between A.D. 1826 and 1843* (London: Longmans, Green, and Co., 1909), 18–19. Again, "the essence of all religion is authority and obedience" (Newman, *Dev.*, 86).

John Paul II affirms the sequence of conscience and magisterium as laid out by Newman:

The authority of the Church, when she pronounces on moral questions, in no way undermines the freedom of conscience of Christians. This is so not only because freedom of conscience is never freedom "from" the truth but always and only freedom "in" the truth, but also because the Magisterium does not bring to the Christian conscience truths which are extraneous to it; rather, it brings to light the truths which it ought already to possess, developing them from the starting point of the primordial act of faith. The Church puts herself always and only at the *service of conscience*, helping it to avoid being tossed to and fro by every wind of doctrine proposed by human deceit (cf. *Eph* 4:14), and helping it not to swerve from the truth about the good of man, but rather, especially in more difficult questions, to attain the truth with certainty and to abide in it.[121]

Because conscience truly so-called is theonomic in nature, the freedom of conscience can only be a freedom in the truth. Rather than being a negative freedom bent on safeguarding sovereign self-determination, freedom in the truth is a positive freedom that—enlightened by the spark of *synderesis*—is realized in seeking the due moral good. The formation of conscience by way of the magisterium serves and facilitates the realization of positive freedom.

Freedom of Conscience as Freedom in the Truth

The natural *habitus* of *synderesis* is an active potency, innate and determined, that requires activation by way of practical reason's concrete judgment (*conscientia*) and operative realization by way of prudence's order (*praeceptum*). The positive freedom characteristic of theonomic conscience always seeks its ongoing formation by way of counsel and instruction. Characteristic of theonomic conscience is the interior forum that gives rise to the inner dialogue of the human being with himself, an inner dialogue that is open—and indeed ordered—to the interior dialogue between the human person and God, who is not only the author of the law but also the triune one in whose image the human being is created and the

---

121. *Veritatis Splendor*, par. 64.

final end of the human being.[122] As Pinckaers observes, conscience truly so-called

makes judgments in the presence of God by listening to his sovereign voice ... [and] lets itself be judged by God and guided by his law through a fruitful, open, and intelligent obedience. One sign that helps us distinguish true from false conscience is certainly that true conscience always presents a challenge, like the steep and narrow way of the Gospel that stands in stark contrast to the broad and easy way that leads to eternal sorrow. At the same time, true conscience gives those who follow it a peace and joy that no external thing can trouble, while false conscience without fail provokes doubt and division, compromise and confusion.[123]

The counterfeit of conscience is indeed nothing but one particularly subtle and powerful instantiation of a false conscience—it is a false conscience in the very act of self-justification as good conscience. As Pinckaers rightly points out, a false conscience has distinctive characteristics, and so does the counterfeit of conscience. Whenever an appeal to the freedom of conscience functions as a conversation stopper—often an emotionally charged last resort that brings to an immediate halt any inquiry into the grounds for judgments made and actions taken—there is a strong indication that we are dealing with the counterfeit of conscience. This simulacrum camouflages the dictates of the sovereign self-determination, for which it can offer no reasons other than its own positing of a decision: theonomic conscience engenders judgments; the counterfeit of conscience posits decisions.[124] The counterfeit of conscience betrays itself in its eagerness to appeal rhetorically to the primacy of conscience in order to defend the sovereignty of one's self-determination from the challenges of the interior dialogue and from the probings of exterior moral interrogation.[125]

122. "The importance of this *interior dialog of man with himself* can never be adequately appreciated. But it is also a *dialog of man with God*, the author of the law, the primordial image and final end of man" (*Veritatis Splendor*, par. 58).

123. Pinckaers, *Morality: The Catholic View*, 57.

124. Decisionism in modern moral and legal philosophy rests on the assumption that neither God nor law (in the sense of natural law participating in the eternal law) exists. Differently put, there seems to obtain a direct correlation in philosophical ethics between the theoretical dismissal of theonomic conscience and the ascendency of decisionism.

125. The flight from theonomic conscience is therefore perfectly compatible with the surprisingly frequent rhetorical appeal in the public life of secularist democratic regimes to conscience—that is, of course, to the counterfeit of conscience.

The dialogue occurring in the interior forum of the human being is, however, a property of mature personhood. The witness of memory stimulated by *synderesis*, its prospective exhortation, and finally its retrospective evaluation (accusatory or excusatory) are essential aspects of this inner dialogue. Thanks to the stratagems of self-will, this dialogue can indeed be repressed or avoided but only at the cost of diminishing one's own personhood and of forgoing the positive freedom that is realized when the theonomic conscience is properly formed and heeded.[126]

What if the negative freedom that characterizes the counterfeit of conscience becomes dominant in a culture—by way of force, law, custom, or prejudice? The sovereign rule of self-will and the concomitant appeal to the counterfeit of conscience might even become concentrated in a political party or symbolically represented in a political leader. To those who grew up in the second half of the twentieth century, Nazism and Communism have taught an important lesson: deny the reality of theonomic conscience, discourage, ridicule, or even attempt to suppress its proper exercise, and the outcome is a system of moral and political barbarity. *Nota bene*: democratic regimes are not in themselves immune to this danger. If democratic regimes embrace as publicly normative a materialist or

126. Thoughtlessness, distraction, negligence, indifference, or subjection to strong passions (fear, lust, hatred) might be proximate causes for avoiding the interior forum and thus muting the inner dialogue. Such consistent muting of the interior dialogue amounts to a culpable self-debasement, a rejection of the *synderistic* root of one's human dignity. In her haunting book *Eichmann in Jerusalem*, Hannah Arendt describes encountering this phenomenon in Eichmann and calls it "thoughtlessness." Hannah Arendt, *Eichmann in Jerusalem: A Report on the Banality of Evil* (New York: Penguin, 1977), 287–88. Aquinas identifies thoughtlessness (*inconsideratio*) as a special sin included in the vice of imprudence (*ST* II-II, q. 53, a. 4). For Aquinas as well as Arendt, thoughtlessness names not a psychological or epistemological defect but rather a profound moral problem. The counterfeit of conscience is so pernicious because, by muting the inner dialogue, it engenders thoughtlessness. In contemporary secularist democratic regimes, there is a dangerous self-congratulatory complacency caused by the erroneous conviction that such thoughtlessness disappeared with the totalitarian regimes of the past century. One can, however, make a reasonable case to the contrary and argue that thoughtlessness has in fact become more widespread since then. Such a case can be, at least indirectly, supported by Neil Postman's far from outdated book *Amusing Ourselves to Death: Public Discourse in the Age of Show Business* (New York: Penguin, 1985). Absorption in the internet, Facebook, Twitter, YouTube, and Netflix hardly encourages attending to the interior forum and the inner dialogue. With few exceptions, a life immersed in cyber-superficiality and digital distraction inculcates routines and habits that are ideal breeding grounds for thoughtlessness. The exercise of theonomic conscience, on the contrary, requires mindfulness, empathy, and moments of interior and exterior silence necessary for recollection, which are prerequisites for the examination of conscience truly so-called.

naturalist secularism and the moral and legal decisionism it entails, and if they are bent on imposing this ideology on the body politic, such secularist democratic regimes will be likely to produce their own subtle and refined versions of barbarity—versions, albeit, most likely devoid of the cynical cruelty that typifies totalitarian regimes. In his 1991 encyclical letter *Centesimus Annus*, John Paul II expressed a warning that has only become more urgent: "Authentic democracy is possible only in a State ruled by law, and on the basis of a correct conception of the human person.... As history demonstrates, a democracy without values turns into open or thinly disguised totalitarianism."[127] Normatively deny the theonomic conscience, as ideological secularism does, and the inherent dignity of the human person from birth to natural death becomes unintelligible, and the reliable and objective perception of the "*rule* of ethical truth, the *standard* of right and wrong" becomes inconceivable.[128] Four years later, John Paul II articulated this looming consequence with even greater clarity in his encyclical letter *Evangelium Vitae*:

When freedom, out of a desire to emancipate itself from all forms of tradition and authority, shuts out even the most obvious evidence of an objective and universal truth, which is the foundation of personal and social life, then the person ends up by no longer taking as the sole and indisputable point of reference for his own choices the truth about good and evil, but only his subjective and changeable opinion or, indeed his selfish interest and whim.[129]

127. Because of its striking relevance, it is worth quoting this passage from *Centesimus Annus* in full: "Authentic democracy is possible only in a State ruled by law, and on the basis of a correct conception of the human person. It requires that the necessary conditions be present for the advancement both of the individual through education and formation in true ideals, and of the 'subjectivity' of society through the creation of structures of participation and shared responsibility. Nowadays there is a tendency to claim that agnosticism and sceptical relativism are the philosophy and the basic attitude which correspond to democratic forms of political life. Those who are convinced that they know the truth and firmly adhere to it are considered unreliable from a democratic point of view, since they do not accept that truth is determined by the majority, or that it is subject to variation according to different political trends. It must be observed in this regard that if there is no ultimate truth to guide and direct political activity, then ideas and convictions can easily be manipulated for reasons of power. As history demonstrates, a democracy without values easily turns into open or thinly disguised totalitarianism." John Paul II, *Centesimus Annus*, Encyclical Letter, May 1, 1991, par. 46; available at www.vatican.va.

128. *Diff.*, ii., 246 (my emphasis).

129. John Paul II, *Evangelium Vitae*, March 25, 1995, par. 19; available at www.vatican.va.

This flight from theonomic conscience has dire political consequences—consequences that become increasingly tangible in the political and social life of Western secularist democratic regimes. John Paul II clearly names the causes of the subtle but pervasive disease and misery that characterize day-to-day life in affluent Western secular societies:

This view of freedom *leads to a serious distortion of life in society*. If the promotion of the self is understood in terms of absolute autonomy, people inevitably reach the point of rejecting one another. Everyone else is considered an enemy from whom one has to defend oneself. Thus society becomes a mass of individuals placed side by side, but without any mutual bonds. Each one wishes to assert himself independently of the other and in fact intends to make his own interests prevail. Still, in the face of other people's analogous interests, some kind of compromise must be found, if one wants a society in which the maximum possible freedom is guaranteed to each individual. In this way, any reference to common values and to a truth absolutely binding to everyone is lost, and social life ventures on to the shifting sands of complete relativism. At that point, *everything is negotiable, everything is open to bargaining*: even the first of the fundamental rights, the right to life.[130]

Not so very long ago it was, of course, quite obvious to every person with a well-formed theonomic conscience that the government of a body politic, in which the laws of the state have a constitutional and *de facto* correlation to the "rule of ethical truth" as reflected in the natural law, cannot be expected to legally exempt individual appeals to conscience that serve as warrants for breaking the law.[131] A convicted murderer is to be punished by law whether or not he appeals to conscience. But that same person with a well-formed theonomic conscience might now ask: what

130. *Evangelium Vitae*, par. 20.

131. G. W. F. Hegel summarizes this matter with great clarity and offers his own method for distinguishing clearly between conscience truly so-called and its counterfeit: "What is right and obligatory is the absolutely rational element in the will's volitions and therefore it is not in essence the particular property of an individual, and its form is not that of feeling or any other private (i.e. sensuous) type of knowing, but essentially that of universals determined by thought, i.e. the form of laws and principles. Conscience is therefore subject to the judgement of its truth or falsity, and when it appeals only to itself for a decision, it is directly at variance with what it wishes to be, namely the rule for a mode of conduct which is rational, absolutely valid, and universal. For this reason, the state cannot give recognition to conscience in its private form as subjective knowing." *Hegel's Philosophy of Right*, trans. T. M. Knox (Oxford: Clarendon Press, 1942), no. 137 (91).

if the laws of an explicitly and consistently secularist democratic regime become unmoored from the natural law and the "rule of ethical truth" and come to encode nothing but the arbitrary will of varying political majorities and their particular predilections—predilections that blatantly contradict the moral law and reflect a flight from theonomic conscience and the identification of the common good with the contingent interests of whatever constitutes a statistical majority in opinion polls? Again, in *Evangelium Vitae* John Paul II foresaw the political consequences inherent in the flight from theonomic conscience, consequences that have become quite tangible in the prevailing political reality of the West: "*When the sense of God is lost, there is also a tendency to lose the sense of man,* of his dignity and his life; in turn, the systematic violation of the moral law, especially in the serious matter of respect for human life and its dignity, produces a kind of progressive darkening of the capacity to discern God's living and saving presence."[132]

Should a secularist democratic regime—unmoored from the natural law and the moral order—impose laws that compel individuals and institutions to cooperate with grave systemic moral evil, such laws will expose the constitutionally guaranteed freedom of religious exercise, so-called, as nothing but an arbitrary function of the regime's institutionalized collective subjectivity severed from the "rule of ethical truth" and policed by the regime's legal machinery.[133]

In such a situation it might be unavoidable and indeed timely to reconsider Aquinas's assertion that "the unjust law is not law" (*lex iniusta non est lex*). Aquinas formulates this position in rather uncompromising terms in two interconnected passages of his teaching on human law in the *Summa theologiae*. He first asks whether every human law is derived from the natural law and answers in the affirmative: human law is derived from the natural law either as a conclusion from principles or as a determination of certain generalities. He then concludes that "if in any point human law departs from natural law, it is no longer a law but a perversion of the law."[134] For in such a case it ceases to be an ordinance of reason

---

132. *Evangelium Vitae*, par. 21.
133. *Diff.*, ii., 246.
134. *ST* I-II, q. 95, a. 2, co. (author's translation).

ordained to the common good. Subsequently, Aquinas asks whether human law binds a person necessarily in the forum of conscience (*in foro conscientiae*).[135] In the *sed contra*, Aquinas quotes the Vulgate text of 1 Peter 2:19 that in translation reads "It is worthy of thanks if, because of his conscience, someone endures sorrows, suffering wrongfully." In his response, he states:

Laws may be unjust in two ways: first, by being contrary to human good … —either in respect of the end, as when an authority imposes on his subjects burdensome laws, conducive, not to the common good, but rather to his own cupidity or vainglory; —or in respect of the author, as when a man makes a law that goes beyond the power committed to him; —or in respect of the form, as when burdens are imposed unequally on the community, although with a view to the common good. The like are acts of violence rather than laws; because, as Augustine says (*De Lib. Arb.* I.5), *a law that is not just, seems to be no law at all.* Wherefore such laws do not bind in conscience, except perhaps in order to avoid scandal or disturbance, for which cause a man should even yield his right, according to Mt 5:40, 41: *If a man … take away thy coat, let go thy cloak also unto him; and whosoever will force thee one mile, go with him another two.* Second, laws may be unjust through being opposed to the Divine good: such are the laws of tyrants inducing to idolatry, or to anything else contrary to the Divine law: and laws of this kind must nowise be observed, because, as stated in Acts 5:29, *we ought to obey God rather than men.*[136]

Laws promulgated by secularist democratic regimes in service of the counterfeit of conscience may fall under Aquinas's first rubric, being contrary to the human good (especially pertaining to the authority of the lawgivers extending beyond the power committed to them); and under the second rubric, being contrary to the divine law.[137] Remember, the divine law, according to Aquinas, is comprised of the revealed aspects of the eternal law that include in the Decalogue a revealed summary of the natural-law principles in their proximate conclusions and that serve as the indispensable guide to the supernatural final end of the human person.[138] Most pertinent

135. *ST* I-II, q. 96, a. 4.
136. *ST* I-II, q. 96, a. 4, co.
137. For a brief discussion of the important principle "an unjust law is not a law," see appendix 7 to this chapter.
138. *ST* I-II, q. 100, a. 3, co.; q. 91, a. 4, a. 5; and qq. 98–108.

to the present discussion is one of Aquinas's arguments for the necessity of the divine law:

On account of the uncertainty of human judgment, especially on contingent and particular matters, different people form different judgments on human acts; whence also different and contrary laws result. In order, therefore, that man may know without any doubt what he ought to do and what he ought to avoid, it was necessary for man to be directed in his proper acts by a law given by God, for it is certain that such a law cannot err.[139]

A conscience that is illumined by divine faith[140] and rightly formed will always be docile to the divine law as interpreted by the ordinary magisterium and will follow the fundamental principle enunciated in Acts 5:29: "We must obey God rather than men" (RSV).

To conclude these considerations of the relationship between human law and divine law, it will be useful to return to one of Newman's hypothetical cases from his Letter: "Suppose, for instance, an Act was passed in Parliament, bidding Catholics to attend Protestant service every week, and the Pope distinctly told us not to do so, for it was to violate our duty to our faith:—I should obey the Pope and not the Law."[141]

The full import of the contemporary analogical case must by now be obvious. Suppose a contemporary secularist democratic regime in the Western Hemisphere were to promulgate laws that would require Catholics who complied with them to violate their faith and morals as taught by the Catholic church and to place themselves in proximity to grave systemic moral evil or even in jeopardy of cooperating with such evil. And let us assume that the pope in unison with the Catholic bishops of this country had spoken out against such laws. Newman's answer to this unfortunately less-than-hypothetical case is clear: "I should obey the Pope and not the Law."[142]

Laws promulgated by secularist democratic regimes that are unmoored

139. *ST* I-II, q. 91, a. 4, co.

140. "Faith, which through assent unites [the human being] to divine knowledge, has God as its principal object, and anything else as a consequent addition." Aquinas, *De veritate*, q. 14, a. 8, co. (*Truth*, 2:245). When in divine faith God engages the human intellect and thus becomes its "object," God engages the intellect as first truth, revealing himself in the person of the Word— scripture and tradition constituting "one single deposit of the Word of God," as *Dei Verbum*, no. 10, teaches.

141. *Diff.*, ii., 240.

142. Ibid.

from the natural law and the moral order have no power to extinguish the spark of *synderesis*; nor do they have the power to suppress the judgments of a properly formed theonomic conscience. But such laws do indeed have the power to inflict grave damage on the body politic—unmooring it evermore thoroughly from the "rule of ethical truth."[143]

Given the sovereign secularism zealously promoted by not a few democratic regimes in the West today, the Catholic church's perennial political vocation as the teacher of conscience becomes simultaneously more difficult and more urgent. Through instruction in and public witness to the divine law, and through public argumentation based on the precepts of the natural law, the church forms consciences and, in doing so, begins to remove the dullness of practical reason that is the consequence of sin.[144]

In whatever political communities the negative freedom of the counterfeit of conscience has achieved dominance in the past and will again become dominant in the future—by way of force, law, custom, or prejudice—the church has suffered and will suffer again discrimination and even persecution. At the same time, as has happened in the past, the positive freedom in the truth that is characteristic of theonomic conscience, the splendor of the dignity of the human being, created in God's image—will be defended by acts of witness that in their heroic extreme are traditionally called martyrdom.[145]

Appendix 1

In 1960 the noted Newman scholar Jan H. Walgrave, OP, made this observation:

We know that, for Newman himself, the existence of God was as evident as his own. In his inmost experience, the presence of God in conscience was so deeply rooted that the twofold evidence of "myself and my Creator" was absolutely indi-

---

143. *Diff.*, ii. 246.

144. This sentence is borrowed from chapter 4, "Democracy after Christendom—Sovereign Secularism, Genuine Liberalism, and the Natural Love of God," of my book *Dust Bound for Heaven: Explorations in the Theology of Thomas Aquinas* (Grand Rapids, Mich.: Eerdmans, 2012), 124.

145. John Paul II states the matter plainly in *Veritatis Splendor*: "Martyrdom, accepted as an affirmation of the inviolability of the moral order, bears splendid witness both to the holiness of God's law and to the inviolability of the personal dignity of man, created in God's image and likeness" (par. 92).

visible.... It was the Providence of God that had inscribed in the very structure of our mind a mission we had the duty to recognize and carry out.... Newman never worked out his proof of the existence of God. Often, however, he indicated that, were he to do so, he would take as his starting-point the fact of conscience.[146]

Consider the famous passage from the *Apologia pro Vita Sua* where Newman states:

Starting then with the being of a God (which, as I have said, is as certain to me as the certainty of my own existence, though when I try to put the grounds of that certainty into logical shape I find a difficulty in doing so in mood and figure to my satisfaction), I look out of myself into the world of men, and there I see a sight which fills me with unspeakable distress. The world seems simply to give the lie to that great truth, of which my whole being is so full; and the effect upon me is, in consequence, as a matter of necessity, as confusing as if it denied that I am in existence myself.... This is, to me, one of those great difficulties of this absolute primary truth, to which I referred just now. Were it not for this voice, speaking so clearly in my conscience and my heart, I should be an atheist, or a pantheist, or a polytheist when I looked into the world.[147]

Then there is Newman's argument from his *Philosophical Notebook*, an argument Terrence Merrigan felicitously summarizes this way: "'*Conscientiam habeo, ergo sum*' is also—and more or less simultaneously— '*Conscientiam habeo, ergo Deus est*' (I have a conscience, therefore God exists')."[148] Here is Newman's line of argumentation:

Now I say that, our consciousness [of thought] is a reflex act implying existence (I think, therefore I am), so this sensation of conscience is the recognition of our obligation involving the notion of an external being obliging, I say this, not from any abstract argument from the force of the terms, (e.g. "a Law implies a Lawgiver") but the peculiarity of that feeling to which I *give* the name of Conscience.[149]

146. Jan II. Walgrave, OP, "The Proof of the Existence of God from Conscience," in *Newman the Theologian*, 358–63, at 358–59. See also the very informative small volume by Adrian J. Boekraad and Henry Tristram, *The Argument from Conscience to the Existence of God According to J. H. Newman* (Louvain: Éditions Nauwelaerts, 1961). The text of Newman's "Proof of Theism" from his *Philosophical Notebooks* is reproduced at 103–25; for useful explanatory notes, see 127–66.

147. Walgrave, *Newman the Theologian*, 23.

148. Terrence Merrigan, "Revelation," in *The Cambridge Companion to John Henry Newman*, ed. Ian Ker and Terrence Merrigan (Cambridge: Cambridge University Press, 2009), 47–72, at 49–50.

149. *The Philosophical Notebook of John Henry Newman*, ed. Edward Sillem and revised by A. J. Boekraad (Louvain: Nauwelaerts Publishing House, 1970), 2:59.

The argument reappears in Newman's *Essay in Aid of a Grammar of Assent*:

It is instinct which impels the child to recognize in the smiles or the frowns of a countenance which meets his eyes, not only a being external to himself, but one whose looks elicit in him confidence or fear. And, as he instinctively interprets these physical phenomena, as tokens of things beyond themselves, so from the sensations attendant upon certain classes of his thoughts and actions he gains a perception of an external being, who reads his mind, to whom he is responsible, who praises and blames, who promises and threatens. As I am only illustrating a general view by examples, I shall take this analogy for granted here. As then we have our initial knowledge of the universe through sense, so do we in the first instance begin to learn about its Lord and God from conscience; and, as from particular acts of that instinct, which makes experiences, mere images (as they ultimately are) upon the retina, the means of our perceiving something real beyond them, we go on to draw the general conclusion that there is a vast external world, so from the recurring instances in which conscience acts, forcing upon us importunately the mandate of a Superior, we have fresh and fresh [*sic*] evidence of the existence of a Sovereign Ruler, from whom those particular dictates which we experience proceed; so that, with limitations which cannot here be made without digressing from my main subject, we may, by means of that induction from particular experiences of conscience, have as good a warrant for concluding the Ubiquitous Presence of One Supreme Master, as we have, from parallel experience of sense, for assenting to the fact of a multiform and vast world, material and mental.... Now certainly the thought of God, as Theists entertain it, is not gained by an instinctive association of His presence with any sensible phenomena; but the office which the senses directly fulfil as regards creation that devolves indirectly on certain of our mental phenomena as regards the Creator. Those phenomena are found in the sense of moral obligation. As from a multitude of instinctive perceptions, acting in particular instances, of something beyond the senses, we generalize the notion of an external world, and then picture that world in and according to those particular phenomena from which we started, so from the perceptive power which identifies the intimations of conscience with the reverberations or echoes (so to say) of an external admonition, we proceed on to the notion of a Supreme Ruler and Judge, and then again we image Him and His attributes in those recurring intimations, out of which, as mental phenomena, our recognition of His existence was originally gained. And, if the impressions which His creatures make on us through our senses oblige us to regard those creatures as *sui generis* respectively, it is not wonderful that the notices, which He indirectly gives us through our conscience, of His own nature are such as to make us understand that He is like Himself and like nothing else.[150]

The editor of the *Philosophical Notebook*, Edward Sillem, observes that Newman's "argument is phenomenological, and from an investigation of what Newman calls 'the phenomena of conscience', and not metaphysical in character. It is not an argument from the nature of law, but from man's experience of himself as a person."[151] Interestingly, in order to make it work as a probative metaphysical demonstration, Philip Flanagan sees the necessity to recast Newman's argument by starting from conscience as a witness to the moral law (and not, as Newman does, starting from conscience as a sense of duty).[152] The nuanced interpretation of the matter that Walgrave advances seems to me the right one:

I agree that the sole absolutely valid proof of the existence of God is the metaphysical one, and that the moral argument, to be strictly conclusive, has to be transformed into the metaphysical one which starts from human contingency, shown specifically in the sphere of morals; but I am certain that this kind of reasoning was foreign to Newman's mentality. For him a certain apprehension of God was among the primary and irreducible facts of conscious existence. From this it follows that a proof of the existence of God amounts to demonstrating, by reflection and analysis, that such indeed is the religious testimony of the spontaneous act of conscience.... Newman's argument has, undoubtedly, the advantage of being eminently practical; it is simple, and thoroughly convincing to those who share the experience he describes; at the same time it brings out clearly the presence of God and our duty towards him. The metaphysical argument, on the other hand, is very difficult to understand perfectly since it presupposes the whole metaphysics of being; its full force is evident only to a metaphysician. Once it is simplified for general use, it becomes more or less defective, and, though it still makes some impression on many, it is not convincing to those versed only in modern methods of philosophy. As it is, experience shows that nowadays there is prevalent a rather unfortunate cast of mind that is not amenable to metaphysical reasoning. In fact, it is this that has led the religious philosophy of our day to prefer Newman's approach.[153]

150. *G.A.*, 62–63 and 103–4.
151. *Philosophical Notebook*, 2:59n2.
152. See "The Conscience Argument for the Existence of God," in Flanagan, *Newman, Faith and the Believer*, 184–92.
153. Walgrave, *Newman the Theologian*, 361–63.

In an important concluding reflection, Walgrave offers a succinct description of how he sees Newman's approach as perfectly compatible with the metaphysical arguments that Aquinas advances for the existence of God. Walgrave echoes here what in the prologue I describe as Newman's approach belonging to the "context of discovery," while Aquinas's argumentation belongs to the "context of justification." Walgrave states:

We are convinced that all consciousness of God is, ultimately, of a metaphysical nature. The metaphysician, when he shows that the "awareness of being," embodied in our consciousness that we are finite, implies a real dependence of finite beings on an Infinite Being, exhibits, in fact, the essential structure of all awareness of God; but this structure is, normally, hidden within the living body of religious experience. Concrete thoughts, by which we apprehend the reality of God, clothes in living tissues the skeleton of metaphysical reason, without whose presence the finely-wrought structure of religious experience would fall apart. Surely, it is unnecessary to oppose the classical ways of theodicy to the modern way of reflection on religious experience, apprehended in its totality and spontaneity. The justification of religious thought, as carried out by Newman, may fittingly be combined with a metaphysical proof that exhibits its structure, a proof so clear in itself, yet so difficult to grasp in the abstract. If metaphysical analysis were put forward as the reconstruction of a framework necessary to that natural religious experience whose actual process has first been described, and which has already been justified as integral to the life of the mind, I think the proof of God's existence would thereby be restored to its natural place; in fact, it would acquire additional force, through the bringing out of its full significance for life. In this way, I believe, we would be in the fullest accord with the spirit of Aristotle, who, no less than St. Thomas, was Newman's master.[154]

Appendix 2

John Calvin's teaching that conscience is the internal witness both to the existence of God and to the law of God is very clear. Newman's pre-1845 reflections on conscience, which echo Calvin's teachings, were most likely influenced by the Calvinist strand in his early evangelical phase. In the *Institutes of the Christian Religion*, Calvin regards conscience as an interior awareness of a divine judgment that engenders (1) the sense of divinity

154. Ibid., 363.

and (2) the distinction between good and evil. According to Calvin (and *pace* Karl Barth's questionable interpretation of Calvin on this matter), every human has an innate knowledge of the natural law as well as the capacity and responsibility to judge whether human laws correspond to the natural law.[155] On the Lutheran side of things, matters were a bit more complicated. After initially adopting the concepts of *synderesis* and *conscientia* in the Scholastic sense (for example in his 1513–15 *Dictata* on the Psalms and in his 1515–16 Romans lectures), Martin Luther discarded *synderesis* completely from his conception of conscience in the years 1517–19. During that period and thereafter for Luther, *conscientia* came to indicate exclusively the human soteriological relationship to God: *Conscientia mala* was the state of estrangement from God under the condition of sin. *Conscientia fidelis* described the restored relationship of being reconciled with God *sola fide*. Reinterpreted in such a radical way, conscience lost its function as the index of the rule of moral truth. It became a strictly soteriological indicator of the human's primordial relationship to God, either as convicted by the law (which God gave to humanity not to be followed but to unmask humanity's sinfulness and thus drive humanity to Christ) or as justified by faith alone.[156]

The Reformer Philip Melanchthon saw this exclusively theological understanding of conscience as a problem and reintroduced the concept of *synderesis* as the relationship to God determined by justifying faith (or the lack thereof).[157] Under the salutary influence of Melanchthon, the Lutheran Scholastic theologian Georg Calixt (1586–1656) finally returned to the Thomistic distinction of *synderesis* and *conscientia* in his *Epitome theologiae moralis* (1634). The anti-Melanchthonian Gnesio-Lutherans and the

155. See John Calvin, *Institutes of the Christian Religion*, II.ii.13, 16, 22, and 24. For this reading of Calvin, I rely on the extensive treatment of conscience in Günter Gloede's classic study *Theologia naturalis bei Calvin* (Stuttgart: Kohlhammer, 1935), 103–331; in so doing, I take a side in what seems to be an interminable controversy. For an instructive summary of this intense intra-Calvinist dispute stretching over the twentieth century about the proper interpretation of Calvin's understanding of conscience and the natural law, see William Klempa, "John Calvin on Natural Law," in *John Calvin and the Church: A Prism of Reform*, ed. Timothy George (Louisville, Ky.: Westminster/John Knox, 1990), 72–95.

156. See Luther's *Disputation Against Scholastic Theology*, in *D. Martin Luthers Werke. Kritische Gesamtausgabe* (Weimar: Hermann Böhlau und Nachfolger, 1883–2009), 1:372; Luther, *Large Catechism*, Part III, fifth petition; and Luther, *Lectures on Galatians* (1531), in *Werke* 40/1:73–74.

157. See Philip Melanchthon's 1540 Commentary on Aristotle's *De anima*.

Lutherans of the early-twentieth-century Luther Renaissance (a return to the young "existentialist" Luther combined with elements of early dialectical theology) continued to insist on a solely *theological* understanding of conscience (*conscientia mala, conscientia fidelis*) at the expense of its function as the index of the rule of moral truth. This has yielded the predictable consequence of modern Lutheran ethics (with a few notable exceptions of theologians returning to the Melanchthon/Calixt adoption of the distinction of *synderesis* and *conscientia*) vacillating interminably between two mutually exclusive alternatives. On the one side, Lutheran ethicists pursued the positivism of the "order of creation" (*Schöpfungsordnung*) or, similarly, the "order of preservation" (*Erhaltungsordnung*) of human existence under the condition of sin (marriage and family; state authority and power; church). On the other side, they favored the situation ethics of "agape-consequentialism" aimed at creating the greatest amount of love in a given moral situation.

Appendix 3

Immanuel Kant, arguably under the ongoing influence of his Pietist upbringing, offers a striking account of the interior forum:

Consciousness of an *internal court* in man ("before which his thoughts accuse or excuse one another") is *conscience*. Every human being has a conscience and finds himself observed, threatened, and, in general, kept in awe (respect coupled with fear) by an internal judge; and this authority watching over the law in him is not something that he himself (voluntarily) *makes*, but something incorporated in his being. It follows him like his shadow when he plans to escape. He can indeed stun himself or put himself to sleep by pleasures and distractions, but he cannot help coming to himself or waking up from time to time; and when he does, he hears at once its fearful voice. He can at most, in extreme depravity, bring himself to *heed* it no longer, but he still cannot help *hearing* it.[158]

But Kant has no account of *synderesis* and consequently ends up with a dangerously unmoored interior forum. He is aware of this problem, of the necessity of a "doubled self" that, if not resolved, leads to the collapse of

---

158. Immanuel Kant, *The Metaphysics of Morals*, ed. and trans. Mary Gregory (Cambridge: Cambridge University Press, 1996), 189.

the interior forum and thus to the infallible decision of the counterfeit of conscience. Hence, Kant postulates: "For all duties a human being's conscience will, accordingly, have to think of *someone other* than himself (i.e., other than the human being as such) as the judge of his actions, if conscience is not to be in contradiction with itself. This other may be an actual person or a merely ideal person that reason creates for itself."[159] Unsurprisingly, there are some requisite qualities that must characterize such an ideal person:

Since such a moral being must also have all power (in heaven and on earth) in order to give effect to his laws (as is necessarily required for the office of judge), and since such an omnipotent moral being is called *God*, conscience must be thought of as the subjective principle of being accountable to God for all one's deeds. In fact the latter concept is always contained (even if only in an obscure way) in the moral self-awareness of conscience.[160]

Kant's *phenomenological* description of theonomic conscience is remarkably accurate and echoes the traditional Christian accounts given in the preceding century by the Catholic Francisco Suárez and the Lutheran Georg Calixt. However, in his *theoretical* account of conscience, Kant replaces *synderesis* with the God-postulate of pure practical reason. In his *Critique of Pure Reason*, Kant argues that the human intellect has no access to supersensible reality. Hence the demonstrability and knowledge of God characteristic of modern rationalist ontotheological metaphysics is called radically into question and, along with it, the theoretical knowledge of human freedom. It is by way of his account of pure practical reason in his *Critique of Practical Reason* that Kant attempts to recover a practical sense of the existence of God, human freedom, and immortality. Pure practical reason that, according to Kant, holds primacy over theoretical reason and is completely independent from human inclinations postulates these supersensible realities as necessary conditions for the possibility of rational moral activity. Kant holds that we must think of moral activity as actually resulting in happiness, the highest good. Yet human agency is nowhere near adequate to this task. Kant argues that we can therefore reasonably hope to produce this highest good only if our will

159. Ibid.
160. Ibid., 190.

is in harmony with that of a holy and beneficent creator. Hence the first and fundamental postulate is the postulate of the existence of God; the second correlated postulate is the immortality of the soul and an afterlife (because happiness may be unattainable in this world); and the third and final correlated postulate is human freedom, the condition of the possibility of moral activity in the first place.

Yet Kant never seemed to feel quite at rest with the line of argumentation he developed in his *Critique of Practical Reason*. Advanced in age, he revisited this question repeatedly in his unfinished *Opus Postumum*. Consider the slightly but markedly different emphases of the existence of God (as in mind only, or in reality) in the following three fragments:

The most important of all the concepts of reason, because it is directed toward the final end (for the concepts of the understanding are only there for the sake of form), is the concept of duty and the legislation relating to it, as a concept of practical reason. The categorical imperative, expressed affirmatively or negatively (in command and prohibition) yet with greater rigor in the latter than in the former (*dictamen rationis moralis*): Thou shalt not steal. (Thou shalt not lie is not in the Decalogue.) Honor thy father and mother. The last are not an expression of proper duties of compulsion. There must also, however, be—or at least be thought—a legislative force (*potestas legislatoria*) which gives these laws emphasis (effect) although only in idea; and this is none other than that of the *highest* being, morally and physically superior to all and omnipotent, and his holy will—which justifies the statement: There is a God.

There is in practical reason a concept of duty, that is, of a compulsion or necessitation according to a principle of the laws of freedom—that is, according to a law which the subject prescribes to itself (*dictamen rationis practicae*) through the categorical imperative, indeed. A command to which everyone must absolutely give obedience, is to be regarded by everyone as from a being which rules and governs over all. Such a being, as moral, however, is called God. So there is a God.

The subject of the categorical imperative in me is an object which deserves to be obeyed: an object of adoration. This is an identical proposition. The characteristic of a moral being which can command categorically over the nature of man is its divinity. His laws must be obeyed as divine commands. Whether religion is possible without the presupposition of the existence of God. *Est deus in nobis.*[161]

161. Immanuel Kant, *Opus postumum*, ed. Eckart Förster, trans. Eckart Förster and Michael Rosen (Cambridge: Cambridge University Press, 1993), 206–7 and 209.

It would not take long after Kant for the deity of the God-postulate of pure practical reason to be deconstructed by Nietzsche and his disciples as a willful pretense of the self, an intentional construal that camouflages the fact that the "doubled self" is a fiction created by those who wish to conceal their will to power behind a mask of moral rectitude. In classical Christian anthropology, represented by Aquinas as well as Newman, conscience signifies the primordial constitution of the human soul in the truth (ontologically as well as epistemologically) by way of the interior presence of the first principles of theoretical as well as practical truth. Kant's attempted reconstruction of this classical account has proven to be notoriously vulnerable to criticism on theoretical counts (from Hegel on one side and Nietzsche on the other) and notoriously unstable on practical counts of the concrete existence of the subject (as shown by Kierkegaard). Kant's colossal prestige and impact on modern philosophy easily distracts from the fact that his critical reconstruction ultimately proved a failure.

Appendix 4

Johann Gottlieb Fichte (1762–1814), the *spiritus rector* of subjective idealism in the Germany of the 1790s, regarded the criterion for the correctness of our convictions to be purely interior to the subjective consciousness. Fichte calls this criterion conscience. In his *System of Ethics* (1798), he states emphatically:

The present deduction has once and for all cancelled and destroyed the evasion of an *erroneous conscience* still present in most systems of ethics. Conscience never errs and is unable to err; for it is the immediate consciousness of our pure, primordial I, which no other consciousness transcends and which cannot be interrogated and corrected by another consciousness; which in and of itself is the judge of all our convictions and which does not acknowledge any higher judge over itself. It [the immediate consciousness of our pure, primordial I] decides as the ultimate authority and cannot be appealed.[162]

162. "Es ist durch die soeben gegebene Deduction auf immer aufgehoben und vernichtet die nach den meisten Moralsystemen noch stattfindende Ausflucht eines *irrenden Gewissens*. Das Gewissen irrt nie und kann nicht irren; denn es ist das unmittelbare Bewusstseyn unseres reinen

In Fichte's account we can observe a radical instantiation of the counterfeit of conscience, the "conscience" of the sovereign self-determination as conceived by a consistent subjective idealism. If the primordial I were God as absolutely different from the created, finite I, a form of *synderesis* (identical with the eternal law) would obtain. However, according to Fichte, the primordial I is the root and origin of my transcendental subjectivity manifesting itself immediately through my consciousness. Thus, *synderesis* and *conscientia* coincide in the infallible decision posited by the Fichtean conscience. The Fichtean conscience cannot be erroneous, because the rule of ethical truth coincides with the immediate consciousness of the primordial I. The interior forum—the precondition for the interior dialogue—collapses into the monologue of a "creative" positing of decisions by the ultimate authority, the immediate consciousness of the primordial I which is the standard of moral truth. The pure primordial I, in its concrete existence, is finite, but in its essential activity is infinite—an infinite longing of the will that is the very root of the primordial I. This longing is the source of the striving that is the essence of freedom, realized in the positing of the decisions of the radically autonomous, self-creating I. In Fichte's account we can observe a radical instantiation of the counterfeit of conscience, the "conscience" of the sovereign self-determination as conceived by a consistent subjective idealism.

Appendix 5

Relatively late in life, Karl Rahner, SJ, published a brief but programmatic and therefore influential essay on conscience. The article appeared in 1983 in German and seven years later in English translation.[163] While very

ursprünglichen Ich, über welches kein anderes Bewusstseyn hinausgeht; das nach keinem anderen Bewusstseyn geprüft und berichtigt werden kann; das selbst Richter aller Ueberzeugungen ist, aber keinen höheren Richter über sich anerkennt. Es entscheidet in der letzten Instanz und ist inappellabel." Johann Gottlieb Fichte, *System der Sittenlehre* [1798], in *Fichtes Werke*, ed. Immanuel Hermann Fichte (Berlin: W. de Gruyter, 1971), 4:173–74.

163. Karl Rahner, "Vom irrenden Gewissen," *Orientierung* 48 (1983): 246B–250A; reprinted as "Vom Gewissen: Gedanken über Freiheit und Würde menschlicher Entscheidung" in Karl Rahner, *Schriften zur Theologie*, vol. 16, ed. Paul Imhof, SJ (Zurich: Benziger, 1984), 11–25. An English translation entitled "Conscience: Freedom and the Dignity of Human Decision" appears in Rahner, *Theological Investigations*, vol. 22: *Humane Society and the Church of Tomorrow*, trans. Joseph Donceel, SJ (New York: Crossroad, 1991), 3–13.

readable, the English translation flattens a delicate three-dimensional and conceptually sophisticated text into a two-dimensional user-friendly English. It abandons much of the precise terminology Rahner uses in the German and seems to be driven by an all-too-transparent agenda of ever so slightly simplifying and thereby radicalizing Rahner's quite nuanced position. For Aquinas as well as Newman, conscience signifies the primordial constitution of the human soul in the truth (ontologically as well as epistemologically) by way of the interior presence of the first principles of theoretical as well as practical truth. Truth thus gives rise to freedom, which, in turn, is rooted in the truth. In the center of Rahner's account, on the contrary, stands the transcendental constitution of the human subject as an essentially free spirit oriented to God. Conscience signifies the subject's transcendental experience of freedom and responsibility in relation to God. Consequently, according to Rahner, theonomy is realized by way of autonomy. Conscience is fundamentally the self-awareness of transcendental subjectivity arising from the experience of being handed over to oneself, the experience of a primordial freedom and responsibility that *qua* creatureliness is essentially, though unthematically, oriented to the theonomic truth. According to this construal of transcendentality, it is not the truth that sets free and thus constitutes freedom. Rather, it is the freedom of a primordial subjectivity of conscience that makes possible the reception of a truth to which the human spirit is oriented. The fundamental problem with this construal is that the first and constitutive moment of the human spirit is the freedom of self-possession and not the innate habitual presence of the theonomic first principle and first precept of moral truth. Rahner's conceptual prioritization of the subject's transcendental experience of freedom inverts the relationship between truth and freedom and thus creates a condition in which his construal in an ever-so-slightly radicalized form becomes a justification for the counterfeit of conscience. *Gaudium et Spes* does not support and *Veritatis Splendor* rejects Rahner's move to root the dignity of conscience in the transcendental experience of freedom and responsibility. His concept of transcendental subjectivity makes impossible the presence of the innate *habitus* of *synderesis*, as the latter would always antecede the self-possession of freedom, would be the truth that sets free, that, in other words, gives rise to freedom in the truth.

Absent *synderesis*, the dignity of conscience must indeed rest in the very constitution of the transcendental subject and the decisions that correspond to the transcendental experience of freedom and responsibility. The step from transcendental freedom to the counterfeit of conscience is minimal. For transcendental freedom is either somehow still aware of its creatureliness and hence its fundamental (even if unthematic) responsibility to the creator—or transcendental freedom becomes "creative" and the dignity of the decisions it produces carry the dignity of being creatures of the self-will. For Rahner, very clearly, conscience is the unconditional call to oneself (being inescapably delivered up to oneself) and as such into radical responsibility (implicitly, at least, always in relation to God). But however one may try to salvage the matter, every decision made by such a subject is ultimately "creative," that is, the subject's own "creation" (of course, in radical responsibility to God). Not acting according to one's conscience seems, according to Rahner, to be the one unforgivable sin—here he echoes Abelard—because in doing so, one would abdicate from the dignity of the transcendental freedom of personhood. Acting according to conscience, thus conceived, does not mean making judgments based on *synderesis* but rather making decisions that are essentially "creative," arising from the abyss of my transcendental freedom. In radical responsibility, I offer these decisions up to God, but they are *my* decisions. Hence, the least that must be stated is that Rahner's account endangers if not makes principally inconceivable the very possibility of an erroneous conscience. If different by intention, there seems to be in place in this essay a rather striking and disturbing *de facto* identity between Rahner's construal of conscience as transcendental subjectivity and any philosophically sophisticated account of the counterfeit of conscience reviewed above. Without the supposition of *synderesis* and the correlated phenomenon of the erroneous conscience, there is the grave danger that "autonomy" and "creativity" become—if not actually intended by Rahner, nevertheless arguably entailed in his construal of conscience—identical with "self-determination" and "sovereignty."

Appendix 6

If one gets clear on Aquinas's understanding of *synderesis* as a natural *habitus*, there is no need in the contemporary consideration of conscience to replace the admittedly *prima facie* unfamiliar technical term of *synderesis* with the by-now equally unfamiliar concept of *anamnesis*, as then-Cardinal Joseph Ratzinger proposed in a very instructive essay on conscience.[164] Ratzinger argues that because the word *synderesis* found its way from Stoicism into the medieval discussion of conscience, the term "remained unclear in its exact meaning, and for this reason became a hindrance to a careful development of this essential aspect of the whole question of conscience."[165] Ratzinger proposes not only to address this problem by replacing the notion of *synderesis* with the Platonic concept of *anamnesis*, a concept he regards as "not only linguistically clearer and philosophically deeper and purer," but also to harmonize "with key motifs of biblical thought and the anthropology derived from it."[166] Based on St. Paul's Letter to the Romans (2:14–15) and guided by St. Basil and St. Augustine, Ratzinger holds:

> The first so-called ontological level of the phenomenon conscience consists in the fact that something like an original memory of the good and the true (they are identical) has been implanted in us, that there is an inner ontological tendency within man, who is created in the likeness of God, toward the divine.... This anamnesis ... is, so to speak, an inner sense, a capacity to recall, so that the one whom it addresses, if he is not turned in on himself, hears its echo from within.[167]

While I regard the overall argument of this important essay as persuasive and of increasing pertinence, I remain unpersuaded by Ratzinger's proposal of replacing *synderesis* with *anamnesis*. I think this matter may be discussed in all due respect to then-Cardinal Ratzinger and now Pope Emeritus Benedict XVI. Because *anamnesis* is the suggested replacement term for *synderesis*, Ratzinger understands, as he explicitly states, *anam-*

---

164. Joseph Ratzinger [Benedict XVI], *On Conscience: Two Essays by Joseph Ratzinger* (San Francisco, Calif.: Ignatius Press, 2007), 11–41, at 30–36.

165. Ibid., 30.

166. Ibid., 31.

167. Ibid., 32.

nesis to pertain to the ontological level of conscience. On the ontological level, *anamnesis* can only be an innate *habitus* (and hence identical with *synderesis*) or an innate act (*actus*).

Let us consider first the option of understanding *anamnesis* as an innate *actus*. This *actus* would need to be conceived as continuous, as an ongoing interior illumination of the human agent with the first principle ("good is that which all things seek after") and the first precept ("good is to be done and pursued, and evil is to be avoided"). Consequently, *anamnesis* would not stand in need of any further reduction to act and would therefore make the interior judgment of *conscientia* superfluous. The virtue of prudence (with its two acts of counsel and command) would suffice to account for the proper realization of the continuous innate *actus* of *anamnesis* in fitting specific exterior acts. On this supposition, there might be either an imprudent realization of the interior illumination of *anamnesis* in the exterior act, or worse, a vicious rejection of the interior illumination by the will (presupposing a strong dichotomy between intellect and will). However, on the supposition that *anamnesis* is an innate *actus* on the ontological level, there could never be an erring conscience—that is, a conscience that is subjectively good but objectively wrong. Because illumination and error are mutually exclusive, the will becomes the fulcrum of "decision" (i.e., decision and not judgment) either to follow the light that *anamnesis* constantly sheds into the intellect or to turn against it. For these reasons, the option of understanding *anamnesis* as an innate *actus* seems unsustainable. Indeed, then-Cardinal Ratzinger does not seem to support this first option either in its full implications. Hence, the second option, construing *anamnesis* as an innate *habitus*, seems to be preferable.

Let us, therefore, now turn to a brief consideration of this option. As mentioned above, its central advantage is that it allows a conceptual account of the erroneous conscience. For in order to maintain the concept of the erring conscience one must uphold, on the one hand, the distinction between (1) the *habitus* of the first principle and the first precept and (2) the interior actualization of a concrete judgment (*conscientia*) and, on the other hand, the distinction between (3) the interior act of judgment and (4) the exercise of the virtue of prudence, which always has its term in an exterior act. Consequently, in order to avoid the problem of the impossibility of an erroneous conscience, one would need to take *anamnesis* not as *actus*—that is, as illumination—but as *habitus*. But in this case *anamnesis* becomes conceptually indistinguishable from *synderesis*. The only remaining question then would be which word would be preferable for pragmatic, prudential, or pedagogical reasons to signify the innate *habitus* of the first principle and precept of practical reason. If one is committed to maintaining the distinction between a natural *habitus* on the ontological level of conscience (*synderesis*) and its reduction to act (*conscientia*), as then-Cardinal Ratzinger himself seems to suggest, the introduction of the concept of *anamnesis* might in the end only complicate the fundamental distinction between the *habitus* and its actualization. In light of the potential misunderstanding of *anamnesis* as an innate *actus*, it seems preferable to keep the initially unfamiliar, but now received technical term *synderesis*. The proposal to adopt *anamnesis* instead seems to open the way to misunderstandings that could undercut the possibility of accounting conceptually for the erroneous conscience.

Appendix 7

Norman Kretzmann offers an instructive analysis of the complex issue condensed in the Thomist principle "an unjust law is not a law."[168] The only authority that Aquinas quotes (and in a subtle way generalizes) in order to back his position is Augustine.[169] As Kretzmann rightly observes, Aquinas has in mind a *"conscientious* conscientious objection" based on a properly formed conscience, which for a Catholic will always entail a genuine docility to the guidance that the ordinary magisterium provides. There is indeed a danger that the counterfeit of conscience can take the moral high ground in the form of a counterfeit moral revivalism that, in the name of an allegedly superior subjectivist morality, takes exception to

168. Norman Kretzmann, "LEX INIUSTA NON EST LEX: Laws on Trial in Aquinas' 'Court of Conscience,'" *American Journal of Jurisprudence* 33 (1988): 99–122.
169. Augustine, *De libero arbitrio* I.5 (PL 32:1227). Kretzmann points out that there are earlier important representatives of Aquinas's position: Plato, *Laws* IV (715b; 712e–713a) and *Statesman* (293d–e); Aristotle, *Politics* III.6 (1282/b12–13) and IV.4 (1292a31–34); and Cicero, *De legibus* II.v.11.

specific or all laws. Allan Bloom describes this danger aptly: "Conscience, a faculty thoroughly discredited in modern political and moral thought and particularly despised by Marx, made a great comeback, as the all-purpose ungrounded ground of moral determination, sufficient at its slightest rumbling to discredit all other obligations or loyalties."[170] Setting aside this particular phenomenon of a "charismatic moral decisionism," a body politic in which theonomic conscience is respected always has the option to acknowledge legally certain forms of conscientious objection, normally based on the principle of religious freedom. In recent years, however, secularist democratic regimes in the West have tended to privilege the full legal protection of the subjectivist counterfeit of conscience and its sovereign self-affirmation over the freedom of religious practice.

170. Bloom, *The Closing of the American Mind*, 326.

CHAPTER 2

FAITH AND ITS COUNTERFEIT

In the first decades of the twenty-first century, an observant spectator might perceive the striking ambiguity that haunts the self-image of late-modern humanity in the Western Hemisphere. The rapidly accelerating progress of the scientific penetration of the natural world and the ensuing technological domination of the whole planet seem to have placed humanity in a quasi-divine position, as a collective Demiurge. Sovereignty, once an exclusive attribute of divinity, seems now to fall to humanity collectively and in far reaching ways to each individual human subject.

Among the affluent in the Western Hemisphere, subjective sovereignty is exercised by the individual through the unfettered rule of his or her will over ideally everything exterior to the will. This includes consumer goods (not only homes and educations, vacations and special experiences, but also partners, children, one's gender, and the specific make-up of one's body), varyingly and multiply defined identities, and last but not least ideological and religious affiliations. The precious and tenaciously defended privilege of subjective sovereignty is, of course, choice. The range of choice available to the individual is seen as directly proportional to the degree of subjective sovereignty he or she enjoys—an increase in the former indicates an increase in the latter.

The interpretation of reality that the natural sciences communicate to the public, however, presents a jarringly different picture. They present an increasingly comprehensive materialist account of the natural world—including the human being. This materialistic account leaves no place for subjective sovereignty. The human mind is understood as an epiphenomenon of the brain's neurological processes; human choices are predicted with statistical precision and unmasked as ultimately driven by the interests of the "selfish gene."[1] In short, humans are nothing more than highly advanced primates that will eventually be completely transparent to the analytic gaze of the natural sciences and therefore open to comprehensive governance through the most advanced psychological and technological means of manipulation.

The late-modern subject vacillates between these two competing self-images. On the one side, the angelism of the putatively disembodied sovereign subject that subjects to its will an absolutely malleable and fluid external world. On the other side, the animalism of a super-primate allegedly determined by its genetic make-up and its particular ecological niche. The extremes touch each other insofar as transhumanism—an outgrowth of the fantasies of the sovereign subject—and posthumanism—the reductive understanding of the human being as super-primate—coincide. In such a context, sovereignty has only two sides, its agent and its object. Angelism and animalism are nothing but the two sides of sovereignty. The only significant struggle in late-modern technologically advanced, economically consumer-capitalist, and politically "liberal" societies of the Western Hemisphere is to avoid at all costs being subjected to the sovereignty of others and simultaneously to maximize one's possibilities of exercising subjective sovereignty.

One of the outcasts of this brave new world is faith. Its detractors regard it, at best, as a benign superstition or, at worst, as pernicious and dangerous nonsense. And faith's Christian practitioners all too often mis-

---

1. See Dawkins, *The Selfish Gene.*

take it for just a strong conviction to be adhered to with heroic persistence, or some existential leap of trust beyond reason, or an exclusively divine act that simply happens in someone, or simply a dogged attachment of the will to certain liturgical, moral, and social practices. It is to be expected that the detractors of the faith, the ones who embrace and celebrate the brave new world of unbelief and irreligion, do not understand properly what they despise. But it is tragic when the practitioners of the faith themselves mistake faith for what might very well belong to it but is not its essence.

The practitioners of the Christian faith rarely if ever commit the crude mistake of understanding their faith through the lens of an evolutionary naturalism. The intellectual, volitional, and existential dynamics of faith instantaneously put the lie to such an interpretive approach. The matter is, however, quite different when it comes to the social imaginary (Charles Taylor) of the sovereign subject. Practitioners of the faith stand in grave danger of mistaking faith for its counterfeit, that is, private judgment in matters of revealed religion. It is for this very reason that in the following, we shall focus on only one of the two dominant self-images of the present age, on the sovereign subject and its most cherished principle, the principle of private judgment.

In the swiftly self-secularizing Great Britain of the nineteenth century, John Henry Newman advanced the highly pertinent distinction between faith and private judgment, a distinction that is crucial for any contemporary recovery of the very nature of faith as it is confronted with the social imaginary of the sovereign subject. Because Newman found himself in a rapidly advancing society in which the imaginary of the sovereign subject was in precipitous ascendancy, his keen analysis of faith and private judgment will serve as our theological "context of discovery." Newman's genius was that of a controversialist and personalist—defending the truth of the Catholic faith in critical engagement with its detractors and recovering the full personal and existential import of the faith, not just its notions, but its reality.[2] Newman neither had patience for nor was properly

2. For an instructive study that documents and analyzes the way Newman in his sermons and tracts aimed at bringing to life in the imagination of his audience the existential import of the faith's substance, see Crosby, *The Personalism of John Henry Newman*.

trained to provide a dogmatic theology. But—especially in his Catholic period—he genuinely respected (although he did not endorse in each instantiation) the careful doctrinal and speculative labor of dogmatic theology. It is therefore neither artificial nor forced to supply Newman's theological "context of discovery" as one of the premier controversialists of his day with an appropriate dogmatic "context of justification," in Thomas Aquinas's treatise on faith in the *Summa theologiae*. Although Newman's and Thomas's approaches, methodologies, temperaments, and respective auxiliary philosophies might to some degree differ, when considered systematically and conceptually, it will become clear that their respective accounts of assent and of divine faith are compatible and, indeed, converging. Their converging accounts of divine faith yield unexpected but important implications—for Catholics and other Christians alike.

Newman on Faith and Private Judgment

Consider the following three brief statements by Newman. These statements are found in the first of the two *Discourses Addressed to Mixed Congregations*, in which Newman discusses, "Faith and Private Judgment" and "Faith and Doubt."[3] Published in 1849, only four years after his conversion from Anglicanism to the Catholic church, Newman addresses in these discourses a mixed audience of Catholics and Protestants with the aim of clarifying central issues of difference between Protestantism and the Catholic church. One of the central topics is, not surprisingly, faith. Here is the first of Newman's brief statements: "The very meaning, the very exercise of faith, is joining the Church."[4] Newman claims that faith and church belong inherently together. Like a cause and its proper effect, the one leads unavoidably to the other. Faith that does not lead to joining the church or is not ordered to it, is not faith but, most likely, its counterfeit. Second: "Men do not become Catholics, because they have not

3. *Discourses Addressed to Mixed Congregations* (London: Longmans, Green, and Co., 1906) [hereafter "*Mix.*"]: Discourse X: "Faith and Private Judgment" (192–213); Discourse XI: "Faith and Doubt" (214–37). See appendix 1 for a brief discussion of the changes in Newman's understanding of the nature of faith after his 1845 conversion to the Catholic faith. The single best book on Newman on the topic of faith is still Philip Flanagan's *Newman, Faith and the Believer* (London: Sands and Co., 1946).

4. *Mix.*, 193.

faith."[5] Here Newman advances the necessary correlate of the first statement. The one and only essential reason that keeps someone from becoming a Catholic is the absence of faith. Newman now makes explicit that the church, the joining of which is the very meaning of faith, is not just any community using the denomination "church"; nor does it denote the infamous Platonic church behind and above all Christian communions. It is, rather, nothing but the Catholic church. Third: "It is vain to discourse upon the beauty, the sanctity, the sublimity of the Catholic doctrine and worship, where men have no faith to accept it as Divine."[6] The property of Catholic doctrine and worship is not their beauty, sanctity, and sublimity, but rather their divinity: Catholic doctrine and worship have their origin in God, lead to God, and communicate the saving presence of God. And it is nothing short of faith that accepts Catholic doctrine and worship as such, as fundamentally divine.

The "ecumenical age" of the twentieth century might very well have reached its apex and therefore end in what Protestant mainline denominations, the successors of the magisterial Protestant Reformation (Lutheran and Reformed), regard—quite contrary to the original meaning of the term—as a state of "differentiated consensus."[7] However important

---

5. *Mix.*, 193.

6. *Mix.*, 207.

7. The phrase "differentiated consensus" was originally put forward by Harding Meyer in the 1990s. See Harding Meyer, "Ecumenical Consensus: Our Quest For and the Emerging Structures of Consensus," *Gregorianum* 77 (1996): 213–25, as well as his "Die Prägung einer Formel: Ursprung und Intention," in *Einheit - Aber Wie? Zur Tragfähigkeit der ökumenischen Formel vom "differenzierten Konsens,"* ed. Harald Wagner (Freiburg: Herder, 2000), 36–58. At its simplest and most straightforward, the phrase formulates the obvious: the doctrinal consensus needed for full communion need not exclude every theological difference. The phrase thus intends originally to eliminate a possible error—that doctrinal consensus means every difference is eliminated—but then sets the decisive task of ecumenical dialogue, that of distinguishing genuine doctrinal difference that must be addressed from school differences that can be allowed to continue even within full reconciliation and the restoration of visible church unity. Such a differentiation was intrinsic to the Christological agreements Pope St. John Paul II signed with the Copts ("Common Declaration of Pope John Paul II and His Holiness Mar Ignatius Zakka I Iwas," 1984) and with the Armenians ("Common Christological Declaration between the Catholic Church and the Assyrian Church of the East," 1994). However, in a situation of widespread doctrinal ignorance and indifference, which arguably is the situation among mainstream Protestantism and all-too-common in North American Catholicism, differentiated consensus has become an excuse for simply abandoning the task of distinguishing doctrinal differences from school differences and settling into an accommodationist state of reconciled (in)difference. I am indebted to Michael Root for an accurate narration of the meaning and intention of the phrase "differentiated consensus" in its original ecumenical "Sitz im Leben."

and useful some notion of "differentiated consensus" has been and still can be in the abstract, it has *de facto* become an excuse for an all too comfortable accommodation to a situation where religions have become consumer goods that simply correspond to our different religious tastes. And, of course, *de gustibus non est disputandum*, in matters of taste, there can be no disputes. Thus, quite contrary to its original ecumenical intention and meaning, "differentiated consensus" has become a sophisticated way of declaring the premature termination of the ecumenical movement as an ecumenical victory—a state of mutual ecclesial recognition in which all remaining doctrinal differences as well as the original ecumenical goal of visible unity are bracketed to a maximal degree. Newman's three statements challenge this "differentiated consensus" in a way that in many ecumenical circles, Protestant and Catholic, would be regarded as jarring, inhospitable, and inopportune, that is, politically incorrect. And, if Newman's statements are true, they unmask the "differentiated consensus" as a lukewarm consensus of reconciled (in)difference and raise the uncomfortable question whether and if so to what degree the consensus of reconciled (in)difference might have its root, at least in part, in the counterfeit of faith, the principle of private judgment in matters of revealed religion. If, as Newman asserts, every exercise of faith is inherently ordered to full communion with the Catholic church, and if indeed someone cannot accept Catholic doctrine and worship as divine if he or she lacks the faith to recognize it as such, the consensus of reconciled (in)difference—which considers the Catholic church to be just one other denominational option—might be a mark of the counterfeit of faith, the principle of private judgment in matters of revealed religion. To sacrifice the notion of divine faith as defended by Newman would be the sacrifice necessary to make possible and to solidify the consensus of reconciled (in)difference. It indeed seems to be the case that many contemporary theologians, including Catholic theologians, of our present ecumenical age are ready to sacrifice the notion of faith proposed by Newman on the altar of ecumenical rapprochement and its putative proximate conclusion, the status quo of "differentiated consensus."[8] Yet in order to understand what is at stake in such

8. This impression imposes itself upon any perceptive observer, for none of the many bilateral ecumenical dialogues between the Roman Catholic church and virtually all major Protestant

a widely supported and welcomed—but ultimately detrimental—sacrifice, it is imperative to understand first what exactly is supposed to be sacrificed, the very reality of divine faith.[9] What exactly is the notion of faith Newman expounds and contrasts with the principle of private judgment in matters of revealed religion?

Faith

Newman holds faith to be "a state of mind, ... a particular mode of thinking and acting, which is exercised, always indeed towards God, but in very various ways."[10] Not a mode of sensing, feeling, or imagining, but rather

---

ecclesial communions has tackled the topic of the nature of faith itself. And even when the bilateral dialogues have taken up the question of authority, the dialogue-groups have proved unwilling to press the question far enough to get at the underlying issue—the issue of the nature of faith itself. If maintained over a longer period of time, such marked unwillingness will eventually only encourage a silent settlement of the question on faith's counterfeit, the tacit premise of the principle of private judgment in matters of revealed religion. Another alternative to tackling the question theologically in a straightforward way is the preemptive theological move made by Karl Rahner. He reconceived faith as a grace-given and freely accepted dynamism of the human spirit toward God, who is the only adequate object of the human spirit's desire and love. Faith, thus reconceived, is an acceptance of the proximity of God as absolute mystery—a faith available to everyone, also atheists: "It can be found in people who consciously believe they are and must be atheists, as long as they are completely obedient to the absolute demands of their conscience, that is, to use our terminology, they accept themselves unconditionally, without self-rejection, fulfilling that primordial capacity of freedom which involves the subject as a whole." "Faith between Rationality and Emotion," 67; see also his articles "Anonymous and Explicit Faith" as well as "The Act of Faith and the Content of Faith." It is hard, if not impossible, to avoid the conclusion that "faith" has thus become fundamentally equivocal. It is furthermore difficult if not impossible to conclude that this reconception of faith can be reconciled with the teaching on faith promulgated in the First Vatican Council's Dogmatic Constitution, *Dei Filius*. It is also difficult if not impossible to conclude, based on a thoughtful reading of Hannah Arendt's *Eichmann in Jerusalem: A Report on the Banality of Evil* and watching the footage of his trial that on the supposition of Rahner's reconceived notion of faith, Adolf Eichmann (a great admirer of Kant's categorical imperative, by the way) indeed had faith. In short, it is difficult if not impossible to conclude that Newman would have submitted Rahner's reconception of faith to one of his rigorous *reductio ad absurdum* treatments. For an instructive analysis of Newman's *reductio ad absurdum* strategy, see John F. Crosby, "A 'Primer of Infidelity' Based on Newman? A Study of Newman's Rhetorical Strategy," *Newman Studies Journal* 8, no. 1 (2011): 6–19. In sum, both alternatives to facing squarely the ecumenically sensitive topic of faith—indefinite ecumenical postponement and its radical reconception—are misjudged.

9. Not all Protestants, of course, endorse the status quo of "differentiated consensus," that is, reconciled (in)difference. Therefore, their inability or unwillingness to recognize the Catholic church as *the* church of Christ is not necessarily an indication of whether they enjoy or are devoid of divine faith.

10. *Mix.*, 193–94.

of thinking and acting, faith is first and foremost exercised in relationship to God. God is the primary object of faith. Furthermore, faith is an act of assent to a teaching that is held because it comes from God who cannot lie. The fact that it comes from God is the sole motive for assenting to the teaching. Crucially, the motive of faith must include in its object also those who serve as God's messengers, as divinely appointed instruments. Consider Newman's concise summary:

[Faith] is assenting to a doctrine as true, which we do not see, which we cannot prove, because God says it is true, who cannot lie. And further than this, since God says it is true, not with His own voice, but by the voice of His messengers, it is assenting to what man says, not simply viewed as a man, but to what he is commissioned to declare, as a messenger, prophet, or ambassador from God.[11]

Because faith unites the mind to the hidden truths about God, truths that God reveals and communicates and because its sole motive is God's veracity and authority, the assent to these truths is rightly called *divine* faith, that is, a divinely infused supernatural virtue. The certitude characteristic of it is an effect of divine grace: "The absolute and perfect certitude of divine faith does not rest on reasoning and human motives, but solely on the fact that God, the Eternal Truth, who cannot deceive nor be deceived, has spoken."[12] Divine faith has two defining characteristics: "It is most certain, decided, positive, immovable in its assent, and it gives this assent

---

11. *Mix.*, 194–95.

12. "Cardinal Newman's Theses de fide and his proposed Introduction to the French Translation of the University Sermons," ed. Henry Tristram, *Gregorianum* 18 (1937): 219–60, here 236, Thesis 10: "Certitudo contra absoluta et perfecta fidei divinae, non ad discursum appellat aut ad motiva humana, sed unice ad hoc quod, locutus est Deus, Aeterna Veritas, qui nec decipere potest nec decipi." Newman refers for support to Aquinas, *ST* II-II, q. 1, a. 1. The Council fathers of the First Vatican Council teach in *Dei Filius*, chap. 3, "On Faith": "Since human beings are totally dependent on God as their creator and lord, and created reason is completely subject to uncreated truth, we are obliged to yield to God the revealer full submission of intellect and will by faith. This faith, which is the beginning of human salvation, the catholic church professes to be a supernatural virtue, by means of which, with the grace of God inspiring and assisting us, we believe to be true what has been revealed not because we perceive its intrinsic truth by the natural light of reason, *but because of the authority of God himself, who makes the revelation and can neither deceive nor be deceived* (*sed propter auctoritatem ipsius Dei revelantis, qui nec falli nec fallere potest*)." *Decrees of the Ecumenical Councils*, vol. 2, *Trent–Vatican II*, ed. Norman P. Tanner, SJ (London / Washington, D.C.: Sheed and Ward / Georgetown University Press, 1990), 807; emphasis added. The Catholic Newman's teaching on faith in his *Theses de fide* and in his sermon "Faith and Private Judgment" fully comports with and finds confirmation in the teaching of Vatican I on faith.

not because it sees with eye, or sees with the reason, but because it receives the tidings from one who comes from God."[13]

Newman insists that if faith is what he understands it to be, it must
"be now the same faculty of mind, the same sort of habit or act, which it
was in the days of the Apostles."[14] For the property of faith in the apostolic age is still the same property now: "Immediate, implicit submission
of the mind," Newman observes, "was, in the lifetime of the Apostles, the
only, the necessary token of faith; then there was no room whatever for
what is now called private judgment."[15] He stresses that divine faith is always apostolic faith, the submission to a living authority: "In the Apostle's
days the peculiarity of faith was submission to a living authority; this is
what made it so distinctive; this is what made it an act of submission at
all; this is what destroyed private judgment in matters of religion. If you
will not look out for a living authority, and will bargain for private judgment, then say at once that you have not Apostolic faith."[16]

The formal characteristic of divine faith in the apostolic age and divine faith now is the submission to a living authority, and this living authority is the same today as in the apostolic age because the present living
authority stands in apostolic, doctrinal, and moral continuity with the
living authority of the apostolic age. The root of divine faith is *fides ex
auditu*, the faith that comes from hearing—not just anybody but the living authority that conveys God's truth: the incarnate Logos first, then the
apostles, then their successors. Newman is not at all interested in advancing a version of the historical argument for apostolic succession. Rather,
he is interested in pointing out the formal contrariety between the principle of divine faith and the principle of private judgment in matters of revealed religion. Wherever divine faith is exercised, the principle of private
judgment in matters of revealed religion is obliterated—and vice versa.
Divine faith and private judgment in matters of revealed religion cannot
coexist in the same person at the same time. But what exactly is private
judgment in matters of revealed religion in the first place?

13. *Mix.*, 195–96.
14. *Mix.*, 206–7.
15. *Mix.*, 197.
16. *Mix.*, 207.

Private Judgment

In an age in which the comprehensive application of the principle of private judgment is the defining mark of the sovereign subject, the dictatorship of relativism in matters of religion and morals becomes seemingly inescapable. The only permissible attitude toward any religion, but especially a religion based on divine revelation, is one reached through private judgment, where one's choice of religious affiliation is ultimately nothing but a consumer choice of a particular commodity that is in principle dispensable or exchangeable at any time. Unsurprisingly, therefore, wherever in the Western Hemisphere the sovereign subject has achieved a hegemonic position, the principle of private judgment in matters of revealed religion takes the position of the conceptual and existential contrary to divine faith. Consider Newman's apt characterization in his *Discourses Addressed to Mixed Congregations*: "I will choose my religion for myself, I will believe this, I will not believe that; I will pledge myself to nothing; I will believe just as long as I please, and no longer; what I believe today I will reject tomorrow, if I choose."[17] Private judgment in matters of revealed religion is a direct function of the subjective sovereignty of the will: "We keep the decision in our own hands, and reserve to ourselves the right of re-opening the question whenever we please."[18] The act of private judgment in matters of revealed religion has its origin in the subject that judges and refers back again to the subject that judges. Like all judgments, private judgments in matters of revealed religion involve the will as well as the intellect and therefore have two characteristic components. First, willfulness in refusing assent to divine testimony. The judgment remains completely contingent upon the subject's willfulness, that is, until the subject happens to replace it with some other judgment. The second component of private judgment pertains to the intellect and is best characterized as a fixed personal *a priori* criterion of what is rational and what is irrational, in short, as a kind of rationalism.

Consider the centrality of doubt in the social imaginary of the sovereign subject. Doubt is a certain reservation of mind in matters of re-

17. *Mix.*, 197.
18. *Mix.*, 195.

vealed truth. Newman rightly stresses that the defenders of the principle of private judgment in matters of revealed religion ought to hold, "if they are consistent, this,—that it is a fault ever to make up our mind once for all on any religious subject whatever; and that, however sacred a doctrine may be, and however evident to us,—let us say, for instance, the divinity of our Lord, or the existence of God,—we ought always to reserve to ourselves the liberty of doubting about it."[19] While the principle of private judgment in matters of revealed religion anticipates the possibility of future doubt, divine faith excludes all doubt. The motive cause of private judgments in matters of revealed religion is the preservation of one's personal sense of sovereignty of will and intellect over against all claims of divine testimony. The motive cause of divine faith is God's authority and veracity. There can obtain only the one or the other motive cause. Divine faith and private judgment in matters of revealed religion are mutually exclusive. It is a strict either-or. As Newman stresses:

Either the Apostles were from God, or they were not; if they were, everything that they preached was to be believed by their hearers; if they were not, there was nothing for their hearers to believe. To believe a little, to believe more or less, was impossible; it contradicted the very notion of believing: if one part was to be believed, every part was to be believed; it was an absurdity to believe one thing and not another; for the word of the Apostles, which made the one true, made the other true too; they were nothing in themselves, they were all things, they were an infallible authority, as coming from God. The world had either to become Christian, or to let it alone; there was no room for private tastes and fancies, no room for private judgment.[20]

Divine faith admits, of course, of innumerable intellectual difficulties to which the mystery of faith gives rise and recognizes objections to the faith. These difficulties and objections are the preoccupations of faith seeking understanding—investigation being its characteristic activity. But they are categorically different from doubt. As Newman famously stated in a letter to his friend Henry Wilberforce: "An objection is not a doubt—ten thousand objections as little make one doubt, as ten thou-

19. *Mix.*, 214–15.
20. *Mix.*, 197.

sand ponies make one horse."[21] It is important to realize that by doubt, Newman always means *real* doubt, not methodical doubt. The activity he correlated with real doubt is inquiry. If persons who have divine faith permit themselves to entertain real doubts by inquiring, the consequences are of a spiritually grave nature.

They have listened to arguments against what they knew to be true, and a deadness of mind has fallen on them; faith has failed them, and, as time goes on, they betray in their words and their actions, the Divine judgment, with which they are visited. They become careless and unconcerned, or restless and unhappy, or impatient of contradiction; ever asking advice and quarreling with it when given; not attempting to answer the arguments urged against them, but simply not believing. This is the whole of their case, they do not believe. And then it is quite an accident what becomes of them; perhaps they continue on in this perplexed and comfortless state, lingering about the Church, yet not of her; not knowing what they believe and what they do not, like blind men, or men deranged, who are deprived of the eye, whether of body or mind, and cannot guide themselves in consequence; ever exciting hopes of a return, and ever disappointing them;—or, if they are men of more vigorous minds, they launch forward in a course of infidelity, not really believing less, as they proceed, for from the first they believed nothing, but taking up, as time goes on, more and more consistent forms of error, till sometimes, if a free field is given them, they even develop into atheism.[22]

The loss of faith is one thing, the loss of charity is quite another. Faith may persist, while love has been forfeit:

A soul which has received the grace of baptism receives with it the germ or faculty of all supernatural virtues whatever,—faith, hope, charity, meekness, patience, sobriety, and every other that can be named; and if it commits mortal sin, it falls out of grace, and forfeits these supernatural powers. It is no longer what it was,

---

21. Ward, *Life of Newman*, 2:250.

22. *Mix.*, 226. Newman comes back to this troubling dynamic in his *Grammar of Assent*: "He who inquires has not found; he is in doubt where the truth lies, and wishes his present profession either proved or disproved. We cannot without absurdity call ourselves at once believers and inquirers also. Thus it is sometimes spoken of as a hardship that a Catholic is not allowed to inquire into the truth of his Creed;—of course he cannot, if he would retain the name of believer. He cannot be both inside and outside of the Church at once. It is merely common sense to tell him that, if he is seeking, he has not found. If seeking includes doubting, and doubting excludes believing, then the Catholic who sets about inquiring, thereby declares that he is not a Catholic. He has already lost faith" (*G.A.*, 191).

and is, so far, in the feeble and frightful condition of those who were never baptized. But there are certain remarkable limitations and alleviations in its punishment, and one is this: that the faculty or power of faith remains to it. Of course the soul may go on to resist and destroy this supernatural faculty also; it may, by an act of the will, rid itself of its faith, as it has stripped itself of grace and love; or it may gradually decay in its faith till it becomes simply infidel; but this is not the common state of a Catholic people. What commonly happens is this, that they fall under the temptations to vice or covetousness, which naturally and urgently beset them, but that faith is left to them.... They have a vivid perception, like sense, of things unseen, yet have no desire at all, or affection, towards them; they have knowledge without love. Such is the state of the many.[23] ...

There is a feeble old woman, who first genuflects before the Blessed Sacrament, and then steals her neighbour's handkerchief, or prayer-book, who is intent on his devotions.... Faith is illuminative, not operative; it does not force obedience, though it increases responsibility; it heightens guilt, it does not prevent sin; the will is the source of action, not an influence, though divine, which Baptism has implanted, and which the devil has only not eradicated. She worships and she sins; she kneels because she believes, she steals because she does not love; she may be out of God's grace, she is not altogether out of His sight.[24]

Hence, to have knowledge without love, that is, to have faith unformed by charity is fundamentally different from entertaining real doubt and from reserving one's right to private judgments in matters of revealed religion. The former is vice, the latter unbelief.

Protestantism and Private Judgment

As I already stated above, Newman stresses that divine faith, that is, genuine apostolic faith comes from hearing (*fides ex auditu*) a living apostolic authority and submitting to it, a living authority that is understood to be authorized and guided by God to communicate God's revelation. But absent the living authority of the church that divine faith entails and for which classical Protestantism substitutes with the principle "Scripture alone" (*sola scriptura*), a state of mind other than divine faith must emerge. Newman puts it thus:

23. *Diff.* i., 273–74.
24. *Diff.* i., 285–86.

Are not these two states or acts of mind quite distinct from each other; —to believe simply at what a living authority tells you, and to take a book, such as Scripture, and to use it as you please, to master it, that is, to make yourself the master of it, to interpret it for yourself, and to admit just what you choose to see in it, and nothing more?[25]

Newman presses that this is the crucial insight: the single reader relies necessarily on his or her private judgment, and a group of readers rely on their collective private judgment. But there can never be a gradual transition from a maximally collective private judgment (as for example the Lutheran *magnus consensus* expressed in the *Confessio Augustana*) to a submission to a living authority. Newman rightly stresses the formal difference: "There is ... an essential difference between the act of submitting to a living oracle, and to his written words; in the former case there is no appeal from the speaker, in the latter the final decision remains with the reader."[26] A living authority can only be rejected or believed as mediator of God's revelation; it is believed in such a way that relinquishes all private judgment in this matter. The principle of an allegedly self-interpreting scripture (*scriptura sua interpres*) can only be maintained if the concomitant principle of private judgment in matters of revealed religion is consistently ignored. Newman draws a startling inference that in our present ecumenical age can sound politically incorrect. Given Newman's notion of faith, the inference is, nevertheless, as conclusive now as it was then: "Protestants, generally speaking, have not faith, in the primitive meaning of that word."[27] And then again: "they know nothing of faith; for they have no authority to submit to."[28] Notably, Newman's qualification "generally speaking" signals that he is referring here not to this or that particular individual, but to a self-styled ideal-type. We might call this ideal-type *principled Protestantism* and differentiate it from what best be called *accidental Protestantism*. "Principled Protestantism" is Protestantism according to its inherent, functioning inner logic, independent both of Catholic concessions individual Protestants make and of the way

25. *Mix.*, 199.
26. *Mix.*, 200.
27. *Mix.*, 201.
28. *Mix.*, 206.

some Reformers thought it could function.[29] Protestants *qua* Protestants according to the ideal-type of principled Protestantism do not have faith in Newman's sense of the term. Differently put, Protestant faith according to the ideal-type of principled Protestantism is not faith but something else. This is different from asserting that no Protestant whosoever has divine faith, a claim that would never occur to Newman to advance.

"Accidental Protestantism" refers to those who might have supernatural faith by virtue of their sacramental baptism and the fact that their Protestant tradition is an accidental vehicle that transmits a divine message which they assent to as divine. One might think of a theologically unschooled Lutheran farmer who gives little thought, if any, to *sola scriptura*, yet who believes that what he reads from the Bible and what he hears preached on Sunday, is God's word to which he assents without understanding the *de facto* deficiency of the purported Lutheran sufficiency of scripture. "Principled Protestantism," on the other hand, is a theologically sophisticated and most often reflectively and explicitly held position that secures the principle of *sola scriptura* with the help of the principle of private judgment in matters of revealed religion. Scripture alone is supposed to yield the *doctrina evangelii*. Because scripture quite obviously does not yield the *doctrina evangelii* on its own, another auxiliary principle is needed, a principle of interpretive authority—in short, a substitute for the living apostolic authority of the Catholic church. This auxiliary principle is the principle of private judgment in matters of revealed religion explicitly defended as at least unavoidable if not as actually desirable (typically found in Liberal Protestantism). This auxiliary principle might be hidden under a pneumatological construal (typically found among Evangelicals): the Holy Spirit interprets scripture that, read in the Spirit,

29. Martin Luther and many of his followers, as well as John Calvin and many of his followers, would have denied any role for something like private judgment in matters of faith. They regarded faith as a matter of trust in and obedience to the clear Word of God delivered by scripture and proclamation true to scripture. What was overlooked first and not acknowledged later was that reading scripture unmoored from any living apostolic authority mandated to distinguish between true and false interpretation of scripture forces these scripture readers, in the long run or even the relatively short run, to fall back some version of the principle of private judgment in matters of revealed religion. History would show what Newman would argue forcefully—that Protestantism is unable to avoid this detrimental development. The canon of scripture was simply never designed to replace a living apostolic authority.

is capable of communicating its authentic divine meaning. If the auxiliary principle turns out to be a tacit acknowledgment of the church as living authority exercised by way of accepting the Trinitarian and Christological dogmas of the Catholic church and by way of acknowledging the New Testament canon as a *de facto* norm then we are faced with a kind of "accidental Protestants" who may be "under the influence of faith" or even have supernatural faith because they tacitly and implicitly submit to some anterior instantiation of the living apostolic authority of the Catholic church. Newman states:

If, however, there are Protestants … who firmly believe in spite of all difficulties, they certainly have some claim to be considered under the influence of faith; but there is nothing to show that such persons, where they are found, are not in the way to become Catholics, and perhaps they are already called so by their friends, showing in their own examples the logical, indisputable connexion which exists between possessing faith and joining the Church.[30]

What Newman adumbrates here in a discourse to a mixed congregation is clarified fully by Vatican II's *Lumen Gentium* and *Unitatis Redintegratio*. *Lumen Gentium* teaches that "this church, set up and organized in this world as a society, subsists in the catholic church, governed by the successor of Peter and the bishops in communion with him, although outside its structure many elements of sanctification and of truth [*elementa plura sanctificationis et veritatis*] are to be found which, as proper gifts to the church of Christ, impel towards catholic unity."[31] These *elementa plura sanctificationis et veritatis* of which the Council fathers speak in *Lumen*

---

30. *Mix.*, 206.

31. *Lumen Gentium*, no. 8, in *Decrees* (ed. Tanner), 2:854. See *Lumen Gentium*, no. 15: "For several reasons the church recognizes that it is joined to those who, though baptized and so honoured with the christian name, do not profess the faith in its entirety or do not preserve the unity of communion under the successor of Peter. For there are many who hold the sacred scripture in honour as the norm for believing and living, and display a sincere religious zeal. They lovingly believe in God the almighty Father and in Christ, the Son of God and savior. They are marked by baptism, by which they are joined to Christ; and indeed there are other sacraments that they recognise and accept in their own churches or ecclesial communities" (ibid., 860–61). *Unitatis Redintegratio* states in no. 3: "Moreover, some, and even most, of the significant elements and endowments which together go to build up and give life to the church itself, can exist outside the visible boundaries of the catholic church: the written word of God; the life of grace; faith, hope, and charity, with the other interior gifts of the holy Spirit, and visible elements too. All of these, coming from Christ and leading back to Christ, properly belong to the one church of Christ" (ibid., 910).

Gentium and which in another context are explicitly called *elementa eccle-siae* are those which tend toward Catholic unity.[32] *Nota bene*: the *eccle-sia* in *elementa ecclesiae* is the Catholic church. That means that in virtue of their baptism and their largely implicit supernatural faith "accidental Protestants" are in a state of partial communion with the Catholic church that objectively tends toward full communion.

Divine Faith Is a Matter of Grace

After having considered the fundamental contrariety between divine faith and the principle of private judgment in matters of revealed religion we must consider how Newman understands divine faith to come about. So far we heard only about "submission to a living authority" as proxi-mate motive cause. This is a necessary but not sufficient cause. Ultimate-ly, divine faith has its origin in God not only formally (as to its motive) and materially (as to its content, the articles of faith), but also effectively. While acts of faith are always genuinely human acts, the disposition that facilitates these acts and the first movement of such acts are caused direct-ly by God. Hence, divine faith is unlike an ordinary conviction or belief. As Newman explains:

Faith is the gift of God, and not a mere act of our own, which we are free to exert when we will. It is quite distinct from an exercise of reason, though it follows upon it.... Faith is not a mere conviction in reason, it is a firm assent, it is a clear certainty greater than any other certainty; and this is wrought in the mind by the grace of God, and by it alone.[33]

Conviction is not divine faith. This is absolutely crucial. A conviction is a very strong, reflexively held opinion.[34] We may hold many convictions,

32. Congregation for the Doctrine of the Faith, "Notification on the book 'Church: Charism and Power' by Fr. Leonardo Boff," *AAS* 77 (1985): 758–59: "the Council chose the word *subsistit* precisely in order to make it clear that there exists a single 'subsistence' of the true Church, while outside her visible structure only *elementa ecclesiae* exist, which—as elements of the Church—tend and lead toward the Catholic Church."

33. *Mix.*, 224. "I may feel the force for the argument for the Divine origin of the Church; I may see that I ought to believe; and yet I may be unable to believe.... It is always indeed his own fault, for God gives grace to all who ask for it, and use it, but still such is the fact, that conviction is not faith" (ibid.).

34. Newman explicates these matters with great acuity in his *Grammar of Assent*: "I shall here

even strong convictions about matters that pertain to the material object of faith, yet the motive cause of all these convictions is nothing but a private judgment or a series of private judgments. The transition from private judgment to divine faith is not one that the subject can engender on his or her own initiative: "You are then what you are, not from any excellence or merit of your own, but by the grace of God who has chosen you to believe."[35] Furthermore, divine faith is formally noncomposite. While it might materially comprise an increasing number of articles of faith, it is formally a simple, undivided faith: "I may love by halves, I may obey by halves; I cannot believe by halves: either I have faith, or I have it not."[36] Because the church is the living apostolic authority to which the believer submits in the act of faith, the church belongs integrally to the mo-

---

use the word to denote an assent, but an assent to a proposition, not as true, but as probably true, that is, to the probability of that which the proposition enunciates; and, as that probability may vary in strength without limit, so may the cogency and moment of the opinion.... Opinion, as being an assent, is independent of premises. We have opinions which we never think of defending by argument, though, of course, we think they can be so defended. We are even obstinate in them, or what is called 'opinionated,' and may say that we have a right to think just as we please, reason or no reason.... Opinion, thus explained, has more connection with Credence than with Inference. It differs from Credence in these two points, viz. that, while Opinion explicitly assents to the probability of a given proposition, Credence is an implicit assent to its truth. It differs from Credence in a third respect, viz. in being a reflex act;—when we take a thing for granted, we have credence in it; when we begin to reflect upon our credence, and to measure, estimate, and modify it, then we are forming an opinion. It is in this sense that Catholics speak of theological opinion, in contrast with faith in dogma. It is much more than an inferential act, but it is distinct from an act of certitude. *And this is really the sense which Protestants give to the word when they interpret it by Conviction; for their highest opinion in religion is, generally speaking, an assent to a probability ... and therefore consistent with toleration of its contradictory*" (*G.A.*, 58–60; emphasis added). Yet Newman also connects conviction with certitude: "There are right and wrong convictions, and certitude is a right conviction; if it is not right with a consciousness of being right, it is not certitude. Now truth cannot change; what is once truth is always truth; and the human mind is made for truth, and so rests in truth, as it cannot rest in falsehood" (*G.A.*, 221). See appendix 2 to this chapter for Newman's astute analysis of the indefectibility of certitude in the paradigmatic instance of changing religious affiliations.

35. *Mix.*, 211. "There are, to be sure, many cogent arguments to lead one to join the Catholic Church, but they do not force the will. We may know them, and not be moved to act upon them. We may be convinced without being persuaded. The two things are quite distinct from each other, seeing you ought to believe, and believing; reason, if left to itself, will bring you to the conclusion that you have sufficient grounds for believing, but belief is the gift of grace. You are what you are, not from any excellence or merit of your own, but by the grace of God who has chosen you to believe" (ibid.).

36. *Mix.*, 216–17. "No one can be a Catholic without a simple faith, that what the Church declares in God's name, is God's word, and therefore true. A man must simply believe that the Church is the oracle of God; he must be as certain of her mission, as he is of the mission of the Apostles" (*Mix.*, 215).

tive cause of the act of faith. The living apostolic authority is not simply joined to God's revelation as an extrinsic human tool, useful for the propagation of the Gospel and subject to the principle of private judgment. It is, rather, integral to God's revelation and hence to the formal motive of divine faith. Newman states: "Nothing is clearer than this, that if faith in God's word is required of us for salvation, the Catholic Church is the only medium by which we can exercise it.... No one should enter the Church without a firm purpose of taking her word in all matters of doctrine and morals, and that, on the ground of her coming directly from the God of Truth."[37] For many a contemporary Catholic or Protestant, Newman's notion of divine faith might come across as too maximalist. Some might wonder whether in Newman we encounter the subtle concoctions of a convert to the Catholic church eager to justify and at the same time camouflage his private judgments that brought him to the threshold of or indeed into the Catholic church. Far from it! Newman formulates, in terms accessible to a modern audience, the teaching on divine faith by numerous Catholic theologians long before the rise of Protestantism. In order to appreciate the depth of the doctrine of divine faith, it is apposite to turn from our modern theological "context of discovery," from Newman's articulation of divine faith as contrasted with the principle of private judgment in matters of revealed religion, to our theological "context of justification," to the comprehensive doctrinal account of the doctrine of divine faith as advanced by Thomas Aquinas in the *Summa theologiae*.

Thomas Aquinas on Divine Faith

Thomas Aquinas, standing in the Augustinian tradition, regards the theological virtues of faith, hope, and charity as the three constitutive virtues of the Christian life. They are not acquired, but infused by God together with sanctifying grace and with the gifts of the Holy Spirit. Unlike the acquired moral virtues that direct us to the common good and unlike the

---

37. *Mix.*, 231. The formal object of faith, its motive, is what makes it divine faith and what differentiates it essentially from strong convictions and beliefs that are the result of the principle of private judgment in matters of revealed religion. The Catholic church as living apostolic authority is integral to the simple, that is, noncomposite motive or formal object of divine faith.

infused moral virtues that guide us on our pilgrimage toward God, the three theological virtues already unite us with God in a certain way. They unite us with God as the distinct "object" of these three virtues. In order to understand Thomas's crucial point here and in order to become an intelligent reader of Thomas, it is necessary to add a new word to our philosophical vocabulary—"object." We think of an "object" as that to which something is done by some "subject." For example, "I open my breviary." "Breviary" is the grammatical object of the verb "to open." That's why under the condition of modernity we want to be subjects—ideally sovereign subjects—and never objects. But this is not how medieval thinkers understood "object" or "obiectum." As Lawrence Dewan has noted, medieval thinkers used the term "object" in connection with apprehensive and appetitive powers to denote that thing from which "the act of apprehension or appetition originates." "In the case of apprehension ["object"] expresses movement from the thing toward the soul. In the case of appetition, ["object"] expresses movement from the soul toward the thing."[38] Let us focus on apprehension. The powers of apprehension and appetition are passive potencies brought into act by their objects. As the noted English Dominican theologian T. C. O'Brien explains, "The term 'object' stands for the reality, thing or person that engages an act."[39] What needs to be highlighted is the verb "engage." The "object" has a causal function in the act of apprehension; it is from the "object" (for example, color) that the act of apprehension (in this case, seeing) receives its specific determination which distinguishes it from other kinds of acts of apprehension (such as hearing or smelling).

---

38. Lawrence Dewan, OP, "'Objectum': Notes on the Invention of a Word," in his *Wisdom, Law, and Virtue: Essays in Thomistic Ethics* (New York: Fordham University Press, 2007), 414: "In the case of apprehension, 'obiectum' expresses movement from the thing toward the soul. In the case of appetition, it expresses movement from the soul toward the thing. This suggests that in using the word 'obiectum' concerning an apprehensive power, one is expected to imagine something moving from the thing apprehended to the one who apprehends: perhaps the best illustration would be sound traveling from the gong or bell to the ear. Color, for example, would be imagined as behaving somewhat similarly. The 'obiectum' would be what is hurled at and strikes the observer. To call something an 'obiectum' would be something like calling it 'striking,' 'a striking thing.' On the other hand, in the case of motive or appetitive powers, the 'obiectum' is 'that which we go for,' the target of our pursuit, that at which we hurl ourselves."

39. T. C. O'Brien, OP, "Appendix 1: Objects and Virtues," in St. Thomas Aquinas, *ST*, vol. 31: *Faith (2a2ae 1–7)*, trans. O'Brien (Cambridge: Cambridge University Press, 2006), 178.

Because the object determines the act, Thomas understands the "object" to operate as a formal principle or a formal cause. Recall: while matter is the principle of potentiality, of the ability of something to become other than it is, form is the principle of actuality and thereby the cause of determination that accounts for something being the kind of thing it is. Why would Thomas now understand the "object" to operate as a formal principle? Here is Thomas's reason: everything acts—that is, has the function of "object" on the passive powers of sense apperception and intellectual apperception—to the degree that it is actual and so through its formal determination. Consequently, that aspect of the object to which a passive power is proportioned (the sense power and the passive intellect) is that which is formal in the object. Color is the formal aspect of the rose in regard to the sense of sight, fragrance is the formal aspect of the rose in regard to sense of smell. It is in respect to these differing formal aspects of the object that the various powers are differentiated from each other.

We can now begin to understand why, for Thomas, the supernatural *habitus* of divine faith is essentially different from something that looks very much like it but is nevertheless its counterfeit. The crucial principle is this: it is the object that specifies the act which in turn specifies the respective *habitus*. This principle is absolutely central: all virtues, whether acquired or infused, are distinguished, that is, specified by their object.[40] It is the formal aspect of the object that is responsible for this specification. Whenever the formal aspect of the object (or, the formal object) changes, the kind or species of the act also changes. Hence, the act of faith and its enabling disposition, the infused *habitus* of faith, are determined by the formal object of faith.[41]

Thomas says that God is the "object" of the theological virtue of faith. This means that God "engages" the human faculty of intellect in such a way that the human can know truths about God. God becoming "object" does not change God but reduces our cognitive and appetitive powers to certain kinds of acts. Consider Thomas's terse statement: "From God

40. Aquinas, *ST* I-II, q. 18, aa. 2 and 5; q. 54, a. 2; q. 63, a. 4.
41. Rather unsurprisingly, therefore, Marie-Dominique Chenu, OP, in one of his very first essays, "Pro supernaturalitate fidei illustrando," *Xenia Thomistica* 3 (1925): 297–307, regards the object of faith to be the very key to Thomas's treatise on faith.

comes forth to us ... the knowing of truth.... Thus faith makes a person cling to God as he is the source of a knowing of truth; for we believe to be true those things that God speaks to us."[42] Those things that God communicates to us constitute the material object of divine faith. These truths about God and things related to God constitute the articles of the faith, its content.[43] But of equal if not greater importance is the fact that by clinging to God himself as the very motive of our assent to the content of faith, faith reaches God in his very being. And so Thomas stresses: "When we believe God by faith, we reach God himself.... This is why I have said ... that God is the object of faith not simply in the sense that we believe in God [*credimus Deum*] but also that we believe God [*credimus Deo*]."[44] We turn now to the crucial distinction between the material object of faith (*credere Deum*), believing in God, and the formal object (*credere Deo*), believing God himself.

The Formal and the Material Object of Faith

By distinguishing between the formal and the material "object" and by also taking "object" as the final end toward which the will is directed, Thomas identifies a threefold relationship between the divine "object" and the act of faith. In order to express this threefold relationship, in *Summa theologiae* II-II, q. 2, a. 2, he adopts the popular Augustinian formula: "Credere Deo, credere Deum et credere in Deum." *Credere Deo*, to believe God, conveys that faith is the reverent submission to God as revealer, the acceptance of God as first truth. This is faith's formal object.

42. *ST* II-II, q. 17, a. 6. Translation from *ST*, vol. 33, *Hope (2a2ae 17–22)*, trans. W. J. Hill, OP (Cambridge: Cambridge University Press, 2006).

43. Thomas uses "article of faith" as a technical term with a precise meaning: "The object of faith is something unseen about the divine. Consequently, there is a particular article of faith wherever there is something being unseen for some distinct reason; where, however, many matters are known or non-known on the same grounds, distinct articles should not be introduced" (*ST* II-II, q. 1, a. 6; Blackfriars edition, 31:29–31). T. C. O'Brien offers this useful commentary: "Because the articles of faith in themselves have the one specific characteristic of being guaranteed by the word of God ... their *contents* to the believer have the distinctive condition of being non-seen, i.e. they are accepted properly and exclusively on the grounds of God's word. The variations of this non-evidence are the basis for the distinction of articles" (ibid., 30).

44. *ST* II-II, q. 81, a. 5. Translation from *ST*, vol. 31, *Faith (2a2ae 1–7)*, trans. T. C. O'Brien, OP (Cambridge: Cambridge University Press, 2006), 190.

Credere Deum, to believe in God, conveys that faith is assent to what God has revealed, first and foremost about himself. This is faith's material object. Both *credere Deo* and *credere Deum* indicate the intellect's relationship to God. Finally, *credere in Deum*, to believe tending toward God, expresses the fact that faith is a dynamic movement into God. This aspect signifies the intellect's act informed by an affective union with its end, charity.

This threefold relationship between the act of faith and its "object" does not designate three distinct acts but rather the three aspects constitutive of every consummate act of divine faith. Hence, while faith is essentially an intellectual act, trust and affectivity are integral to "living" or "formed" faith.[45] When God engages the human intellect and thus becomes its "object," God engages the intellect first formally, as first truth (*prima veritas*), also known as first truth speaking (*prima veritas loquens*), who reveals himself in the person of the Word in scripture and tradition constituting "one single deposit of the Word of God."[46] For our present purposes, this sketch of the distinction between the formal and the material objects of the act of faith suffices. I shall focus now on one all-important aspect of the formal object of faith, what Newman called its motive. Consider the formal object of color that engages your sense of sight. You see the color only in virtue of the light that shines on the

45. *ST* II-II, q. 4, a. 3: "The act of faith is directed to the object of the will, i.e., the good, as to its end: and this good which is the end of faith, viz., the Divine Good, is the proper object of charity. Therefore charity is called the form of faith in so far as the act of faith is perfected and formed by charity." O'Brien states, as tersely as rightly: "Only in one who loves God does faith reach its fully intended meaning as the beginning of eternal life." *ST*, vol. 31, *Faith (2a2ae 1–7)*, 125. For a brilliant and exacting study of the precise correlation between the theological virtues of faith and charity in Thomas's theology, see Michael S. Sherwin, OP, *By Knowledge & By Love: Charity and Knowledge in the Moral Theology of St. Thomas Aquinas* (Washington, D.C.: The Catholic University of America Press, 2005).

46. So teaches *Dei Verbum*, no. 10. We do not have to go all too far into the theological past in order to find a clear allusion to the *obiectum fidei* under the title of "first truth." In his 1910 "Sacrorum antistitum," Pope Pius X states: "Faith is ... the genuine assent of the intellect to a truth that is received from outside by hearing [*ex auditu*]. In this assent, given on the authority of the all-truthful God, we hold to be true what has been said, attested to, and revealed by the personal God, our Creator and Lord." Heinrich Denzinger, *Compendium of Creeds, Definitions, and Declarations on Matters of Faith and Morals*, Latin-English, ed. Peter Hünermann; English version, ed. Robert Fastiggi and Anne Englund Nash, 43rd ed. (San Francisco, Calif.: Ignatius Press, 2012), no. 3542.

material object, for example, a rose. The color is the formal object *which* (*obiectum formale quod*) engages you; the light is the formal object *by which* (*obiectum formale quo*) you are able to see the color. By analogy, we can distinguish the formal object of faith *which* engages the intellect from the formal object *by which* we believe. In faith, the formal object "which" is God the first truth revealing, and the formal object "by which" is the authority of the first truth in revealing; it is the medium by reason of which the term is attained, the personal God who is supreme and first truth.[47]

What happens when this formal object "by which" is abjured? What happens when the distinct motive of divine faith is renounced?

On Abjuring the Formal Object "by which" of Faith

In the fifth question of his treatise on faith in the *Summa theologiae*, Thomas addresses four special cases of those who do and do not have divine faith.[48] In the third article, he asks whether someone who persistently disbelieves one article of faith can retain at least a faith in the other articles that is unformed by charity. One commentator helpfully articulates what is at stake in this article:

This article of the *Summa* throws light on the Thomistic doctrine concerning the formal motive of faith. The disbeliever in question is one who deliberately withholds his assent from a dogma after it has been sufficiently explained. His

47. Consider the crisp formulation of the matter penned by America's foremost Catholic theologian, Avery Dulles, SJ, in his commendable theology of faith, *The Assurance of Things Hoped For: A Theology of Faith* (New York: Oxford University Press, 1997): "In adhering to God as revealer the believer accepts God as the one whose word is supremely deserving of assent, trust, and obedience. The authority of God who speaks is inseparable from the authority of God's word, but the word as created reality cannot be the formal object, or motive, of faith" (188). For a clear and penetrating theological meditation according to the mind of St. Thomas of divine faith and of the reality of the theological life that divine faith affords, see Romanus Cessario, OP, *Christian Faith and the Theological Life* (Washington, D.C.: The Catholic University of America Press, 1996).

48. First he attends to angels and humans in the original state, then he attends to the fallen angels, who in the letter of James are said to believe but tremble. See *ST* II-II, q. 5, a. 2, "Whether the devils have faith." The *sed contra* states: "The devils believe and tremble" (Jas 2:19). In the last of the four questions, he asks whether divine faith can be greater in one than in another.

pertinacity may take the form of open denial or be hidden beneath some alleged protestation of nonacceptance. The two positions are: first, "it is not true"; secondly, "I am non-committal."[49]

The Latin term used for this kind of person is *haereticus*. In the contemporary post-ecumenical context this term occludes rather than clarifies what is at stake in this article. Our commentator's rendition (in his Latin original as well as in the English translation) of "haereticus" as "pertinacious disbeliever" captures better the thrust of Thomas's question for our own time in which the principle of private judgment in matters of revealed religion makes indeed everyone a virtual heretic.

The *sed contra* tersely summarizes Thomas's position: "As one mortal sin goes counter to charity, so disbelief in one article goes counter to faith. Charity does not survive after one mortal sin. Neither, then, does faith after disbelief in one article," that is, in one of the twelve articles of the Apostles' Creed. Thomas takes these articles and the truths implicit in these articles to be the material object of divine faith. With all desirable clarity, Thomas restates his position in the first sentence of his response, "[a person who pertinaciously disbelieves] one article of faith possesses the habit neither of formed nor of [unformed] faith."[50] The pertinacious disbeliever of one article of the faith has lost the infused *habitus* of the theological virtue of faith, whether formed or unformed by charity, for the formal object "by which" such a person holds the other articles of the faith is not the authority of the first truth revealing but his or her own private judgment. Thomas makes his case by a *reductio ad absurdum* of the contrary: to deny the conclusion Thomas draws is to deny the fundamental principle that the formal object specifies the act as well as the *habitus* that facilitates the act. To deny Thomas's conclusion is thus to rob the act

---

49. Reginald Garrigou-Lagrange, OP, *The Theological Virtues. Volume One: On Faith. A Commentary on St. Thomas' Theological Summa I*-*II*^{ae}, *qq. 62, 65, 68: II*-*II*^{ae}, *qq. 1–16*, trans. Thomas a Kempis Reilly, OP (St. Louis, Mo.: Herder, 1965), 331.

50. Blackfriars translation. Significantly, this is one of the relatively rare occasions where the *sed contra* does not include a reference to an authority, be it scriptural, doctrinal, or theological. Incidentally, the respective *sed contra* in articles 1, 2, and 4 all include references to the scripture. In the case of question 3, however, we encounter a genuine theological inference typical of *sacra doctrina* as a *scientia argumentativa* (*ST* I, q. 1, a. 8). The inference Thomas draws in the *sed contra* and in the body of his response is a direct and necessary consequence of the formal object "by which" specifying the act of divine faith.

of divine faith of its very intelligibility. For as soon as the formal object or motive that specifies an act is removed, the act ceases. As soon as it is replaced by another formal object or motive the act it elicits is of a different kind. Shut off the light (the formal object by which we see), and the color (the formal object which we see), visible only in virtue of the light, cannot be seen anymore. The act of sight ceases because the formal object that specifies the act ceases. Thomas applies this principle to faith and states:

The essence of any habit depends on the formal [object] of that habit; once that is taken away the essence of the habit can no longer perdure. The formal [object] of faith is the first truth as this is made known in Scripture and in Church teaching. Anyone, therefore, who does not hold as the infallible and divine rule of faith Church teaching that derives from divine truth as handed down in Scripture, does not have the habit of faith.[51]

Such a person may very well accept the things of the faith, but significantly, "in a way other than by faith." A person who knows the middle term of a syllogism holds the conclusion in the form of strict demonstrative knowledge (*scientia*), while a person ignorant of the middle term might hold the same conclusion as a true opinion, but nevertheless just as an opinion. In a syllogism the middle term is equivalent to the formal object "by which" a conclusion is known. Hence the former person resembles a person who has divine faith in virtue of the formal object "by which," the first truth, God, while the latter person resembles a pertinacious disbeliever in one article of faith, the person who has rejected the formal object "by which" faith is held. Let me emphasize that the adjective "pertinacious" or "obstinate" is crucial, because a person might simply be in error. Such a person, displaying the docility proper to divine faith, is eager, upon proper instruction, to have their error corrected.

T. C. O'Brien rightly emphasizes that Thomas's argument "underlines the connexion between the formal objective of faith and the definite message to which God's word attests. This is what makes the message taught an infallible rule of faith."[52] Rejecting the formal object "by

51. *ST* II-II, q. 5, a. 3 (Blackfriars translation).
52. *ST*, vol. 31, *Faith (2a2ae 1–7)*, 158, note c.

which" of divine faith, that is, the first truth, results necessarily in the tacit adoption of a contrary principle. Thomas states that a person who pertinaciously disbelieves one article of faith "does not have faith in the other articles, but some sort of opinion that suits his own will"—which is nothing but another way of describing what Newman later identified as the principle of private judgment in matters of revealed religion. And Newman's notion of faith could not be captured better than in the lucid summary Thomas offers in the response to the second objection: "Faith … holds to all the articles of faith on the basis of the one single motive, the divine truth set before us in Scripture understood, rightly, i.e. in conformity with Church teaching."[53] Newman means nothing else when he distinguishes divine faith from private judgment.[54] The only difference is that Thomas offers a detailed theoretical account of the nature of divine faith, its object, act, and agent, while Newman offers a phenomenological analysis of how divine faith and private judgment differ as subjective attitudes. As I explained in the prologue, Newman's phenomenology of faith is understood best as belonging to the theological context of discovery

---

53. *ST* II-II, q. 5, a. 3, ad 2 (Blackfriars translation).

54. But one might justifiably wonder whether it might not be a rather stark anachronism to assume that when Thomas dictated this response he had on his mind the phenomenon of the sovereign subject applying the rule of private judgment in matters of revealed religion? Did medieval Christendom not make such a phenomenon in principle impossible? Does Thomas's teaching not simply consider the case of the educated person, philosopher, or theologian who conscientiously and, after instruction and correction, pertinaciously rejects one particular article of faith? Must we not distinguish clearly between the medieval "haereticus" and the modern sovereign subject? While Thomas clearly anticipates the principle of private judgment in matters of revealed religion as succinctly formulated much later by Newman, does Thomas not necessarily lack awareness of the reality Newman was faced with—the reality of the sovereign subject, at least as an increasingly hegemonic social imaginary, in concrete political and cultural operation? Nothing, I would submit, could be further from the truth. Thomas arguably had the paradigmatic instantiation of the sovereign subject right in front of his eyes, a single sovereign subject exercising the hegemony of a tyrant, the "stupor mundi," the one who allegedly called Moses, Jesus, and Mohammed the three greatest impostors of the world—the infamous Emperor Frederick II (1194–1250). If there is a high medieval exemplar that celebrates the sovereign subject as a new mode of existence it is Emperor Frederick II. In him Thomas encountered the counterfeit Newman by his time saw afloat all over in admittedly much smaller currency. As the life of Emperor Frederick II teaches, the birth of the sovereign subject coincides with abjuring divine faith. For two studies of his extraordinary life, see Paul Wiegler, *The Infidel Emperor and His Struggle against the Pope* (London: Routledge, 1930), and Thomas Curtis Van Cleve, *The Emperor Frederick II von Hohenstaufen:* Immutator Mundi (Oxford: Oxford University Press, 1972).

while Thomas's theoretical account of the act of faith is best understood as belonging to the theological context of justification.

Conclusion: Divine Faith and Its Counterfeit

What is lost when under the intensifying spell of the social imaginary of the sovereign subject divine faith becomes virtually indistinguishable from its counterfeit? The categorical distinction between divine faith and private judgment and with it the divine character and absolute gratuity of divine faith. We can bring about our private judgments, and our act of assent is intrinsic to divine faith. However, we do not bring about divine faith; it is, rather, a gift of grace. But we are able to forfeit divine faith by replacing its formal object or motive cause with our own private judgment. According to Thomas, such forfeiture requires the pertinacious rejection of at least one article of faith; but for Newman the matter presents itself in a considerably more dramatic way.

In the hegemonic ambience of the sovereign subject, the formal object of divine faith, the first truth which includes the living apostolic authority of the Catholic church, becomes unacceptable in principle—because the self's sovereignty and its submission to a living authority are mutually exclusive. More than 170 years ago, Newman held the mirror before the face of his contemporaries and unmasked the tacit but real pretentions of the sovereign subject: "Let them speak plainly; our offence is that of demanding faith in the Holy Catholic Church; it is this, and nothing else. I must insist upon this: faith implies a confidence in a man's mind, that the thing believed is really true; but, if it is once true, it never can be false."[55] Today, the hegemonic sovereign subject imposes what the sociologist Peter Berger felicitously called "the heretical imperative" not only on Protestants, but also on Catholics.[56] Whenever the heretical imperative is internalized as an integral component of the social imaginary of the sovereign subject and wherever it receives theological justification, modernism or neo-modernism celebrates its return. As soon as the heretical im-

55. *Mix.*, 216.
56. Peter Berger, *The Heretical Imperative: Contemporary Possibilities of Religious Affirmation* (New York: Anchor Press, 1979).

perative begins to hold sway by extending the rule of private judgment to matters of revealed religion and thereby substituting divine faith, "church membership" in the Catholic church turns into a conditional affiliation, with a future change of mind always possible—whether in response to perceived magisterial intransigence or narrow-mindedness regarding the putative advances of the spirit of the age, or in response to real or alleged past and present injustices committed by members of the church, or in response to real or alleged scandals (priestly abuse of minors, corruption, infidelity, duplicity, etc.) by individual church leaders.[57] Resisting the heretical imperative and thereby rejecting the principle of private judgment in matters of revealed religion and thus preserving the gift of divine faith requires holding fast in one's assent of faith to the formal object or motive cause, the first truth, which includes the living apostolic authority of the Catholic church.

The doctrine of divine faith as taught by Aquinas and Newman (among many other important Catholic theologians) is far from anti-ecumenical—as some might fear. It is, rather, the *conditio sine qua non* for genuine ecumenism. If Thomas Aquinas and John Henry Newman are right, it is clear that divine faith indeed can but should not be forfeited by Catholics and replaced with the principle of private judgment in matters of faith and morals. On the other hand, if Aquinas and Newman are right, divine faith may obtain among Protestants. All who are baptized according to the triune formula and the intention of the church, do not knowingly and intentionally reject irreversible doctrines of the Catholic church, and who simultaneously submit to the living voice of a shared doctrinal consensus (the doctrinal consensus of the first five centuries— the *consensus quinquesaecularis*) expounded authoritatively in their par-

57. If "church membership" is the intentional result of a distinct act of private judgment contingent upon revision, one only remains a member of the visible Catholic church and that only accidentally, provisionally, until better advisement. Yet one has relinquished one's membership of the mystical body of Christ. One becomes a member of the mystical body of Christ, and thereby necessarily and irreversibly also a member of the visible church only by way of baptism and divine faith and one remains a member of the mystical body only if one does not forfeit divine faith for unbelief or replace divine faith with beliefs held on the basis of private judgments alone. Based solely on an act of private judgment one can become or remain a member of the visible church; but only baptism and divine faith makes one a member of the mystical body of Christ (or—in the case of "accidental Protestants"—order one objectively to full communion with the Catholic church).

ticular ecclesial communions and on the basis of which scripture is read, may have divine faith—albeit often mixed with erroneous beliefs held by human faith.[58] This admixture of human faith is successively relinquished by those who eventually find themselves on the path Newman took and described so well—the path, as *Lumen Gentium* and *Unitatis Redintegratio* would put it, from partial to full communion with the Catholic church.[59] But divine faith is gravely endangered wherever the social imaginary of the sovereign subject holds sway. Here there is imminent danger that divine faith may be replaced with the deliveries of its counterfeit, the conclusions in matters of revealed religion afforded by the principle of private judgment.

There obtains one further implication if Thomas Aquinas and John Henry Newman are right. It seems to be the case that the spiritual danger to forfeit divine faith is highest with theologians, philosophers, and in general with persons of intellectual formation and sophistication. Such persons often acquire over a long period of time a deep-seated proclivity to loathe submission of intellect to anything else but their own judgments. In a day and age when Kant's imperative, *sapere aude* ("dare to

---

58. This, of course, can also happen among Catholics, because of the possibility of error in believing when particular expositions of the faith are inexact or incorrect—as patently during the Arian crisis, brilliantly narrated and analyzed doctrinally by Newman in his first major theological work, *The Arians of the Fourth Century*. Concerning Thomas's nuanced position on this matter and its implications for the contemporary ecumenical situation, Reginald Garrigou-Lagrange, OP, offers this succinct commentary: "The faithful thus deceived believe in error based on human authority only; hence, the faith they profess in it can be only a human faith. They do not assent to what is asserted and proposed by their bishops because God has revealed it. They assent only because they wrongly believe that God has revealed it. Their inability to distinguish between what, among themselves, they accept on divine authority and what they accept on human authority, makes them like numerous others whose limitations keep them tied up in knots in spite of themselves.... The good faith of many Protestants is of a kindred mixture. Because of an unsuspecting ignorance, which can be fully involuntary and furthermore invincible, they see no difference between their belief in the Incarnation of the Word of God, derived ulteriorly from infused faith, and whatever else their ministers teach them. Accordingly, they are led to uphold various positions, guided only by human faith in their leaders. Outstanding among the miscellanies is the denial of infallibility as a papal prerogative, even when the Sovereign Pontiff speaks *ex cathedra*. Good faith, so palliated, is not infused faith. It is either ignorance or error—for the most part invincible and perhaps totally involuntary. Sincerity is not lacking, but truth. 'The unleavened bread' of Christians needs both (cf. 1 Cor 5:8). Therefore, wherever there is question of genuine infused supernatural theological faith, there can be no trace of intrinsic error. It is excluded by reason of the formal motive, namely, Prime Truth revealing." *The Theological Virtues. Volume One: On Faith*, 97–98.

59. See notes 31 and 32 above.

know") and his program of liberation from a self-incurred tutelage seem to have become part of the collective subconscious, the full assent of faith looks too much like an unjustifiable sacrifice of reason (*sacrificium intellectus*) on the altar of a putatively arbitrary religious authority and blind faith—a sacrifice to be avoided by means of an acquired disposition of the will that secures the exceptionless application of the principle of private judgment in matters of revealed religion.[60] Acquiring and maintaining this disposition of the will is incompatible with the infused, that is, grace-given disposition of divine faith. Adopting the former is to forfeit the latter. Holding firmly on to the latter is to forego the former.

Newman and Aquinas argue consistently and convincingly that divine faith, the motive cause of which is the authority of the first truth, must necessarily include the divinely willed and guided mediation of divine truth, that is, faith in the apostolicity of the Catholic church and its teaching as divinely authorized, guided, and protected as the continuation of the apostolic witness. For this very reason divine faith necessarily leads to joining "the Church of the living God, the pillar and bulwark of the truth" (1 Tm 3:15)—which, as the fathers of the Second Vatican Council have taught, subsists in the Catholic church.[61] The magisterium has specified this article of faith in the following way: "The Catholic faithful *are required to profess* [*fideles profiteri tenentur*] that there is a historical continuity—rooted in the apostolic succession—between the Church founded by Christ and the Catholic Church" such that "the Church of Christ ... continues to exist fully only in the Catholic Church."[62] This article of faith is no cause for triumphalism but rather an invitation to

60. Immanuel Kant, "An Answer to the Question: 'What Is Enlightenment?,'" in Immanuel Kant, *Political Writings*, 2nd ed., ed. Hans Reiss, trans. H. B. Nisbet (Cambridge: Cambridge University Press, 1991), 54–60. See also Immanuel Kant, *Religion within the Boundaries of Mere Reason: And Other Writings*, ed. and trans. Allen Wood and George di Giovanni (Cambridge: Cambridge University Press, 1998). Kant's famous essay "An Answer to the Question: 'What Is Enlightenment?'" begins with these programmatic words: "Enlightenment is man's release from his self-incurred tutelage. Tutelage is the incapacity to use one's own understanding without the guidance of another. Such tutelage is self-imposed if its cause is not lack of intelligence, but rather a lack of determination and courage to use one's intelligence without being guided by another."

61. *Lumen Gentium*, no. 8; see notes 31 and 32 above.

62. Congregation for the Doctrine of the Faith, "Declaration *Dominus Iesus* on the Unicity and Salvific Universality of Jesus Christ and the Church," August 6, 2000, par. 16; available at www.vatican.va.

ecumenical authenticity in charity, that is, an invitation not to hide or compromise the gift of apostolic truth, the *depositum fidei* and its authentic and homogeneous development in dogma and the doctrine of faith. Rather, this article held by divine faith is nothing but an invitation to the way of the cross, to give witness in humility and charity to the gift of truth the Catholic church has no authority to compromise, sell short, let alone, abandon. "From everyone to whom much has been given, much will be required; and from the one to whom much has been entrusted, even more will be demanded" (Lk 12:48; NRSV).

Divine faith cannot be attained by oneself. It is a gift of grace. But divine faith can be forfeited by oneself—not just by obvious apostasy or heresy but by exchanging the motive cause of faith from the authority and veracity of God as represented by the living apostolic authority of the church for the principle of private judgment in matters of revealed religion. Christ's own words according to the Gospel of Luke may serve as a salient warning in this regard: "When the Son of Man comes, will he find faith on earth?" (Lk 18:8; NRSV). He will, it is certain, find all kinds of deliveries of private judgment in matters of revealed religion. Their name is legion. But will he find divine faith? It is the church's prayer in union with the prayer of the Virgin Mary that every member of the mystical Body be preserved in the gift of divine faith and that this gift may be offered to all. As the church prays, so she teaches in *Lumen Gentium*: "Therefore to this catholic unity of the people of God, which prefigures and promotes universal peace, all are called, and they belong to it or are ordered to it in various ways, whether they be catholic faithful or others who believe in Christ or finally all people everywhere who by the grace of God are called to salvation."[63]

Appendix 1

Newman's understanding of faith changed considerably during his stay in Rome (1846–47) under the influence of Jesuit dogmatic theologian Giovanni Perrone (1794–1876). In his *Oxford University Sermons* on faith

---

63. *Lumen Gentium*, no. 13, in *Decrees* (ed. Tanner), 2:860.

and reason from his Anglican period, Newman takes faith to be simply a higher reason and a gifted inference. Important clarifications about the nature of faith occurred in dialogue with Perrone and found their first echo in Newman's Latin *Theses de fide* and in the new introduction he wrote for the French translation of the *Oxford University Sermons* as well as in the important introduction and footnotes added by the Catholic Newman to the 1870 re-edition of the *Oxford University Sermons*.[64]

Only four years after the publication of the *Discourses Addressed to Mixed Congregations*, Newman in his 1853 papers on the certainty of faith advances a sketch of an analysis of the process of supernatural faith, what the theologians in the centuries after the Council of Trent would call the *analysis fidei*. In this sketch Newman considers the positions of major post-Tridentine Catholic theologians—as a matter of fact, all of them Jesuit theologians—Suárez, Bellarmine, Lugo, Tanner, and Perrone:

On the process of supernatural faith, and the portion of it which is supernatural.

Every step of the process, from the very first up to the assent to the credibilitas of the supernatural revelation *inclusive* is natural.

Every step then of that process, including the judgment of the prudentia declaring the credibilitas of the revelation may be mastered by a mind destitute of the grace of Christ.

Every step then of that process may be made a matter of natural consideration and reason, and may be taught the natural man, in the same way medicine or farming is taught him.

The process is as follows:

A body of proof exists for the credibilitas of Revelation which make that credibilitas evidens, and which viewed as one is the motivum credibilitatis to the individual.

This body of proof is substantially the same to all men, but it is variously represented, with various relative prominences of its portions to various minds.

This body of proof is the formal cause of the conclusion, or the shape in which the conclusion comes to us.

---

64. See *Theses de fide*; for Newman's early Catholic period in Rome and the years following, see the instructive study by C. Michael Shea, *Newman's Early Roman Catholic Legacy 1845–1854* (Oxford: Oxford University Press, 2017).

It consists of all the facts and truths of the case, each in its right place as the prudentia sees and arranges them, conspiring to the conclusion of the credibilitas of Revelation.

It exists and is present to the mind of every one who has prudentia; it is not present to those who have not.

This prudentia is simply a natural acquisition, in the subject matter of revelation, as well as in the subject matter of medicine or farming.

This prudentia, not only arranges and forms the body of proof, or motiva of the credibilitas of Revelation, but carries on the mind to a distinct judgment of, or assent to, that credibilitas, <but only an assent with *fear*.>

And this assent to, or speculative evident judgment of, the credibilitas of Revelation is followed by the act of reflexion upon, or recognition, of, that assent, which I have called certainty.

The whole of this is within the powers of natural reason. An infidel may get as far as this. A mind which gets as far as this does not yet believe. It only sees that Revelation is credibile....

But again on the other hand, supposing *no* grace, can the unaided mind go *further* than the judicium speculativum? Yes, it can go to a *human faith*, which does not exclude fear etc....

The steps which follow are all rational, according to human reason, but supernatural also, or require grace. They consist of

1. A practical judgment, as it is called, accompanying the speculative—viz. an assent to the proposition that it is right and fitting and excellent to believe what is credible.
2. A pia affectio, or voluntas credendi, determining and commanding the intellect to believe.
3. The act of faith, in the intellect, thus commanded; the object being at once Revelation and the Res Revelata, viz. that God has spoken, and that he has spoken thus.

Hence there are three supernatural habits involved in the act of faith,

1. the assent to the fitness of believing,
2. the wish to believe,
3. the act <habit> of faith distinctly embracing and holding as true, the fact of the Revelation, and the thing revealed.[65]

65. *Theological Papers on Faith and Certainty*, 36–37.

John R. Connolly ably summarizes Newman's clarified and deepened understanding of faith, especially the distinction between human faith and divine faith, thus:

By 1853 Newman arrived at a position in which he saw human faith and divine faith as being distinguished in terms of both their material and formal objects. The material object of human faith is the *revelatio*, the fact of revelation. The formal object of human faith is the acceptance of the credibility of the fact of revelation as a conclusion of a process of informal reasoning. On the other hand, the material object of divine faith is the revealed truths themselves. The formal object of divine faith is the acceptance of the revealed truths as true through grace on the authority of the Word of God revealing.[66]

After almost another twenty years of reflection on this topic, in his late masterwork, the *Essay in Aid of a Grammar of Assent*, Newman offers this compelling description of divine faith in its full and authentic Catholic scope:

If we believe in the revelation, we believe in what is revealed, in all that is revealed, however it may be brought home to us, by reasoning or in any other way. He who believes that Christ is the Truth, and that the Evangelists are truthful, believes all that He has said through them, though he has only read St. Matthew and has not read St. John. He who believes in the *depositum* of Revelation, believes in all the doctrines of the *depositum*; and since he cannot know them all at once, he knows some doctrines, and does not know others; he may know only the Creed, nay, perhaps only the chief portions of the Creed; but, whether he knows little or much, he has the intention of believing all that there is to believe whenever and as soon as it is brought home to him, if he believes in Revelation at all. All that he knows now as revealed, and all that he shall know, and all that there is to know, he embraces it all in his intention by one act of faith; otherwise, it is but an accident that he believes this or that, not because it is a revelation. This virtual, interpretative, or prospective belief is called a believing *implicitè*; and it follows from this, that, granting that the Canons of Councils and the other ecclesiastical documents and confessions, to which I have referred, are really involved in the *depositum* or revealed word, every Catholic, in accepting the *depositum*, does *implicitè* accept those dogmatic decisions.

66. John R. Connolly, "Newman on Human Faith and Divine Faith: Clarifying Some Ambiguities," *Horizons* 23, no. 2 (1996): 261–80, at 279.

I say, "granting these various propositions are virtually contained in the revealed word," for this is the only question left; and that it is to be answered in the affirmative, is clear at once to the Catholic, from the fact that the Church declares that they really belong to it. To her is committed the care and the interpretation of the revelation. The word of the Church is the word of the revelation. That the Church is the infallible oracle of truth is the fundamental dogma of the Catholic religion; and "I believe what the Church proposes to be believed" is an act of real assent, including all particular assents, notional and real; and, while it is possible for unlearned as well as learned, it is imperative on learned as well as unlearned. And thus it is, that by believing the word of the Church *implicitè*, that is, by believing all that that word does or shall declare itself to contain, every Catholic, according to his intellectual capacity, supplements the shortcomings of his knowledge without blunting his real assent to what is elementary, and takes upon himself from the first the whole truth of revelation, progressing from one apprehension of it to another according to his opportunities of doing so.[67]

Appendix 2

Certitude is, according to Newman, a crucial feature of the human mind, because, as Newman holds with Aristotle and Thomas Aquinas, the human mind is made for truth:

It is the characteristic of certitude that its object is a truth, a truth as such, a proposition as true. There are right and wrong convictions, and certitude is a right conviction; if it is not right with a consciousness of being right, it is not certitude. Now truth cannot change; what is once truth is always truth; and the human mind is made for truth, and so rests in truth, as it cannot rest in falsehood. When then it once becomes possessed of a truth, what is to dispossess it? but this is to be certain; therefore once certitude, always certitude. If certitude in any matter be the termination of all doubt or fear about its truth, and an unconditional conscious adherence to it, it carries with it an inward assurance, strong though implicit, that it shall never fail. Indefectibility almost enters into its very idea, enters into it at least so far as this, that its failure, if of frequent occurrence, would prove that certitude was after all and in fact an impossible act, and that what looked like it was a mere extravagance of the intellect. Truth would still be truth, but the knowledge of it would be beyond us and unattainable. It is of great importance

---

67. *G.A.*, 152–53.

then to show, that, as a general rule, certitude does not fail; that failures of what was taken for certitude are the exception; that the intellect, which is made for truth, can attain truth, and, having attained it, can keep it, can recognize it, and preserve the recognition.[68]

Furthermore, *pace* any recurring rumors of Newman's alleged leanings toward skepticism, Newman holds together with Aristotle and Thomas Aquinas the indefectible certitude of primary truths: "The initial truths of divine knowledge ought to be viewed as parallel to the initial truths of secular: as the latter are certain, so too are the former."[69] Newman continues:

This is the true parallel between human and divine knowledge; each of them opens into a large field of mere opinion, but in both the one and the other the primary principles, the general, fundamental, cardinal truths are immutable. In human matters we are guided by probabilities, but, I repeat, they are probabilities founded on certainties. It is on no probability that we are constantly receiving the informations and dictates of sense and memory, of our intellectual instincts, of the moral sense, and of the logical faculty. It is on no probability that we receive the generalizations of science, and the great outlines of history. These are certain truths; and from them each of us forms his own judgments and directs his own course, according to the probabilities which they suggest to him, as the navigator applies his observations and his charts for the determination of his course. Such is the main view to be taken of the separate provinces of probability and certainty in matters of this world; and so, as regards the world invisible and future, we have a direct and conscious knowledge of our Maker, His attributes, His

68. *G.A.*, 221–22.

69. *G.A.*, 237. In his reflections on certitude in the *Grammar of Assent*, Newman not only relies heavily on Aristotle, but also on the Anglican theologian Bishop Joseph Butler's famous *Analogy of Religion*. For a useful discussion of these matters, see James W. Lyons, *Newman's Dialogues on Certitude* (Rome: Officium Libri Catholici, 1978). On Thomas Aquinas's limited but still important impact on Newman's *Grammar of Assent*, see also G. R. Evans, "Newman and Aquinas on Assent," *The Journal of Religious Studies, New Series* 30, no. 1 (1979): 202–11. Evans rightly observes that Thomas Aquinas "has suggested to him the idea of constructing such a ladder of certainty; and he has enabled him to do so in terms which do not altogether contradict his arguments later in the *Grammar* against Locke's theory that there are 'degrees of assent'" (ibid., 209). For Newman's famous exposition and critique of Locke's error of attributing degrees of assent, see the section "Simple Assent" of chap. 6, "Assent Considered as Unconditional," in *G.A.*, 159–87. John Locke's own influential account of the purported degrees of assent is to be found in Book IV, chap. XVI, "Of the Degrees of Assent," of his *magnum opus*, *An Essay concerning Human Understanding*, ed. Peter H. Niddich (Oxford: Clarendon Press, 1975), 657–68.

providences, acts, works, and will, from nature, and revelation; and, beyond this knowledge lies the large domain of theology, metaphysics, and ethics, on which it is not allowed to us to advance beyond probabilities, or to attain to more than an opinion.[70]

One of the immediate objections to the most important instance of Newman's understanding of certitude—religious certitude—is the obvious phenomenon of persons changing from one religion to another or forfeiting religious beliefs altogether. Consider Newman's astute analysis of the indefectibility of certitude in the paradigmatic instance of changing religious affiliations:

The real difficulty lies not in the variety of religions, but in the contradiction, conflict, and change of religious certitudes. Truth need not be universal, but it must of necessity be certain; and certainty, in order to be certainty, must endure; yet how is this reasonable expectation fulfilled in the case of religion? On the contrary, those who have been the most certain in their beliefs are sometimes found to lose them, Catholics as well as others; and then to take up new beliefs, perhaps contrary ones, of which they become as certain as if they had never been certain of the old....

When, then, we are told that a man has changed from one religion to another, the first question which we have to ask, is, have the first and the second religions nothing in common? If they have common doctrines, he has changed only a portion of his creed, not the whole: and the next question is, has he ever made much of any doctrines but such as are if otherwise common to his new creed and his old? what doctrines was he certain of among the old, and what among the new?

Thus, of three Protestants, one becomes a Catholic, a second a Unitarian, and a third an unbeliever: how is this? The first becomes a Catholic, because he assented, as a Protestant, to the doctrine of our Lord's divinity, with a real assent and a genuine conviction, and because this certitude, taking possession of his mind, led him on to welcome the Catholic doctrines of the Real Presence and of the Theotocos, till his Protestantism fell off from him, and he submitted himself to the Church. The second became a Unitarian, because, proceeding on the principle that Scripture was the rule of faith and that a man's private judgment was its rule of interpretation, and finding that the doctrine of the Nicene and Athanasian Creeds did not follow by logical necessity from the text of Scripture, he said

70. *G.A.*, 239–40.

to himself, "The word of God has been made of none effect by the traditions of men," and therefore nothing was left for him but to profess what he considered primitive Christianity, and to become a Humanitarian. The third gradually subsided into infidelity, because he started with the Protestant dogma, cherished in the depths of his nature, that a priesthood was a corruption of the simplicity of the Gospel. First, then, he would protest against the sacrifice of the Mass; next he gave up baptismal regeneration, and the sacramental principle; then he asked himself whether dogmas were not a restraint on Christian liberty as well as sacraments; then came the question, what after all was the use of teachers of religion? why should any one stand between him and his Maker? After a time it struck him, that this obvious question had to be answered by the Apostles, as well as by the Anglican clergy; so he came to the conclusion that the true and only revelation of God to man is that which is written on the heart. This did for a time, and he remained a Deist. But then it occurred to him, that this inward moral law was there within the breast, whether there was a God or not, and that it was a roundabout way of enforcing that law, to say that it came from God, and simply unnecessary, considering it carried with it its own sacred and sovereign authority, as our feelings instinctively testified; and when he turned to look at the physical world around him, he really did not see what scientific proof there was there of the Being of God at all, and it seemed to him as if all things would go on quite as well as at present, without that hypothesis as with it; so he dropped it, and became a *purus, putus* Atheist.

Now the world will say, that in these three cases old certitudes were lost, and new were gained; but it is not so: each of the three men started with just one certitude, as he would have himself professed, had he examined himself narrowly; and he carried it out and carried it with him into a new system of belief. He was true to that one conviction from first to last; and on looking back on the past, would perhaps insist upon this, and say he had really been consistent all through, when others made much of his great changes in religious opinion. He has indeed made serious additions to his initial ruling principle, but he has lost no conviction of which he was originally possessed.

I will take one more instance. A man is converted to the Catholic Church from his admiration of its religious system, and his disgust with Protestantism. That admiration remains; but, after a time, he leaves his new faith, perhaps returns to his old. The reason, if we may conjecture, may sometimes be this: he has never believed in the Church's infallibility; in her doctrinal truth he has believed, but in her infallibility, no. He was asked, before he was received, whether he held all that the Church taught, he replied he did; but he understood the question to mean, whether he held those particular doctrines "which at that time the Church in matter of fact formally taught," whereas it really meant "whatever the Church then or at any future time should teach." Thus, he never had the indispensable and elementary faith of a Catholic, and was simply no subject for reception into the fold of the Church. This being the case, when the Immaculate Conception is defined, he feels that it is something more than he bargained for when he became a Catholic, and accordingly he gives up his religious profession. The world will say that he has lost his certitude of the divinity of the Catholic Faith, but he never had it.[71]

One important implication of Newman's understanding of certitude, as unfolded in this long passage, is the fact that "certitude does not admit of an interior, immediate test, sufficient to discriminate it from false certitude."[72] Yet the more important insight to which Newman's reflections on certitude yields is that divine faith, when enjoyed by a baptized Christian in only partial communion with the Catholic church, already has the central characteristic of certitude, its indefectibility—because of the knowing acceptance of the revealed truths as true on the authority of the Word of God revealing—and when rightly acted upon by that person will lead eventually into full communion of the Catholic church—without any diminishment of the certitude enjoyed before entering into full communion. At the point of entering into the full communion of the Catholic church this person's religious certitude has expanded, following "on investigation and proof, that it is accompanied by a specific sense of intellectual satisfaction and repose," such that it extends now also to the church's infallibility.[73] It is for this very reason that this person upon reception into the full communion of the Catholic church, after joining with the faithful in reciting the Nicene Creed, is able to make with perfect certitude the profession of faith: "I believe and profess all that the holy Catholic Church believes, teaches, and proclaims to be revealed by God."

71. *G.A.*, 242–48.
72. *G.A.*, 255.
73. *G.A.*, 258.

CHAPTER 3

THE DEVELOPMENT
OF DOCTRINE AND ITS
COUNTERFEITS

In the opening pages of his seminal *Essay on the Development of Christian Doctrine* Newman famously states: "To be deep in history is to cease to be a Protestant."[1] Yet lest we immediately misunderstand Newman's statement, we must realize that the history he refers to is not the history presented by the History Channel on contemporary television in the United States; nor is it the sum total of random historical facts that some are eager to learn by heart in order to shine at games of Trivial Pursuit. Nor is it the supposed "history" craftily insinuated to the reader's unguarded imagination in the wave of recent anti-Catholic novels, like Dan Brown's *The Da Vinci Code* or Colm Tóibín's *The Testament of Mary*. Nor is it even the substantive history taught at American colleges and universities in

1. *Dev.*, 8.

the days when they still maintained an authentic liberal arts curriculum before its recent replacement by social studies. Rather, the history Newman refers to with his evocative expression "to be deep in history" is the Spirit-guided and Spirit-filled history of salvation that the living church holds in her memory. It is the church's memory of the living Christ, the bridegroom, who guides his bride, the church by means of the Comforter he promised to send.

The church's memory is deeply informed by Christ's words as communicated in the Gospel of John: "I have yet many things to say to you, but you cannot bear them now. When the Spirit of truth comes, he will guide you into all the truth" (Jn 16:12–13; RSV). It is for this reason that a Catholic is "deep in history." It is the history of the unfolding truth of the divine Word, the incarnate and risen Lord, and it is into this ever-unfolding truth that the Spirit guides the church that continuously passes it on in its teaching in such a way that it constantly informs the divine faith of all the faithful.[2] For the same reason, a Catholic is also deep in the Christ-rooted and Spirit-filled present, God's living Word in history, which realizes itself in the mind of the church. Salvation history necessarily entails "the Church of the living God, the pillar and bulwark of the truth" (1 Tm 3:15), in its visible unity, holiness, catholicity, and apostolicity; and to be deep in history in this precise sense of salvation history means to be deep in the church. Protestantism by its own self-understanding has adopted a fundamentally different understanding of church. To enter deep into salvation history with all its essential implications is to encounter the church and enter into full communion with her and thus cease to be a Protestant.[3]

For the same reason a Catholic is deep in history, he is also deep in

2. For an excellent account of Newman's understanding of the Spirit-guided church in history as received and developed by Yves Congar, see Andrew Meszaros, *The Prophetic Church: History and Doctrinal Development in John Henry Newman and Yves Congar* (Oxford: Oxford University Press, 2016), esp. chaps. 4–6.

3. See note 31 in chapter 2 (above) for the church's important teaching about the partial communion of the church that in fact all baptized Christians enjoy. This truth, strongly emphasized by the fathers of the Second Vatican Council in *Lumen Gentium* and *Unitatis Redintegratio* takes, however, nothing away from Newman's provocative claim—a claim that in its core does nothing but anticipate the teaching of *Lumen Gentium* on the interpenetration of salvation history and the church.

the Christ-rooted and Spirit-filled present, God's living Word in history, which realizes itself in the mind of the church. From the perspective of the recipient, the church, this unfolding truth takes the form of what Newman calls a real idea, the "idea of Christianity," imprinting itself first inchoately and then with ever greater precision on the mind of the church and thereby forming the living tradition which continuously bears upon the church's present. In the last and arguably most famous of his fifteen Oxford University sermons, "The Theory of Developments in Religious Doctrine," Newman observes that "the great idea takes hold of a thousand minds by its living force," so that it "may rather be said to use the minds of Christians, than to be used by them."[4] And insofar as this "idea of Christianity" is the object of the church's progressive growth in insight, it becomes a concrete body of defined teaching handed on in an explicit way. Yet, at the same time, precisely because the animating principle of the idea of Christianity is God's living Word in history, Christ, this body of teaching is really one idea. As Newman explains in the *Essay on the Development of Christian Doctrine*, "this body of thought, thus laboriously gained, will after all be little more than the proper representative of one idea, being in substance what that idea meant from the first, its complete image as seen in a combination of diversified aspects, with the suggestions and corrections of many minds, and the illustration of many experiences."[5]

The Christ-rooted and Spirit-filled church, the visible representative of the ever-unfolding truth of revelation, has a *sacramental* expression, first and foremost in the sacrifice of the Mass, in the Eucharist, and in the priestly vocation, an *institutional* expression, the episcopal hierarchy in apostolic succession in union with the See of Peter. It has a *charismatic* expression in the monastic orders, the ecclesial movements, and the daily Spirit-guided witness of all the faithful. It has a *prophetic* expression in its theologians and a *doctrinal* expression in revelation by way of the scripture and tradition, being continuously made explicit and thus being ever alive in the ongoing development of doctrine. Finally, the church has a *magisterial* expression, related to the doctrinal expression, in the college

4. *Oxford Sermons*, 316–17.
5. *Dev.*, 38.

of bishops in union with the pope. All of these expressions of the unfolding truth of revelation—sacramental, institutional, charismatic, prophetic, doctrinal, and magisterial—are integral parts of the visible representative of God's living Word in history, Christ's church. In *Lumen Gentium*'s memorable words, "This church, constituted and organized as a society in this present, world, subsists in the Catholic Church, governed by the Successor of Peter and by the Bishops in communion with him" (no. 8). A Catholic is simultaneously deep in history and deep in the Christ-rooted and Spirit-filled present, because they are the two aspects of one single, "tensed" reality: the living, Christ-rooted, and Spirit-filled church that encompasses the past, the present, and in her risen head, the incarnate Lord—together with the Virgin Mary, assumed into heaven, body and soul, and the communion of saints—already its eschatological fulfillment.

To all of these integral expressions of the unfolding truth of revelation, strong opposition has arisen at one time or another in the life of the church. This has also been the case with the church's doctrinal expression, taking the form of an authentic development of doctrine. In the wake of the reception of the Second Vatican Council two types of opposition arose to the idea of an authentic development of doctrine.[6]

First, there is the opposition of the ecclesial antiquarian. The antiquarian is a purist of origins. Antiquarians are eager to locate the true Gospel of Christ behind the various portraits advanced by the four Evangelists, or in St. Paul's original message without the later accretions of his disciples, or in the church of the New Testament canon and the earliest pre-Nicene theologians without all the later doctrinal additions and complications, or in some other, authentic tradition that at some identifiable point in history was jettisoned. For ecclesial antiquarianism, all developments beyond some allegedly pure origin or some purportedly undistorted temporally limited expression of the origin are nothing but a fall from the original truth, an amassment of both light and grave corruptions that more and more pollute the clear spring water the further it is car-

---

6. In the following, I understand ecclesial antiquarianism and ecclesial presentism as ideal types, heuristic devices for identifying theologically detrimental attitudes, tendencies, and programs. In concrete lived reality they occur often in mixed forms, are qualified by other factors, and appear in varying degrees of intensity.

ried away from its pristine source. Return to and union with this origin, or at least with the latest state of its authentic expression, is the ultimate goal of ecclesial antiquarianism. *Nota bene*: the ecclesial antiquarian does not oppose the authentic development of doctrine, but rather simulates it. Authentic development, for the antiquarian, is nothing but the latest state of the origin's authentic expression. Anything beyond this state is to be rejected as a corruption of doctrine. This distinct ersatz version of the authentic development of doctrine makes antiquarianism one of its current counterfeits.

Second, there is the opposition of the ecclesial presentist. For ecclesial presentists all that counts are the collective convictions we hold right now in the present as we move into the future. Ecclesial presentism holds the church to be a self-actuating and self-norming body empowered by the Spirit. Rupture is an inbuilt moment of this dynamic. It is the Spirit-granted liberation from a past that once was the self-actuation of what is now the church of the past. The dynamic, rupture-filled, and spontaneous fluidity of ongoing ecclesial self-actuation is the ideal of ecclesial presentism—the interminable process of shaking off the shackles of past ecclesial self-actuations and bringing about the self-actuation of the new church of the present. The notion that differentiates between the outgoing and the incoming church of the present is "future." The shape the future is supposed or desired to take on the basis of the purportedly collective convictions of the present becomes the blueprint for the self-actualization of the emergent church of the present and the criterion by which the outgoing church, now the church of the past, is purged, corrected, and remodeled. For ecclesial presentism the necessity of the constant reform of the church (*ecclesia semper reformanda est*) does not arise from the fact that the visible church is a *corpus permixtum*, a mixed body, and that its personnel—to use the philosopher Jacques Maritain's term—are fragile, sinful, and at times corrupt.[7] On the contrary, for ecclesial presentism, the principle *ecclesia semper reformanda* simply articulates the very dynamic of the church's ongoing self-actuation. *Nota bene*: the ecclesial presentist does not oppose the authentic development of doc-

---

7. See Jacques Maritain, *On the Church of Christ: The Person of the Church and Her Personnel*, trans. Joseph W. Evans (Notre Dame, Ind.: University of Notre Dame Press, 1973).

trine, but rather simulates it. Authentic development, for the presentist, is nothing but the dynamic, rupture-filled, and spontaneous fluidity of ongoing ecclesial self-actuation. This distinct ersatz of the authentic development of doctrine make presentism the other of its current counterfeits.

An authentic ecclesial existence, faithful to Catholic teaching, excludes ecclesial antiquarianism and ecclesial presentism as seductive counterfeits that are at best reductive and, at worst, distortive errors. Instead, an authentic ecclesial existence simultaneously integrates what is true in each of these tendencies into a higher synthesis: without being rooted in the original deposit of faith, without a constant return to revelation received in scripture and in sacred tradition, the church would cease to be apostolic in its doctrinal substance; she would betray the teaching of the Gospel. Yet without living constantly in the Christ-centered and Spirit-filled present, the church would turn into a museum, a vast display of precious architectural, liturgical, and intellectual antiques, a display of cold memories instead of the Christ-rooted and Spirit-filled living tradition of the church.

Antiquarianism and presentism are constant dangers in the contemporary post-Vatican II church, dangers that are counteracted best by a robust understanding of the development of doctrine. Such a robust understanding matters greatly because it helps to avoid two dangers—becoming stuck in the past for the past's sake and getting rid of the past for the sake of an ever-changing present. Such a robust understanding clarifies the meaning of Christ's promise that "when the Spirit of truth comes, he will guide you into all the truth" (Jn 16:13; RSV). If the Spirit sent by Christ indeed guides the church into all the truth and if the mission of the Spirit indeed is one single divine act encompassing all created time, then this is true—in the Christ-rooted and Spirit-filled church to be deep in history and to be deep in the present are two aspects of the selfsame reality. The present is the fruit of history and history is the root of the present. What connects the one with the other is the development of doctrine.

I shall unpack these initial claims about the development of doctrine in three steps. First, I shall attend to the voice of the recent magisterium to ascertain its teaching on the development of doctrine. In a second step, I shall attend to John Henry Newman's notes of an authentic development of doctrine, and then apply them, in a third step, to a test case, the arguably most controversial document of the Second Vatican Council, the Declaration on Religious Freedom, *Dignitatis Humanae*. In the decades since the Council theologians from both ends of the spectrum, antiquarians as well as presentists, have argued that this declaration represents a severe rupture with the church's traditional teaching. By drawing upon Newman's notes of an authentic development of doctrine and the case Ian Ker makes in his noteworthy book, *Newman on Vatican II*, I shall argue that the Second Vatican Council's Declaration on Religious Freedom, *Dignitatis Humanae*, does not constitute such a rupture, but rather an authentic development of doctrine. Finally, I shall offer some concluding reflections on why the development of doctrine matters, reflections that come back to the dangers of ecclesial antiquarianism and ecclesial presentism as two attitudes that presuppose rupture, the one as a cataclysmic event to be circumvented in the search of some authentic original state, the other as the principle of liberation from the alienating and oppressive impact of the past on the present.[8]

Development of Doctrine: The Voice of the Magisterium

We find the first important statement of the modern magisterium on the development of doctrine in *Dei Filius*, the First Vatican Council's Dogmatic Constitution on the Catholic Faith:

The doctrine of the faith which God has revealed is put forward not as some philosophical discovery capable of being perfected by human intelligence, but as a divine deposit committed to the spouse of Christ to be faithfully protected and infallibly promulgated. Hence, too, that meaning of the sacred dogmas is ever to be maintained which has once been declared by holy mother church, and there must never be any abandonment of this sense under the pretext or in the name of a more profound understanding. May understanding, knowledge, and wisdom increase as ages and centuries roll along, and greatly and vigorously flourish, in

8. For an analysis of the post-conciliar "camps" second to none, see the first chapter, "Interpreting the Interpreters," in Gavin D'Costa, *Vatican II: Catholic Doctrines on Jews and Muslims* (Oxford: Oxford University Press, 2014), 10–58.

each and all, in the individual and the whole church: but this only in its own proper kind, that is to say, in the same doctrine, the same sense, and the same understanding.[9]

The fathers of the First Vatican Council emphasize the ongoing identity of meaning between a defined teaching and the original deposit of faith. What has been implicit in the deposit may become increasingly explicit and thus afford an ever-deeper understanding. But what must be secured is the ongoing identity of sense and meaning in this process of an ongoing unfolding, a making explicit of what has been implicit.

In the close to one hundred years between the First and Second Vatican Council falls an extremely rich harvest of Catholic theological reflection on the development of doctrine. John Henry Newman, Maurice Blondel, Francísco Marín-Sola, Ambrose Gardeil, Léonce de Grandmaison, Henri de Lubac, Yves Congar, Karl Rahner, and other theologians composed significant works on the development of doctrine.[10] In a small but significant volume with the English title *What Is Dogma?* the eminent Swiss theologian and cardinal Charles Journet offers a condensed summary of the best of these efforts, a summary that finds a clear echo in the Second Vatican Council's Dogmatic Constitution on Divine Revelation, *Dei Verbum*. Cardinal Journet published the original French version in 1963; *Dei Verbum* was promulgated in 1965. Cardinal Journet aptly states:

On the one hand that which was contained in the original deposit explicitly is ever kept in mind by the living authority of the Church, while, on the other hand, that which was contained in the original deposit implicitly, still in a preconceptual, unformulated way, obscure, yet forceful and unavoidable, is explained and put forward in a conceptual and formulated way by the living authority of the Church.[11]

The development of doctrine lies in the dynamic of unfolding what is implicit in the original deposit of faith into explicit affirmations. The instru-

---

9. *Dei Filius*, no. 4, in *Decrees* (ed. Tanner), 2:809.

10. One of the most informative presentations of this rich and complex discussion is Aidan Nichols, OP, *From Newman to Congar: The Idea of Doctrinal Development from the Victorians to the Second Vatican Council* (Edinburgh: T and T Clark, 1990).

11. Charles Journet, *What Is Dogma?*, trans. Dom Mark Pontifex (London: Burns and Oates, 1964), 54.

ment that moves the understanding of the deposit of faith from implicit to explicit is the authority of the Christ-rooted and Spirit-filled church. Only two years after the publication of Journet's book, *Dei Verbum* states:

This tradition which comes from the apostles progresses in the church under the assistance of the holy Spirit. There is growth in understanding of what is handed on, both the words and the realities they signify. This comes about through contemplation and study by believers, who "ponder these things in their hearts" (see Lk 2:19 and 51); through the intimate understanding of spiritual things which they experience; and through the preaching of those who, on succeeding to the office of bishop, receive the sure charism of truth. Thus, as the centuries advance, the church constantly holds its course towards the fullness of God's truth, until the day when the words of God reach their fulfillment in the church.[12]

While the fathers of the First Vatican Council emphasized the ongoing identity of the meaning of dogma with the original deposit, the fathers of the Second Vatican Council emphasize the ongoing dynamic explication of doctrine toward the plenitude of divine truth. Far from being contradictory, the two statements simply differ in emphasis and scope, Vatican I focusing on the transition from what is preconceptual and therefore implicit to what takes explicit conceptual form, with Vatican II stressing the complex and manifold dynamics that are integral to this process involving in various ways all of the faithful. Hence, the development of doctrine is not simply a historical fact—merely an accident of the church's ongoing reception of the deposit of faith, interesting only to historians of dogma as a feature of the church's historically extended and embedded reality. It is, rather, first and foremost a reality that is integral to the church's life, a reality that the church has become aware of only slowly, but now holds and teaches explicitly.

How Is an Authentic Development of Doctrine to Be Discerned?

But how do we distinguish between authentic developments of doctrine and developments that are actually corruptions of doctrine? Not every

---

12. *Dei Verbum*, no. 8, in *Decrees* (ed. Tanner), 2:974.

development is necessarily an authentic development. Arguably, a most fruitful resource for gaining clarity on this matter is still the great classic that initiated the modern theological reflection on the development of doctrine, John Henry Newman's *Essay on the Development of Christian Doctrine*. Newman originally published this work in 1845 while he was, as Aidan Nichols put it, "in the throes of reception into the Catholic Church."[13] In 1878, after Newman had been made a cardinal by Pope Leo XIII, he published a second, Catholic, and better organized version. This is the version usually reprinted in current editions of Newman's works.

In a very instructive book on Newman's thought, the late Cardinal Avery Dulles calls Newman's *Essay of the Development of Christian Doctrine* "one of the most seminal works of nineteenth-century theology."[14] He observes that "Newman gave no quarter to dogmatic relativism. He argued vigorously for the irreversibility of dogmas, not necessarily in their wording, but in their meaning. His balanced position represents a middle course between a fluid historicism and a rigid dogmatism."[15] Dulles continues:

From the very outset Newman opposes the "transformist" view that Christianity is ever in flux and accommodates itself to the times. For him it is axiomatic that the faith of the apostles must perdure. But in order to retain its vitality and ward off new errors, the living Church will sometimes have to articulate its faith in new ways. Granted that development must occur, it must still be asked whether the new formulations are in accord with the ancient faith. To respond to this difficult question he proposed seven notes or tests for authentic development.[16]

These seven notes of an authentic development of doctrine are preservation of type, continuity of principles, power of assimilation, logical sequence, anticipation of its future, conservative action on its past, and finally, chronic vigor.

---

13. Nichols, *From Newman to Congar*, 45.
14. Dulles, *John Henry Newman*, 79.
15. Ibid.
16. Ibid., 74.

Newman's Seven Notes of an Authentic Development of Doctrine

The first note is *preservation of type* which Newman illustrates with the help of an analogy from biological life:

This is readily suggested by the analogy of physical growth, which is such that the parts and proportions of the developed form, however altered, correspond to those which belong to its rudiments. The adult animal has the same make, as it had on its birth; young birds do not grow into fishes, nor does the child degenerate into the brute, wild or domestic, of which he is by inheritance lord. Vincentius of Lerins adopts this illustration in distinct reference to Christian doctrine: "Let the soul's religion," he says, "imitate the law of the body, which, as years go on, develops indeed and opens out its due proportions, and yet remains identically what it was. Small are a baby's limbs, a youth's are larger, yet they are the same."[17]

Monasticism, for example, emerged as the first charismatic and ascetic movement in the early church both East and West and has grown into many diverse branches and still exists and flourishes in the Catholic church, but is not found among Methodist, Presbyterian, or Baptist ecclesial communities. Thus, the Catholic church passes the test of preservation of type, while these Protestant ecclesial communions do not.

The second note is *continuity of principles*. It is intimately connected to the first note. In order to preserve its type, the church must be faithful to its foundational principles. Newman proposes nine such principles: the principle of dogma, the principle of faith, the principle of theology, the sacramental principle, the principle of the spiritual sense of scripture, the principle of grace, the principle of asceticism, the principle of the malignity of sin, and the principle that matter and the mind are capable of sanctification. At the end of the list he adds a tenth principle, the principle of the development of doctrine.[18] Abandon any one of these principles and Christianity will be diminished and even distorted in one or the other respect. Accepting all of these principles and assuring their continuity is essential to the life and vigor of the church.

---

17. *Dev.*, 171–72.
18. For the complete list, see *Dev.*, 325.

The third note is *power of assimilation*, which Newman explains pithily: "Development is a process of incorporation."[19] Cardinal Dulles offers a helpful image to understand this note: "As a healthy organism builds itself up by ingesting food, so the Church takes in what is assimilable in the cultures it meets, and transforms what it appropriates. The Church and its faith have matured by interaction with the great civilizations of Greece and Rome."[20]

The fourth note is *logical sequence*. Here Newman has in mind the fact that in retrospect "the process of development ... [is] capable of a logical expression."[21] "A doctrine ... professed in its mature years by a philosophy or religion, is likely to be a true development, not a corruption, in proportion as it seems to be the *logical issue* of its original teaching."[22] There is, for example, undoubtedly a logical sequence—broadly conceived—between the dogma of Mary as *Theotokos*, as God-bearer, promulgated at the Council of Ephesus and the Dogmas of the Immaculate Conception of the Mother of God and of her Assumption more than a millennium later.

The fifth note is *anticipation of its future*. An ultimate development may be authentic when there is a "*definite anticipation* at an early period in the history of the idea to which it belongs."[23] The veneration of relics of the martyrs might come to mind as an anticipation of and prelude to the invocation of the saints.

The sixth note is *conservative action on its past*. "A true development ... may be described as one which is conservative of the course of antecedent developments being really those antecedents and something besides them: it is an addition which illustrates, not obscures, corroborates, not corrects, the body of thought from which it proceeds; and this is its characteristic as contrasted with a corruption."[24] The doctrine of the Trinity, for example, rightly understood, does not undermine, but rather affirms the prior and more fundamental doctrine of monotheism. Equally,

19. *Dev.*, 186–87.
20. Dulles, *John Henry Newman*, 75.
21. *Dev.*, 191.
22. *Dev.*, 195.
23. *Dev.*, 199.
24. *Dev.*, 200.

the Marian dogmas of the Immaculate Conception and of the Assumption do not undermine the absolute and surpassing centrality of the incarnate Logos and his exclusive and universal role as savior, but rather affirm it.

The seventh note is *chronic vigor*. By retaining its youthful vigor despite its antiquity, the church with its development of doctrine may be presumed to be authentic. By contrast, "a corruption, if vigorous, is of brief duration, runs itself out quickly, and ends in death; on the other hand, if it lasts, it fails in vigor and passes into a decay."[25] Ongoing reform, ongoing charismatic renewal, and ongoing development of doctrine are signs of the church's chronic vigor.

Newman understands "development" across all seven notes as the sign and characteristic of ongoing, but deepening and more explicit identity. Against the danger of ecclesial antiquarianism, Newman famously maintains:

It is indeed sometimes said that the stream is clearest near the spring. Whatever use may fairly be made of this image, it does not apply to the history of a philosophy or belief, which on the contrary is more equable, and purer, and stronger, when its bed has become deep, and broad, and full.... In a higher world it is otherwise, but here below to live is to change, and to be perfect is to have changed often.[26]

Authentic change is a function of the ongoing identity of meaning, of faithfulness to the principles given in the one single and selfsame deposit of faith.

At the same time, it should be noted, Newman saw his notes as applicable to the "actual decisions of authority," that is, to a promulgated teaching.[27] The seven notes of authentic development are not at all meant to help project, predict, or even somehow encourage and bring about future developments. Against the danger of presentism, Newman insists that the development of doctrine is not the tool of ongoing change managed by self-appointed developers of doctrine in view of a desired future church

25. *Dev.*, 437.
26. *Dev.*, 40.
27. *Dev.*, 78.

whose teaching is to be designed in advance by the self-authenticating church of the ongoing present. Such a grave misunderstanding of the development of doctrine could, according to Newman, only lead to doctrinal corruptions, but not to authentic developments of doctrine.[28]

Now we can turn to the proposed test case for an authentic development of doctrine, the Second Vatican Council's Declaration on Religious Freedom, *Dignitatis Humanae*.[29]

A Test Case of Authentic Development of Doctrine: *Dignitatis Humanae*

The famous American Catholic theologian John Courtney Murray, theological architect of *Dignitatis Humanae*, observes rather dryly that it "was, of course, the most controversial document of the whole Council, largely because it raised with sharp emphasis the issue that lay continually below the surface of all the conciliar debates—the issue of the development of doctrine."[30] The warrant for his judgment can easily be found in the first

28. It should, however, be noted as a fact of history that Catholic theologians have used the theory of the development of doctrine in general and of notes in particular to seek out the viability of future teaching, i.e., whether Newman would approve or not (e.g., Giovanni Perrone on the Immaculate Conception of the Blessed Virgin Mary or John Courtney Murray in the preparation of *Digniatis Humanae*, to name just two prominent cases). It seems indeed quite impossible in the contemporary theological context, therefore, completely to avoid appealing to development theory when disputed questions are under debate. What is indispensable in this context—lest one give in to the error of presentism—is to understand the notes as principles of continuity, not of change. The notes serve to identify points of continuity, not justify change. It is for this very reason that a return to a largely forgotten Thomist theologian is apposite, one who tackled in a deep way the challenge of the homogeneity of development. His work complements in a salutary way in the dogmatic context of justification what Newman unfolds in his inimitable approach in the context of discovery. See the appendix at the end of this chapter for a brief introduction to Francísco Marín-Sola's *The Homogeneous Evolution of Catholic Dogma*.

29. For a lucid and instructive commentary on this next to *Nostra Aetate* most controversial document of the Second Vatican Council, see F. Russell Hittinger, "The Declaration on Religious Freedom, *Dignitatis Humanae*," in *Vatican II: Renewal within Tradition*, ed. Matthew L. Lamb and Matthew Levering (New York: Oxford University Press, 2008), 359–82, and for the best edition, translation, introduction, and interpretation of *Dignitatis Humanae*, see David L. Schindler and Nicholas J. Healy Jr., *Freedom, Truth, and Human Dignity: The Second Vatican Council's Declaration on Religious Freedom. A New Translation, Redaction History, and Interpretation of Dignitatis Humanae* (Grand Rapids, Mich.: Eerdmans, 2015).

30. *The Documents of Vatican II*, ed. Walter M. Abbott, SJ (London: Geoffrey Chapman, 1966), 673.

article of *Dignitatis Humanae*: "In treating of this religious freedom the synod intends to develop the teaching [*evolvere doctrinam intendit*] of more recent popes on the inviolable rights of the human person and on the regulating of society by law."[31] Consider the teaching that stands at the very center of *Dignitatis Humanae*, as it is articulated in no. 2 of the document. Because of its significance, it deserves to be cited in full:

This Vatican Council declares that the human person has a right to religious freedom. This freedom means that all [human beings] are to be immune from coercion on the part of individuals or of social groups and of any human power, in such wise that no one is to be forced to act in a manner contrary to his own beliefs, whether privately or publicly, whether alone or in association with others, within due limits. The council further declares that the right to religious freedom has its foundation in the very dignity of the human person as this dignity is known through the revealed word of God and by reason itself. This right of the human person to religious freedom is to be recognized in the constitutional law whereby society is governed and thus it is to become a civil right. It is in accordance with their dignity as persons—that is, beings endowed with reason and free will and therefore privileged to bear personal responsibility—that all [human beings] should be at once impelled by nature and also bound by a moral obligation to seek the truth, especially religious truth. They are also bound to adhere to the truth, once it is known, and to order their whole lives in accord with the demands of truth. However, [human beings] cannot discharge these obligations in a manner in keeping with their own nature unless they enjoy immunity from external coercion as well as psychological freedom. Therefore the right to religious freedom has its foundation not in the subjective disposition of the person, but in his very nature. In consequence, the right to this immunity continues to exist even in those who do not live up to their obligation of seeking the truth and adhering to it and the exercise of this right is not to be impeded, provided that just public order be observed.[32]

In the years after the Council intense conflict erupted over the interpretation of *Dignitatis Humanae*. The issue at stake in the interpretation of *Dignitatis Humanae* has been and continues to be this: is it possible to receive the teaching of *Dignitatis Humanae* as an authentic development of doctrine or must this teaching rather be understood as a contradiction of

31. *Decrees* (ed. Tanner), 2:1002.
32. *Dignitatis Humanae*, no. 2.

teachings advanced by Popes Gregory XVI, Pius IX, and Leo XIII? Consider Thomas Pink's precise characterization of the dilemma from which the interpretive conflict takes its departure:

In the nineteenth century, in encyclicals from Gregory XVI's *Mirari Vos* in 1832 to Leo XIII's *Libertas* in 1888, the Catholic Church taught that the state should not only recognize Catholic Christianity as the true religion, but should use its coercive power to restrict the public practice of, and proselytization by, false religions—including Protestantism. Yet in its declaration on religious freedom, *Dignitatis Humanae*, the Second Vatican Council declared that the state should not use coercion to restrict religion—not even on behalf of the true faith. Such coercion would be a violation of people's right to religious liberty. This looks like a clear change in Catholic doctrine.[33]

The *change* in the church's teaching is obvious. One might characterize this change as a change in the church's prudential decision or as a change in non-infallible teaching. Yet a change in the church's teaching it plainly is. The intense conflict of interpretation rages over whether this change of the church's teaching is an authentic development of doctrine or a rupture with the church's teaching and hence what Newman would call a corruption of doctrine. On the one end of the spectrum, there emerged the eventually schismatic Lefebvrists, and those in the Catholic church sympathetic to their position, often referred to as "traditionalists."[34] They regard the document as a significant rupture with the church's past teaching that error had no rights and that, therefore, there could be no general freedom of religion. Consequently, the Levebvrists and their Catholic supporters regard the teaching of *Dignitatis Humanae* as a corruption of what they regard to be the teaching of the authentic tradition. On the opposite side of the spectrum emerged those, often referred to as "progressives," who also hold the Declaration's teaching to constitute a rupture with past teaching, but for them it is a welcome rupture.[35] It is

33. Thomas Pink, "Conscience and Coercion," *First Things* (August/September 2012): 45–51, at 45.
34. Marcel Lefebvre, *Religious Liberty Questioned* (Kansas City, Mo.: Angelus Press, 2002); Michael Davies, *The Second Vatican Council and Religious Liberty* (Long Prairie, Minn.: Neumann Press, 1992).
35. Charles Curran, *Catholic Moral Theology in Dialogue* (Notre Dame, Ind.: Fides Publications, 1972); Richard A. McCormick, *The Critical Calling* (Washington, D.C.: Georgetown University

not hard to discern antiquarianism on the one end of the spectrum and presentism on the other end. Notably, on this particular issue, the assessment of *Dignitatis Humanae*, antiquarians and presentists—despite their glaring differences otherwise—share a common perception: *Dignitatis Humanae* represents a break with earlier papal teaching. Antiquarians loathe and condemn this perceived rupture as a fateful and detrimental self-unmooring of the Council from the tradition of the Catholic church and a capitulation to the heresy of modernism; presentists praise and welcome it as affording them the justification to bring about more ruptures in order to separate the present church ever-more thoroughly from what they regard to be an utterly outdated and therefore alienating and consequently spiritually stultifying and oppressive tradition.

Yet Newman's seven notes of an authentic development of doctrine make rather plain that the antiquarians as well as the presentists are wrong in their shared assumption that *Dignitatis Humanae* constitutes a rupture with the church's past teaching. On the contrary, Newman's seven notes afford a cumulative argument that the teaching of *Dignitatis Humanae* is an authentic development of doctrine. Here, I am in complete agreement with Ian Ker and in the following I largely rely on the case he makes in his recent book, *Newman on Vatican II*.[36]

Press, 1989); John T. Noonan, *A Church That Can and Cannot Change: The Development of Catholic Moral Teaching* (Notre Dame, Ind.: Notre Dame University Press, 2005).

36. Ian Ker, *Newman on Vatican II* (Oxford: Oxford University Press, 2014), 65–71. In the following discussion, I abstain from the academic temptation to be original and rather gratefully rely on Ker's astute analysis and argumentation that strikes me as just right. For theologians who do not draw upon Newman's notes to make their case yet based on different arguments interpret *Dignitatis Humanae* as an authentic development of doctrine, see especially Basile Valuet, *La liberté religieuse et la tradition catholique: Un cas de développement doctrinal homogène dans le magistère authentique*, 3 vols. (Le Barroux: Abbaye Sainte-Madeleine, 1998); Avery Dulles, SJ, "*Dignitatis Humanae* and the Development of Catholic Doctrine," in *Catholicism and Religious Freedom: Contemporary Reflections on Vatican II's Declaration on Religious Liberty*, ed. Kenneth L. Grasso and Robert P. Hunt (Lanham, Md.: Rowman and Littlefield, 2006), 43–67; Brian W. Harrison, *Religious Liberty and Contraception* (Melbourne: John XXIII Fellowship, 1988); F. Russell Hittinger, "The Declaration on Religious Freedom, *Dignitatis Humanae*," in *Vatican II: Renewal Within Tradition* (ed. Lamb and Levering), 359–82; Martin Rhonheimer, "Benedict XVI's 'Hermeneutic of Reform' and Religious Freedom," in *The Common Good of Constitutional Democracy*, ed. William F. Murphy (Washington, D.C.: The Catholic University of America Press, 2013), 429–54; David L. Schindler, "Freedom, Truth, and Human Dignity: An Interpretation of *Dignitatis Humanae* on the Right to Religious Freedom," in Schindler and Nicholas J. Healy Jr., *Freedom, Truth, and Human Dignity:*

Regarding the first note, *preservation of type*, Newman emphasizes that "preservation of type" does not rule out all variations, and, in fact, anticipates "considerable alteration of proportion and relation, as time goes on, in the parts or aspects of an idea."[37] How might *Dignitatis Humanae* display this first note? Ker rightly observes that "the fact ... that *Dignitatis Humanae* may appear to contradict previous teaching does not in itself mean that it is not a genuine development. Before the Second Vatican Council, the condemnation of religious liberty meant that people were not free to choose whatever religion they pleased."[38] For it is, after all, the case that the Declaration itself rejects the liberty "to choose whatever religion one might please" as a false idea of religious freedom. It states: "We believe that this one true religion subsists in the Catholic and Apostolic Church, to which the Lord Jesus committed the duty of spreading it abroad among all men," that furthermore "on their part, all men are bound to seek the truth, especially in what concerns God and His Church, and to embrace the truth they come to know, and to hold fast to it," and that finally "it is upon the human conscience that these obligations fall and exert their binding force. The truth cannot impose itself except by virtue of its own truth, as it makes its entrance into the mind at once quietly and with power" (no. 1). Ker observes that "nowhere does the document speak about 'freedom of conscience,' implying that a person has the right to do whatever their conscience tells them to do, simply because their conscience tells them to. Consciences can be erroneous and need to be informed."[39] For *Dignitatis Humanae* explicitly states that "every man has the duty, and therefore the right, to seek the truth in matters religious in order that he may with prudence form for himself right and true judgments of conscience, under use of all suitable means" (no. 3). All of this is in accord with the fundamental principle that the true idea of religious freedom as taught by the Council "leaves untouched traditional Catholic doctrine on the moral duty of men and societies toward the true

---

The Second Vatican Council's Declaration on Religious Freedom. A New Translation, Redaction History, and Interpretation of Dignitatis Humanae (Grand Rapids, Mich.: Eerdmans, 2015), 39–209.

37. *Dev.*, 173.

38. Ker, *Newman on Vatican II*, 66.

39. Ibid.

religion and toward the one Church of Christ" (no. 1). In light of Newman's first note, Ker draws from all this the following conclusion: "Had the Council failed to embrace the idea of religious freedom expressed in *Dignitatis Humanae*, there would have been a very real danger of a corruption arising in Catholic theology, since, as Newman points out, 'one cause of corruption … is the refusal to follow the course of doctrine as it moves on, and an obstinacy in the notions of the past.'"[40]

Recall that *Gaudium et Spes* explicitly and unequivocally recognizes the church's doctrine on conscience as taught by Thomas Aquinas, namely that it is a participation in the divine law.[41] Now, it would have been quite impossible for the Council to uphold and reaffirm the church's teaching on conscience in *Gaudium et Spes* and, in the context of pluralist societies, not to draw the right inference from this teaching in *Dignitatis Humanae*. *Gaudium et Spes* lays down the central tenets that *Dignitatis Humanae* merely unfolds:

In fidelity to conscience, Christians are joined with the rest of men in the search for truth, and for the genuine solution to the numerous problems which arise in the life of individuals from social relationships.… Only in freedom can man direct himself toward goodness. Our contemporaries make much of this freedom and pursue it eagerly; and rightly to be sure.… For its part, authentic freedom is an exceptional sign of the divine image within man. For God has willed that man remain "under the control of his own decisions," (cf. *Sir.* 15:14) so that he can seek his Creator spontaneously, and come freely to utter and blissful perfection through loyalty to Him. Hence man's dignity demands that he act according to a knowing and free choice that is personally motivated and prompted from within, not under blind internal impulse nor by mere external pressure. Man achieves such dignity when, emancipating himself from all captivity to passion, he pursues his goal in a spontaneous choice of what is good, and procures for himself through effective and skillful action, apt helps to that end.[42]

40. Ibid.

41. *Gaudium et Spes*, no. 16: "In the depths of his conscience, man detects a law which he does not impose upon himself, but which holds him to obedience. Always summoning him to love good and avoid evil, the voice of conscience when necessary speaks to his heart: do this, shun that. For man has in his heart a law written by God; to obey it is the very dignity of man; according to it he will be judged. (Cf. Rom 2:15–16.) Conscience is the most secret core and sanctuary of a man. There he is alone with God, Whose voice echoes in his depths. (Cf. Pius XII, *Radio address on the correct formation of a Christian conscience in the young*, March 23, 1952: *Acta Apostolicae Sedis* [1952], 271)."

42. *Gaudium et Spes*, nos. 16–17.

Recall also that the two documents were, after all, promulgated on the same day, December 7, 1965. Had the Council refused to promulgate *Dignitatis Humanae*, it would have been, according to Newman, guilty of "an obstinacy in the notions of the past," in short, guilty of antiquarianism.[43] Rather, the Council had to teach the difference between authentic freedom, freedom for the truth, and its corruption, indifferentism regarding the truth. And precisely by doing this in *Dignitatis Humanae*, the Declaration displays the note of the preservation of type.

Regarding the second note, *continuity of principles*, Newman recognizes that the difference between doctrines and principles sometimes depends on how we look at them; he states that the "life of doctrines may be said to consist in the law or principle which they embody."[44] Ker quite appropriately puts the matter into a wider picture by recalling the two relevant principles. He characterizes the first one thus:

The first is that at any moment in her history certain aspects of what Newman called the Christian "idea" are inevitably stressed more than others.... The Church must constantly be seeking to balance the different "aspects" without excessive imbalances. In the case of religious freedom two doctrines are involved: the duty of all human beings to seek the true religion which is Catholicism, and on the other hand the sovereignty of conscience.[45]

Because *Dignitatis Humanae* in fact holds both doctrines, Ker argues, it is a fitting example of the first relevant principle put into practice. Pertaining to the second relevant principle he states that

the Church has to take account of changing circumstances and to apply her doctrines accordingly.... In the case of religious freedom, the first of the two doctrines … was assumed in a totally Catholic context like Italy to require the legal exclusion of all other erroneous religions, if only to ensure that, as the Declaration itself allows for, "the just requirements of public order are observed" (art. 2).[46]

But it is the case, Ker adds significantly, that "Newman recognized that even in the nineteenth century Italy was less than completely Catholic and that the Church would be better off not using coercion through legal

43. *Dev.*, 177.
44. *Dev.*, 178.
45. Ker, *Newman on Vatican II*, 67.
46. Ibid., 67–68.

and political means."[47] Thus, in order to remain truthful to the guiding principle, in a pluralist society the church does have to interpret the doctrine differently from the way Pius IX did. Therefore, precisely by insisting on the continuity of the underlying principles that inform its teaching, *Dignitatis Humanae* displays the note of the continuity of principles.

Newman's third note is *power of assimilation*, or *unitive power*. He observes that "doctrines and views which relate to man are not placed in a void, but in the crowded world, and make way for themselves by interpenetration, and develope [sic] by absorption,"[48] and concludes that the Catholic church "can consult expedience more freely than other bodies, as trusting to her living tradition, and is sometimes thought to disregard principle and scruple, when she is but dispensing with forms."[49] Ker is quick to observe that right in its opening paragraph the Declaration explicitly recognizes "that the Council is responding to external influences when it refers to the growing sense of the dignity of the human person and the importance of responsible freedom as opposed to state coercion."[50] Precisely by being "willing to absorb ideas emanating from secular thought without fear of compromising her own essential doctrines," the Council fathers display the third note, the power of assimilation.[51]

Newman's fourth note is *logical sequence*. This note does not necessarily mean, as Newman is quick to warn, "a conscious reasoning from premises to conclusions."[52] All that is required is that a doctrine should seem to be "the *logical issue* of its original teaching."[53] Recall that the church's traditional teaching was that the Catholic religion is the one true religion and that all human beings are bound in conscience to embrace the truth. The logical issue from this teaching is this: in order to be able to follow one's conscience and thereby to fulfill one's duty one must have the freedom to do so. Hence, the Declaration calls in a new way attention to the fact that "the truth cannot impose itself except by virtue of its own truth" (no. 1), and that therefore religious freedom is indeed necessary for hu-

47. Ibid., 68.
48. *Dev.*, 186.
49. *Dev.*, 189.
50. Ker, *Newman on Vatican II*, 68.
51. Ibid.
52. *Dev.*, 189.
53. *Dev.*, 195.

man beings in order "to fulfill their duty to worship God" (no. 1). For after all, "It is one of the major tenets of Catholic doctrine that man's response to God must be free" (no. 10). The logical issue of the church's ongoing freedom is the full uncovering of the ontological bond of freedom with truth and vice versa. With this conciliar teaching, David L. Schindler persuasively argues, the church "signals a development in her understanding of the inherent unity of truth with freedom and freedom with truth. While still affirming that the *truth alone* frees, she now affirms at the same time, in a more explicit way, that truth itself presupposes freedom, and that truth *really does free*."[54] Precisely this—the ontological bond of freedom with truth and vice versa—is the logical sequence of the church's constant teaching on conscience as "the most secret core and sanctuary of a human being."[55]

What about Newman's fifth note, *anticipation of its future*?[56] Ker points out that "it would be hard to imagine a better example of 'such early … intimations of tendencies which afterwards are fully realized' than the example of Jesus Christ himself, who 'bore witness to the truth, but … refused to impose the truth by force on those who spoke against it.'"[57] Ker's point is fair enough. Yet it is arguably the church's constant teaching on conscience, a doctrine profoundly expounded by Thomas Aquinas and central to Newman's own thought, affirmed in *Gaudium et Spes*, and rightly applied in *Dignitatis Humanae*, that most clearly instantiates the fifth note, anticipation of the future.[58]

Newman's sixth note, *conservative action on its past*, identifies an authentic development as one "which is conservative of the course of antecedent developments being really those antecedents and something be-

---

54. David L. Schindler, "Freedom, Truth, and Human Dignity: An Interpretation of *Dignitatis Humanae* on the Right to Religious Freedom," 43. Already in 1976, the French Dominican theologian Philippe André-Vincent, OP, in his book *La Liberté religieuse: Droit fundamental* (Paris: Téqui, 1976), argued that the idea most central to the teaching of *Dignitatis Humanae* was the ontological bond of the freedom of the person with the truth, the same idea that stands at the center of Pope John Paul II's 1993 encyclical letter *Veritatis Splendor*.

55. *Gaudium et Spes*, no. 16: "Conscience is the most secret core and sanctuary of a man. There he is alone with God, Whose voice echoes in his depths."

56. *Dev.*, 195–96.

57. Ker, *Newman on Vatican II*, 69. Quotations within this quotation are drawn from *Dev.*, 189, 195–96, and *Dignitatis Humanae*, no. 11, respectively.

58. See the book chapter by Hittinger referred to above in note 36.

sides them: it is an addition which illustrates, not obscures, corroborates, not corrects, the body of thought from which it proceeds.... a *tendency conservative* of what has gone before it."[59] Considering the Declaration in light of this note, Ker astutely argues:

Discussion of the first note has already shown that *Dignitatis Humanae* preserves the two teachings that human beings are not free to choose whatever religion they choose but that they have a duty to seek and hold the true religion, and that the true religion is to be found in the Catholic Church. The Declaration only *seemed* to be a departure from the previous teaching because of the way it was taken to apply in a homogeneous Catholic context. But the teaching is one thing, its interpretation and implementation another. The essential teaching has been preserved and therefore the Declaration passes Newman's sixth test.[60]

Antiquarians as well as presentists fail to appreciate the distinction Ker draws between a teaching on the one side and, distinct from it, on the other side its interpretation and implementation.[61] Assuming absolute

59. *Dev.*, 200 and 203.

60. Ker, *Newman on Vatican II*, 69.

61. Arguably, this distinction could be abused in order to justify all sorts of innovative ruptures. Yet the distinction may not be isolated from the criteria the other notes afford. To maintain the church's teaching "in the same doctrine, the same sense, and the same understanding," as the Council fathers of the First Vatican Council insist in *Dei Filius*, especially when such teaching pertains to prudential matters and involves therefore non-infallible teaching, that is, "doctrines" in Newman's wider sense of term as used in his *Essay on the Development of Christian Doctrine*, ongoing interpretation is precisely the way to secure what the Council fathers insist upon in *Dei Filius*. It is "doctrine" in this wider sense pertaining especially also to prudential matters and involving non-infallible teaching, to which Newman's famous statement is rightly to be applied: "An idea not only modifies, but is modified, or at least influenced, by the state of things in which it is carried out, and is dependent in various ways on the circumstances which surround it. Its development proceeds quickly or slowly, as it may be; the order of succession in its separate stages is variable; it shows differently in a small sphere of action and in an extended; it may be interrupted, retarded, mutilated, distorted, by external violence; it maybe enfeebled by the effort of ridding itself of domestic foes; it may be impeded and swayed or even absorbed by counter energetic ideas; it may be coloured by the received tone of thought into which it comes, or depraved by the intrusion of foreign principles, or at length shattered by the development of some original fault within it. But whatever be the risk of corruption from intercourse with the world around, such a risk must be encountered if a great idea is duly to be understood, and much more if it is to be fully exhibited. It is elicited and expanded by trial, and battles into perfection and supremacy. Nor does it escape the collision of opinion even in its earlier years, nor does it remain truer to itself, and with a better claim to be considered one and the same, though externally protected from vicissitude and change. It is indeed sometimes said that the stream is clearest near the spring. Whatever use may fairly be made of this image, it does not apply to the history of a philosophy or belief, which on the contrary is more equable, and purer, and

identity between a teaching and its interpretation would indeed entail that only the very origin itself, the apostolic deposit of faith, was ever-pristine and that subsequent to it we only encounter an interminable sequence of ruptures.

Last but not least there is *chronic vigor*, the seventh note of an authentic development of doctrine. *Dignitatis Humanae* would seem clearly to pass this test if some fifty years are anything to go by. While there are still schismatic Lefebvrists who reject it as contrary to the constant teaching and tradition of the church, the Catholic church as a whole has received the teaching as authentic and any reversal of it seems out of the question. Popes John Paul II, Benedict XVI, and Francis have continuously affirmed the teaching of *Dignitatis Humanae*.

In sum, a reading of *Dignitatis Humanae* in light of Newman's notes yields a veritable line of converging probabilities. In accumulation they constitute a robust, indeed "irrefragable" argument demonstrating that the teaching advanced by *Dignitatis Humanae* does indeed represent an authentic development of doctrine.[62] Ker rightly concludes that Newman's seven notes do very usefully "serve as answers to objections brought against the ... decisions of authority," that is, the Lefebvrists and those

---

stronger, when its bed has become deep, and broad, and full. It necessarily rises out of an existing state of things, and for a time savours of the soil. Its vital element needs disengaging from what is foreign and temporary, and is employed in efforts after freedom which become more vigorous and hopeful as its years increase. Its beginnings are no measure of its capabilities, nor of its scope. At first no one knows what it is, or what it is worth. It remains perhaps for a time quiescent; it tries, as it were, its limbs, and proves the ground under it, and feels its way. From time to time it makes essays which fail, and are in consequence abandoned. It seems in suspense which way to go; it wavers, and at length strikes out in one definite direction. In time it enters upon strange territory; points of controversy alter their bearing; parties rise and fall around it; dangers and hopes appear in new relations; and old principles reappear under new forms. It changes with them in order to remain the same. In a higher world it is otherwise, but here below to live is to change, and to be perfect is to have changed often" (*Dev.*, 39–40). In the case of the teaching of *Dignitatis Humanae*, David L. Schindler has persuasively identified (see note 54 above) the constitutive underlying principle as "the inherent unity of truth with freedom and freedom with truth."

62. Newman gave one of the best explanations for his method in a letter to Canon Walker from July 6, 1864: "The best illustration of what I hold is that of a *cable*, which is made up of a number of separate threads, each feeble, yet together as sufficient as an iron rod. An iron rod represents mathematical or strict demonstration; a cable represents moral demonstration, which is an assemblage of probabilities, separately insufficient for certainty, but, when put together, irrefragable" (Ward, *Life of Newman*, 2:43).

sympathetic to their position.[63] Yet they also answer those on the opposite side of the spectrum "who hold also that the document constitutes a rupture with past teaching, albeit in their view a welcome rupture."[64] Avery Dulles's assessment comports well with Ker's judgment. Dulles states that "the Church has applied the unchanging principles of the right to religious freedom and the duty to uphold religious truth to the conditions of an individualist age, in which almost all societies are religiously pluralist. Under such circumstances the establishment of religion becomes the exception rather than the rule. But the principle of noncoercion of consciences in matters of faith remains constant."[65]

Conclusion: Two Counterfeits of the Authentic Development of Doctrine

The development of doctrine gives concrete witness to the continuous mission of the Holy Spirit to guide the church into all the truth. Truth cannot contradict truth and the Holy Spirit does not contradict itself. Consequently, antiquarianism and presentism resist the mission and work of the Holy Spirit, the one by absolutizing allegedly pristine origins in blatant disregard of the Spirit's continuing guidance into an ever-deeper and fuller reception of the truth of revelation in the mind of the church, the other by severing the Spirit's present guidance from the Spirit's past guidance, thereby undercutting the identity of the Spirit's mission, past, present, and future. Antiquarianism and presentism, two unfortunate post-Vatican II counterfeits of the authentic development of doctrine, are static, reductive, and eventually unsustainable; in short, *they lack chronic vigor.* They therefore lack ecclesial authenticity and tend to display the characteristics Newman would regard as typical for corruptions of doctrine. Precisely for this reason, in order to identify and repel antiquarianism and presentism whenever they raise their heads, a robust understanding of the development of doctrine greatly matters.

63. *Dev.*, 78, cited by Ker, *Newman on Vatican II*, 70.

64. Ker, *Newman on Vatican II*, 70.

65. Avery Cardinal Dulles, SJ, "Development or Reversal?," *First Things* (October 2005): 53–61.

Yet the usefulness of Newman's teaching on the development of doctrine for the purposes of identifying and repelling the most notorious post-Vatican II counterfeits of an authentic development of doctrine is only one small aspect of Newman's insight into the development of doctrine. It is vastly more important to realize and hold before the inner eye of one's mind Newman's realization that the development of doctrine is nothing less than pneumatology and ecclesiology in their doctrinal expression. "To be deep in history is to cease to be a Protestant." History shows us that the church, at times, displays her infallible magisterial authority to judge: this is true, that is not. Hence, the dogmas we all hold dear, even Protestants, are inherently ecclesial. The Catholic is deep in history, the history of salvation, stored in the doctrinal memory of the church. The truth into which the Holy Spirit guides has a living history—namely, the development of doctrine—and a concrete living body, with a hierarchical and magisterial expression, "the church of the living God, the pillar and bulwark of the truth" (1 Tm 3:15).

Appendix: Francísco Marín-Sola's Thomist Reception of Newman

Instead of drawing upon Aquinas's thought as the proper "context of justification" for the insights that Newman gains in the complex "context of discovery" of his *Essay on the Development of Doctrine*, I shall introduce in this appendix an unjustly forgotten Thomist theologian, Francísco Marín-Sola, who more deeply and acutely than any other Thomist theologian in the twentieth century tackled the theological problems that the development of doctrine presents when considered in the "context of justification" according to authentic Thomistic principles. Simultaneously, Marín-Sola developed a deep understanding of and appreciation for John Henry Newman's *Essay on the Development of Doctrine*.[66] As the noted fundamental theologian and Newman scholar Jan H. Walgrave states:

---

66. The monograph by Sylvester P. Juergens, *Newman on the Psychology of Faith in the Individual* (New York: Macmillan, 1928), emerged from a doctoral dissertation written under the guidance of Marín-Sola.

There is no book on the question of development that met with more response among Catholic schoolmen than that of Marín-Sola.... Even A. Gardeil, the most original and powerful innovator in the domain of neo-Thomistic fundamental theology, abandoned his own somewhat forced theory and adopted with enthusiasm the views of the great Spanish theologian. But, as was to be expected, all possible objections were urged against him, and the history of the controversy could fill a book. But within the general frame of scholastic thought most difficulties could be either easily solved or rejected as having no point.[67]

Insofar as Francísco Marín-Sola is virtually unknown to the contemporary generation of theologians, a brief sketch of his life is called for in order properly to situate his famous dogmatic work on the development of doctrine. He was born on November 22, 1873, in Cárcar, a town located in the Spanish province of Navarra. On December 9, 1888, at age 15, he took the Dominican habit at Ocaña (Toledo). This priory belonged to the missionary province of the Spanish Dominicans, the province of the Holy Rosary. Judicially in Spain, the province was centered with its activities on the Philippines but also covered China and Japan. On December 10, 1889, he took his simple vows and on December 10, 1892, his solemn vows. After completing his philosophical and theological studies in Toledo and Avila with great distinction, he was assigned in 1897—still a deacon—to Manila where he was ordained a priest later that year. Due to his frail health he was sent the same year to the province of Cagayán into the parish in Amulung. There he was surprised by the Philippine Revolution of 1898. After his release from prison in 1900, he returned to Manila where he first taught mathematics at the Colegio de San Juan de Letrán and from 1904 on philosophy at the University of Santo Tomás. Because of his extraordinary success as a teacher he was sent back to Spain in 1906 in order to teach scripture and theology at the province's study house in Avila.

During Marín-Sola's first years of teaching theology back in Spain, two factors converged to occasion his preoccupation with the problematic of the development of doctrine in the years to come. The first was the simple fact that in Avila he had to teach Melchior Cano's *De locis theo-*

67. Jan H. Walgrave, OP, *Unfolding Revelation: The Nature of Doctrinal Development* (London / Philadelphia: Hutchinson / Westminster, 1972), 173–74.

logicis and the second that his first years of teaching theology fell into the period when modernism was at its peak. In the crucible between Cano's demanding treatise on theological method and modernism's unbridled historicism, the question became ever-more urgent to him as to whether all doctrinal development is unavoidably transformist and thus ultimately heterogeneous or whether authentic doctrinal development can indeed be shown to be homogeneous. After two years of teaching theology in the study house in Avila, he was sent back to Manila in 1908 where he obtained in 1909 the licentiate and the doctorate in sacred theology at the University of Santo Tomás, the Dominican university under the immediate oversight of the missionary province of the Holy Rosary. In 1910 he returned to Spain in order to occupy the chair in theology at the province's study-house in Avila. Prompted by political changes in the Far East, the province judged it to be advantageous for the missionary friars to be fluent in English and therefore transferred the Province's study house from Avila to Rosaryville (Ponchatoula) in the state of Louisiana. From 1911 to 1913 he was sent to the University of Notre Dame to obtain proficiency in English and to teach philosophy there; subsequently, from 1913 until 1918, he taught theology in Rosaryville. In 1917 the University of Notre Dame conferred on Marín-Sola the doctorate in civil law *honoris causa*. It was during his years at the University of Notre Dame and at the study house in Rosaryville that he finally began to publish what he had been working on for a number of years. From 1911 to 1922 his articles under the general title *La homogeneidad de la doctrina católica* appeared in the theological journals *La Ciencia Tomista* and *Revue Thomiste*.

After the death of the Dominican theologian Norberto del Prado, Marín-Sola was asked to fill the vacancy at the University of Fribourg, Switzerland, where he taught dogmatic theology from 1919 until 1927 and for a time acted as dean of the theological faculty. During this period, he not only published his last articles on doctrinal development in *La Cienca Tomista* and the *Revue Thomiste* but collected and recast all of them into one large tome which appeared in 1923 in Spain under the title *La evolución homogénea del dogma católico*. The book became the first title of the Biblioteca de Tomistas Españoles in honor of St. Thomas Aquinas on the sixth centenary of his canonization and was widely acclaimed by reviewers. A significantly enlarged French edition appeared the following year in Fribourg under the title *L'Evolution homogène du dogme catholique*. Failing health and an ongoing controversy surrounding his subtle proposal on the concord between the divine motion and created freedom forced him to retire to the convent of Ocaña in Spain, where his religious life as a Dominican had begun. After his health was somewhat restored, he returned to Manila in 1929 and taught at the University of Santo Tomás until his death in 1932.

Further editions of *The Homogeneous Evolution of Catholic Dogma* appeared posthumously—a Spanish edition that incorporates the significant additions made to the French edition in 1952 (reprinted in 1963), and an English translation based on the 1963 Spanish edition in 1988. The 1963 Spanish re-edition suggests an ongoing interest in this work in the Spanish-speaking theological world up to and into the Second Vatican Council, while the 1988 English translation marks the commendable effort of Marín-Sola's disciples at the University of Santo Tomás in Manila to give access to his demanding work in the landscape of post-Vatican II Catholic theology.

No Catholic theologian working on the inherently complex and ongoingly contested question of the development of doctrine could afford to ignore Marín-Sola's *magnum opus*, especially during the period leading up to the Second Vatican Council. After Vatican II, this attitude changed considerably. With the exception of Jan H. Walgrave, Aidan Nichols, and a few others, most Catholic theologians still dealing with the development of Catholic doctrine embrace the notion of a radical paradigm shift initiated by Vatican II. This purported paradigm shift makes possible the unexamined dismissal of Marín-Sola's theory as belonging to an outdated "neo-Scholastic" past. Theologians who uncritically adopt this possibly premature dismissal become oblivious of a nuanced, profound, and coherent tradition of discourse on the development of doctrine stretching from the sixteenth century right up to the threshold of the Second Vatican Council. It is this very oblivion that makes post-Vatican II theologies of doctrinal development vulnerable to the very pitfalls and dead-ends Marín-Sola astutely identifies and ably navigates around in *The Homogeneous Evolution of Catholic Dogma*.

With *The Homogeneous Evolution of Catholic Dogma*, Marín-Sola responds to two different theological accounts of the development of Catholic doctrine most prominent in the early decades of the twentieth century, each one problematic in its own specific way: on the one hand, the a-rational and heterodox conception of Catholic doctrine that modernism advanced and, on the other, a theory that took the development of Catholic doctrine to be a primarily affective and mystical process. Marín-Sola intended to overcome the error of the former and to integrate the legitimate insights of the latter into a comprehensive and balanced system that accounted for the intellectual as well as the intuitive aspects of the process of an homogeneous evolution of doctrine. His central question concerns the way a proposition or truth is contained in or related to the deposit of faith. According to Marín-Sola, as Walgrave aptly states, "a development is homogeneous when the transition does not entail in the *terminus ad quem* a concept different from the *terminus a quo*.... A transition that entails different or contrary concepts is not homogeneous but transformistic or heterogeneous."[68]

In *The Homogeneous Evolution of Catholic Dogma*, Marín-Sola expands upon the theory of Ambrose Gardeil, OP (1859–1931), and restores the correct notion of Melchior Cano, OP (1509–60), on the subject of theological conclusions. There are two central but tacit suppositions operative in his theory. The first supposition is that revelation has cognitive content which can only be apprehended when it is expressed in propositions or, as Thomas Aquinas puts it, in articles of faith. The second supposition is that sacred theology is not merely the hermeneutical effort of understanding and communicating divine revelation as expressed in scripture and tradition, but is rather also, and first and foremost, a science of conclusions. If divine revelation indeed issues in true propositions, in articles of faith, true inferences can be drawn from them. The normative point of departure for Marín-Sola's profound exercise in dogmatic and speculative theology is, of course, the teaching of the First Vatican Council on the development of doctrine:

The doctrine of the faith which God has revealed is put forward not as some philosophical discovery capable of being perfected by human intelligence, but as

68. Walgrave, *Unfolding Revelation*, 169.

a divine deposit committed to the spouse of Christ to be faithfully protected and infallibly promulgated. Hence, too, that meaning of the sacred dogmas is ever to be maintained which has once been declared by holy mother church, and there must never be any abandonment of this sense under the pretext or in the name of a more profound understanding. May understanding, knowledge, and wisdom increase as ages and centuries roll along, and greatly and vigorously flourish, in each and all, in the individual and in the whole church: but this only in its own proper kind, that is to say, in the same doctrine, the same sense, and the same understanding.[69]

Marín-Sola advances an interpretation of the normative lead given by Vatican I with the help of the concept of the "implicitly revealed": everything that is implicit in the revealed principles is homogeneous to the same. When considering what is "implicitly revealed," he identifies three modes of implication: (1) *formal and implicit*, which obtains when the difference between the original and the later proposition is one of terms only; (2) *virtually implicit*, which obtains when the relation between the original and the later proposition implies a difference in explicative concepts; and (3) *simply virtual*, which obtains when the difference implies a real distinction, but in such a way that the concepts are still only explicative. He emphasizes an important subdivision of the second and the third modes of implication: *virtual-inclusive* in contrast with *virtual-connective*. For Marín-Sola, "the distinction is of the utmost importance because the line that separates what may become defined dogma from what may not runs between the virtual-inclusive and the virtual-connective."[70] The distinction rests on the difference between metaphysical and physical causes: "Inferences from metaphysical causes are virtually included in those causes; inferences from physical causes are virtually connected with them. There are, then, only two kinds of implication that are virtual-connective; deductions of facts from pure essences and deductions of effects from real physical causes. Truths derived after that manner from explicitly revealed propositions cannot become part of defined dogma."[71]

Consider the central thesis of Marín-Sola's theory: what is virtually

69. *Dei Filius*, no. 4, in *Decrees* (ed. Tanner), 2:809.
70. Walgrave, *Unfolding Revelation*, 169–70.
71. Ibid., 171.

implicit in certain principles entails a real identity with these principles. Consequently, the virtually implicit is included in the revealed principles themselves. Hence, while any conclusions validly drawn from these principles are only virtually and implicitly true, they are nevertheless still revealed, and if revealed therefore definable, and when defined by the church are to be believed with divine faith. One of the important entailments of his theory is that "the domain of ecclesiastical definition and the range of doctrinal development are coextensive with divine faith. There is no *fides ecclesiastica*."[72]

Marín-Sola understood his project as a retrieval of the undiluted doctrine of Thomism as it pertains to the development of doctrine. At the same time, Marín-Sola was interested in integrating genuine new insights, especially central aspects of John Henry Newman's insights from the *Essay on the Development of Christian Doctrine*. He regarded the following two theses to be central to an authentic Thomist theory of the development of doctrine. First, all virtual revelation is logically implicit. Its explication is an unfolding from within revelation; this explication is neither an addition to nor a transformation of revelation. Second, in order to be *de fide*, what is virtually revealed must be proposed by the church and until the church proposes it as such, the virtually revealed is not *de fide*.

Marín-Sola saw the rudiments of this position most clearly developed in Melchior Cano's *De locis theologicis*. On Marín-Sola's supposition every truly theological conclusion is implicitly revealed and can be defined as a truth of faith and after the church proposes it as such it is be believed by divine faith. With his actualization and development of Cano's theory, Marín-Sola stands in critical opposition to a range of proposals advanced in the course of and subsequent to the Catholic reform of the sixteenth century: Vásquez and Vega held that an inference could be *de fide* even before the church declared it. Molina, on the contrary, did not think that such an inference was *de fide* even after the church proposed it. In opposition to Molina, Suárez and Lugo admitted as acceptable some additions that could not be called strictly implicit but rather "formal confused" and that were to be held only by ecclesiastical faith.

72. Ibid., 169.

What is unique and crucial about Marín-Sola's theory is this: while numerous other Catholic theologians objected to transformist theories of doctrinal development, they—as opposed to Marín-Sola—confined all development to that contained in "ecclesiastical," that is, human faith. By implication they denied that there could be any development in divine faith or at least that what the church went on to teach should be held by divine faith. It was his unique achievement to show that the kind of development Suárez and Lugo defended was that of a merely physical or virtual connection. The "virtual implicit" that they had erroneously eclipsed had to be restored to its proper prominence. Based on it, one could conceive of a homogeneous evolution of doctrine that—supposing the church proposes it—is to be held by divine faith. Although this was a new argument and genuinely his own, he nevertheless returned with it to the tradition antecedent to Molina, Suárez, and Lugo.

Marín-Sola identifies two authentic paths of homogeneous theological, doctrinal, and dogmatic evolution, two distinct but interrelated processes by way of which what is virtually implicit in revelation is explicated: one is the way of the intellect and of study, the other is the way of the will and of connaturality, of the experience of the divine. In the latter case there obtains a virtual connatural contact with these truths, a kind of experience of them. Marín-Sola takes the very source of this approach to be the infused divine principle that elevates human nature—sanctifying grace. Together with the theological virtues of faith, hope, and charity and the gifts of the Holy Spirit, sanctifying grace confers on the person who possesses it a divine mode of being, which is nothing but a principle of intuition or appreciation of things divine. Analogous to the natural habits that, in virtue of their conformity to right reason, impart a natural sense of estimating the rational rectitude of things, the infused virtues and gifts of the Holy Spirit impart a supernatural sense of appreciating the divine character of things proposed by God and also things opposed to God. Consequently, what Newman would have called strictly illative theological reasoning can, according to Marín-Sola, discover truths capable of being defined as dogmas of the faith.

Quite obviously, even a masterwork is not free from shortcomings and hence not beyond criticism. Walgrave achieves the probably best balance between appreciation and critique when he observes that Marín-Sola's *magnum opus*

is the most comprehensive work on the subject, not only presenting an amply elaborated and perfectly articulated theory but also embracing in its view the whole history of the question, widely discussing all the opinions of contemporary authors. Marín-Sola is a speculative genius, and his erudition is prodigious; but strictly speaking he is no historian. He does not look at the data of history in a strict historical perspective, and he often accommodates them to fit into his own system. He systematizes history. In itself this is not a bad thing, but it is a most dangerous enterprise.[73]

One might readily agree with Walgrave about the danger concomitant with any theological theory of the development of doctrine, but it might be an unavoidable danger given the very nature of the enterprise—*which is ultimately not a historical one*. Yet the reason for the "systematization of history" is not Marín-Sola's alleged "Scholasticism" or, worse, a worrisome "propositionalism" (which he indeed does hold). The reason for his "systematization of history" is rather the "dogmatic principle," the fundamental supposition that revelation—*pace* modernism's and historicism's tenets—has a distinct cognitive content virtually implicit in the deposit of faith and eventually explicated in propositions that one can apprehend and assent to. Accounting for the development of doctrine on the supposition of the dogmatic principle leads unavoidably to a certain and quite legitimate "systematization of history." The most obvious example can be found in the first ecumenical councils. In order to be faithful to the dogmatic principle, the Council fathers had to be engaged in a certain "systematization of history." A strictly historical reconstruction and interpretation of what the Council fathers would have regarded to be the works of orthodox theologians would have resulted in just another interpretation, but not the grasp of the essence of the truth of revelation, articulated as dogma. All relativism, of which historicism is but a variant, denies the grasp of the essential. Walgrave rightly emphasizes one danger, the omission of historical nuance; but is not the opposite danger not only much worse but also much more pressing—that in the eagerness to do

73. Ibid., 168.

justice to all historical nuances, complexities, and ambiguities, one loses sight of the essential?

Walgrave and others group Marín-Sola with the "logical theories" of development, in contrast with "transformist theories" and more recent "theological theories" which, according to the common post-Vatican II theological consensus, have overcome the weaknesses of the two earlier kinds of theories. While there are good reasons for subsuming Marín-Sola's work under the "logical theories," it has a grave disadvantage. For this categorization occludes Marín-Sola's novel and sustained effort to integrate the insights of Newman's *Essay on the Development of Christian Doctrine* into the established tradition of Catholic dogmatic discourse on the development of doctrine. Marín-Sola saw his own position and that of Reginald-Maria Schultes, OP, as analogous to the positions of Newman and Bossuet: while Bossuet and Schultes emphasize the immutability of dogma, Newman and Marín-Sola stress the vitality and homogeneous evolution of it. Marín-Sola regarded it as perfectly compatible to stress the immutability of dogma and its homogeneous evolution.[74]

Even an only superficial familiarity with this monumental work of dogmatic and speculative theology suggests immediately that Marín-Sola's *magnum opus* deserves an unrivaled place next to John Henry Newman's *Essay on the Development of Christian Doctrine*. The renowned Anglican church historian Owen Chadwick regards Marín-Sola's work as "probably the most able, and perhaps the most influential thesis upon the theory of development written during the twentieth century."[75] While *The Homogeneous Evolution of Catholic Dogma* is informed quite obviously by a different philosophical tradition and theological method than Newman's *Essay on the Development of Christian Doctrine*, it is crucial to understand that Marín-Sola as well as Newman hold revelation to have cognitive content expressed in propositions that can be apprehended and assented to, and that neither of them gives any quarter to the kind of dogmatic

---

74. For Marín-Sola's explicit discussion of Newman, and especially his *Essay on the Development of Christian Doctrine*, see *The Homogeneous Evolution of Catholic Dogma*, 396–400 (*La evolución homogénea del dogma católico*, 355–59).

75. Owen Chadwick, *From Bossuet to Newman: The Idea of Doctrinal Development* (Cambridge: Cambridge University Press, 1957), 204.

relativism characteristic of a preconceptual historicist understanding of revelation. Both Newman and Marín-Sola achieve a level of theological penetration and conceptual sophistication that has not been reached by Catholic theology in the post-Vatican II period. Even the commendable *ressourcement* in the patristic patrimony can only for so long circumvent and postpone the questions that Marín-Sola treated with great profundity and rigor in his theological masterwork.

After the more recent flirtations by avowedly late-modern or post-modern Catholic theologians with philosophical historicism and constructivism have exhausted themselves, the opportune time might have arrived for a new generation to tackle again the profound and substantive theological as well as conceptual issues involved in the development of doctrine and in this course rediscover the treasure that Marín-Sola's work is. To label Marín-Sola's account as purportedly merely "logical" and to dismiss it due to its alleged lack of "historical consciousness" might be nothing but an all-too-facile way of ignoring the perennial challenges he addresses as well as, possibly, unreflective and unwarranted historicist premises at play in such a critique.[76] In order to arrive at a sound theologi-

76. There obtains a categorical difference between the new awareness of history reflected in the important Spanish Dominican theologian Melchior Cano's *De locisi theologicis* (1563) and the principled historicism advanced in the latter part of the nineteenth century by the German thinkers Wilhelm Dilthey (1833–1911), Ernst Troeltsch (1865–1923), and Friedrich Marheinecke (1862–1954), and developed further in the twentieth century by the German sociologist Karl Mannheim (1893–1947). Despite their sharp distinction between historicism and relativism, they admitted as a consequence of historicism the high probability of relativism. Recall that in his *De locis theologicis*, Melchior Cano, next to the seven *loci proprii* of theology (scripture; the oral tradition of Christ and the apostles; the universal church; the councils; the Apostolic See; the saints of the early church; Scholastic theology and canonist thought) identifies three *loci alieni* of theology: (1) human reason expressed in the sciences, (2) human reason expressed in philosophy and in the history of philosophy, and—last but not least—(3) human history. Not only because of his unique vocation as a friar preacher that led him to work on three continents, Asia, America, and Europe, but also because of his deep familiarity with Cano's *magnum opus* and especially its last *locus alienus* of theology, human history, we should rightly expect that the categorization of the *Homogeneous Evolution of Catholic Dogma* under "logical theories" of development fails to do justice to the complexity and nuance of his achievement. Marín-Sola is as little a "logicist" in matters of doctrinal development as Newman is a "modernist." For an astute analysis and demonstration of the theoretical inadequacy of philosophical historicism, see Carl Page, *Philosophical Historicism and the Betrayal of First Philosophy* (University Park: Pennsylvania State University Press, 1995). This book should be required reading for presentists who characteristically invoke in intellectually all-too-facile ways the purportedly obvious inevitability of an intellectually and culturally historicist reading of past and present as the normative *locus primus* of the *loci proprii* of theology in the twenty-first

cal understanding of the inherently erroneous positions of the two characteristic contemporary counterfeits of the development of doctrine—antiquarianism and presentism—and in order to have a conceptually and dogmatically sound criteriology for authentic doctrinal development (lest Pope Benedict XVI's "hermeneutic of reform" become instrumentalized by presentists), Marín-Sola's *The Homogeneous Evolution of Catholic Dogma* remains an indispensable supplement in the dogmatic context of justification for the insights that a contemporary rereading of Newman's *Essay on the Development of Doctrine* yields in the theological context of discovery.

---

century. For one concrete application of such a subtle, albeit programmatic presentist view, see Hans-Joachim Sander's extensive commentary on Vatican II's Pastoral Constitution *Gaudium et Spes*, where he argues that the "signs of the times" originating outside the church should—in alleged accord with *Gaudium et Spes*—be accorded a privileged place in shaping the future course of doctrine and pastoral practice. Hans-Joachim Sander, "Theologischer Kommentar zur Pastoralkonstitution über die Kirche in der Welt von heute," in *Herders theologischer Kommentar zum Zweiten Vatikanischen Konzil*, ed. Bernd Jochen Hilberath and Peter Hünermann (Freiburg i.B.: Herder, 2005), 5:581–886. For an instructive study on Melchior Cano's *De locis theologicis*, see Bernhard Körner, *Melchior Cano, De locis theologicis: Ein Beitrag zur theologischen Erkenntnislehre* (Graz: Styria-Medienservice, 1994), and for a thoughtful and nuanced contemporary application of Cano's approach, see Bernhard Körner, *Orte des Glaubens—loci theologici: Studien zur theologischen Erkenntnislehre* (Würzburg: Echter, 2014).

CHAPTER 4

THE UNIVERSITY AND
ITS COUNTERFEIT

John Henry Newman's life spanned the nineteenth century, a time of tremendous social, political, cultural, scientific, and technological change. The time of his birth was still part of the age of carriages, front-loaded muskets, and sailboats, the time when Napoleon began to export the sociopolitical program of the French Revolution all over continental Europe; the time of his death was the age of transcontinental express trains, machine guns, ocean-steamers, the time when England was the leading industrial nation of Europe and the British Empire approached its widest global extension. Despite the two world wars and the other horrors of the twentieth century, as well as the ever-accelerating computer-technological and biotechnological revolution of the early twenty-first century, Newman remains our contemporary in more than one sense, especially in matters pertaining to the institution of the university and university education. For even the most superficial perusal of his classic *The Idea of a University* makes it abundantly plain that our time shares with Newman's the dominant ideology of secularism.[1] What Newman discerned and exposed in its still nascent state has since become a global reality. As the noted historian Brad Gregory aptly puts it: "Regardless of the academic discipline, knowledge in the Western world today is considered secular by definition. Its assumptions, methods, content, and truth claims are and can only be secular, framed not only by the logical demand of rational coherence, but also by the methodological postulate of naturalism and its epistemological correlate, evidentiary empiricism."[2] The ideological premises of secularism were honed in the sixteenth and seventeenth centuries, became politically and socially explicit in the eighteenth century, imperial in the nineteenth and the first half of the twentieth century, and global in the second half of the twentieth and the early twenty-first century.[3]

1. Invited by Archbishop Cullen, Newman became founding rector of the planned Catholic University of Ireland. Between May 10 and June 7, 1852, he delivered five discourses to the Catholic clergy and intelligentsia of Dublin. By the end of November 1852, Newman had finished writing five more discourses. On February 2, 1853 (although with an 1852 imprint) all ten lectures, together with a lengthy appendix of supporting documentation, appeared in print under the title *Discourses on the Scope and Nature of University Education. Addressed to the Catholics of Dublin.* Omitting the original fifth discourse, "General Knowledge Viewed as One Philosophy" as well as the appendix, Newman eventually published a considerably edited version of the remaining nine discourses together with the 1859 "Lectures and Essays on University Subjects" under the well-known title *The Idea of a University.* For a comprehensive account of the textual history of the volume and for the reasons that led Newman to repress the original fifth discourse and also the appendix, see Ian Ker's "Editor's Introduction," in John Henry Newman, *The Idea of a University Defined and Illustrated. I. In Nine Discourses Delivered to the Catholics of Dublin. II. In Occasional Lectures and Essays Addressed to the Members of the Catholic Church,* ed. I. T. Ker (Oxford: Clarendon Press, 1976), xi–lxxxv. This edition also contains as appendices the fifth discourse and the Appendix of the original 1852 edition [hereafter "*Idea,* 1852 Discourse V"]. For two instructive accounts of John Henry Newman's work as founder and first rector of the Catholic University in Dublin, see Fergal McGrath, SJ, *Newman's University: Idea and Reality* (London: Longmans, Green, and Co., 1951), and Paul Shrimpton, *The "Making of Men": The Idea and Reality of Newman's University in Oxford and Dublin* (Leominster: Gracewing, 2014), and for an informative account of the ecclesial and secular historical context, see Colin Barr, *Paul Cullen, John Henry Newman, and the Catholic University of Ireland, 1854–1864* (Notre Dame, Ind.: University of Notre Dame Press, 2011).

2. Brad Gregory, *The Unintended Reformation: How a Religious Revolution Secularized Society* (Cambridge, Mass.: Belknap Press of Harvard University Press, 2012), 299.

3. For the currently magisterial account and analysis of this development, see Charles Taylor's *magnum opus, A Secular Age* (Cambridge, Mass.: Belknap Press of Harvard University Press, 2007). For the complex process of the accommodation of the university to the "immanent frame" and its consequent functionalization by its varying immanent ends, see the following works. It is far from accidental that for the late eighteenth and the nineteenth century, primarily German authors come to mind: Johann David Michaelis, *Raisonnement über die protestantischen Universitäten in Deutschland,* 4 vols. (Frankfurt/Leipzig, 1768–76). As there does not exist an English transla-

In the American and European consumer capitalist societies of the twenty-first century, secularism presents itself typically as "hyperpluralism."[4] In its nascent state, hyperpluralism was already quite familiar to Newman. He describes the state of his society as one "in which authority, prescription, tradition, habit, moral instinct, and the divine influences go for nothing,

tion of it, the interested reader might turn for a helpful summary and discussion of major aspects of Michaelis's *magnum opus* to Michael Legaspi, *The Death of Scripture and the Rise of Biblical Studies* (New York: Oxford University Press, 2010), 33–37. Other important works the interested reader might want to consult are Immanuel Kant, *The Conflict of the Faculties* [1798], trans. Mary J. Gregor (New York: Abaris Books, 1979); Johann G. Fichte, *The Purpose of Higher Education: Also Known as the Vocation of the Scholar* [1794], trans. John K. Bramann (Mt. Savage, Md.: Nightsun Books, 1988); F. W. J. von Schelling, *On University Studies* [1803], trans. E. S. Morgan, ed. Norbert Guterman (Athens: Ohio University Press, 1966); Friedrich Schleiermacher, *Occasional Thoughts on Universities in the German Sense, With an Appendix Regarding a University Soon to Be Established* [1808], trans. Terrence N. Tice and Edwina G. Lawler (Lewiston, N.Y.: Edwin Mellen Press, 1991); Max Weber, "Science as Vocation" [1919], in *From Max Weber: Essays in Sociology*, trans. and ed. H. H. Gerth and C. Wright Mills (New York: Oxford University Press, 1946), 129–56; and the infamous inaugural Rectorial Address at the University of Freiburg by Martin Heidegger, "The Self-Assertion of the German University" [1933], trans. Karsten Harries, *Review of Metaphysics* 38 (1985): 467–502. For a lonely and unheeded voice critical of all these more or less subtle forms of subjecting the university to purposes extrinsic to its idea, see Friedrich Nietzsche, *On the Future of Our Educational Institutions* [1872], trans. J. M. Kennedy (London: T. N. Foulis, 1910). By transforming strategically and organizationally the Baconian university of utility into a consistent and effective institution of advanced research, the German university of the nineteenth century became the paradigm of the modern research university. Legaspi puts it well: "In the nineteenth century, there were two kinds of universities: German universities and those that wanted to be German" (*The Death of Scripture*, 28). For an excellent study of the German university in the nineteenth century, see Thomas Albert Howard, *Protestant Theology and the Making of the Modern German University* (New York: Oxford University Press, 2006).

    4. In *The Unintended Reformation*, Brad Gregory employs this term in order to characterize "the overwhelming pluralism of proffered religious and secular answers to [the so-called life questions]" (74). Gregory understands as these questions: "'What should I live for, and why?' 'What should I believe, and why should I believe it?' 'What is morality, and where does it come from?' 'What kind of person should I be?' 'What is meaningful in life, and what should I do in order to lead a fulfilling life?'" (74). I offer a longer passage from Gregory's analysis, not only because I think it is accurate but also because it forms the very background in which I regard Newman's insights to be of pressing relevance: "In Western society at large, the early twenty-first-century basis for most secular answers to the Life Questions seems to be some combination of personal preferences, inclinations, and desires: in principle truth is whatever is true to you, values are whatever you value, priorities are whatever you prioritize, and what you should live for is whatever you decide you should live for. In short: whatever. All human values, meanings, priorities, and morality are contingent, constructed, and subjective. In principle you are your own basis, your own authority, in all these matters, within the boundaries established by the law.... You can change the basis for your answers, as well as their content, at any time, any number of times, and for any reason or without any reason. You are *free*—hence, whatever" (77).

in which patience of thought, and depth and consistency of view, are scorned as subtle and scholastic, in which free discussion and fallible judgment are prized as the birthright of each individual."[5] Newman's nineteenth-century England and our twenty-first-century Western societies are haunted by the pervasive presence of hyperpluralism's central protagonist—the sovereign subject and its infinitely varied and insatiable desires.

What was in Newman's day its nascent state has become today a pervasive reality: university education and university sciences deliver goods that are seen as commodities to be purchased in order to satisfy the desires of the sovereign subject, be it in its individual or collective expression. The commodification and the instrumentalization of the university are two sides of the same coin, where supply and demand, branding and competition, determine the life of universities and colleges. The knowledge gained in the modern research university is a production or making, a *technē* that is a means to ends extrinsic to the institution itself. The American Association of Universities (AAU), the exclusive club of the leading research universities in the United States of America, characterizes a research university as an institution that advances a great variety of expertise to be applied to real-world problems. Cutting-edge faculty research is combined with undergraduate training for such research, often in highly specialized programs.[6]

Taking the officially promoted understanding of the AAU at its word means to conclude that the modern research university is essentially a highly advanced polytechnical institute, or put into one word, a polytechnicum. At the time when he delivered his university lectures in Dublin, Newman discerned this polytechnicum in its nascent state and named it after the person he took to be its *spiritus rector*—the English philoso-

---

5. *Idea*, 37.

6. The AAU's "White Paper" puts it thus: "The raison d'être of the American research university is to ask questions and solve problems. Together, the nation's research universities constitute an exceptional national resource, with unique capabilities: America's research universities are the forefront of innovation; they perform about half of the nation's basic research. The expert knowledge that is generated in our research universities is renowned worldwide; this expertise is being applied to real-world problems every day. By combining cutting-edge research with graduate and undergraduate education, America's research universities are also training new generations of leaders in all fields." American Association of Universities, "White Paper," available at www.aau.edu/research/article.aspx?id=4670.

pher Francis Bacon. Newman pointedly observed that Bacon "abundantly achieved what he proposed. His is simply a Method whereby bodily discomforts and temporal wants are to be most effectually removed from the greatest number."[7] And the ability to fulfill a wide range of material and social desires makes the Baconian polytechnicum almost irresistible. Questioning it puts the critic immediately under the suspicion of being an enemy of material progress. The modern research university is the Baconian polytechnicum in a highly advanced state. It has had a stunning global career, such that, as Brad Gregory puts it, "leading scientists and scholars at research universities are the societal and indeed the global arbiters of what counts as knowledge and what does not in the early twenty-first century."[8]

Yet the very success of the Baconian polytechnicum carries the seed of its own undoing. If the dynamic of the Baconian polytechnicum were to be carried to the full term of its interior logic, each of its advanced research competencies might eventually—for the sake of greater immediate applicability—be moved to private and state labs for bioengineering, or to the various branches of the military-industrial and medical-industrial complex. For the ends the Baconian polytechnicum serves can quite obviously be achieved in other, possibly more efficient ways. These ends are not intrinsically dependent upon the interior unity of such an institution. To still call it a university is undoubtedly useful for reasons of branding and marketing but at the same time profoundly deceptive. With good reasons, the philosopher Benedict Ashley, OP, educated in the great early years of the University of Chicago's extraordinary undergraduate program developed in the 1930s under university president Robert Maynard Hutchins, observes about the university's counterfeit: "The very term 'university' means many-looking-toward-one, and is related to the term 'universe,' the whole of reality. Thus, the name no longer seems appropriate to such a fragmented modern institution whose unity is provided only by a financial administration and perhaps a sports team."[9] Ashley presses the crucial point: the university is a *per se* unity that carries its end or purpose in its very practices of

7. *Idea*, 119.

8. Gregory, *The Unintended Reformation*, 299.

9. Benedict M. Ashley, OP, *The Way toward Wisdom: An Interdisciplinary and Intercultural Introduction to Metaphysics* (Notre Dame, Ind.: University of Notre Dame Press, 2009), 20.

education and inquiry; it is categorically different from the Baconian poly-technicum that merely is a unity *per accidens*, a contingent agglomeration of means in service of changing extrinsic ends.[10] Precisely because "university" entails *per se* unity, the Baconian polytechnicum cannot rightfully claim the title "university." By doing so nevertheless, the Baconian polytechnicum be-comes the university's counterfeit. It insists on this denomination because "university" is commonly regarded as the objective gold standard for the institutional pursuit of intellectual excellence and most advanced forms of education. It is for this very reason that none of the leading global research universities would ever seriously consider calling itself by that term that most effectively describes what it indeed is, a polytechnicum that might sustain a curricular appendix, a skill-producing propaedeutic that for rea-sons of public relations still is called "the liberal arts" or "the humanities." It is for the same reason that colleges are eager to upgrade themselves to the rank of "university," despite the fact that they do nothing but expand them-selves into "polytechnic utiliversities" by adding programs in sports man-agement, forensics, law enforcement, accounting, business administration, and every technological skill imaginable and marketable.[11]

10. In his eventually repressed 1852 Discourse V, "General Knowledge Viewed as One Philoso-phy," Newman observes with characteristic clairvoyance and formidable force: "At the present day, they knock the life out of the institutions they have inherited, by their alterations and adaptations. As to their own creations, these are a sort of monster, with hands, feet, and trunk moulded respec-tively on distinct types. Their whole, if the word is to be used, is an accumulation from without, not the growth of a principle from within. Thus ... their notion of a University, is a sort of bazaar or hotel, where every thing is showy, and self-sufficient, and changeable.... The majestic vision of the Middle Age, which grew steadily to perfection in the course of centuries, the University of Paris, or Bologna, or Oxford, has almost gone out in night. A philosophical comprehensiveness, an orderly expansiveness, an elastic constructiveness, men have lost them, and cannot make out why. This is why: because they have lost the idea of unity: because they cut off the head of a living thing, and think it is perfect, all but the head. They think the head an extra, an accomplishment, the *corona operis*, not essential to the idea of the being under their hands. They seem to copy the lower speci-mens of animated nature, who with their wings pulled off, or a pin run through them, or eaten out by parasitical enemies, walk about, unconscious of their state of disadvantage. They think, that, if they do but get together sufficient funds, and raise a very large building, and secure a number of able men, and arrange in one locality ... a suite of distinct lecture-rooms, they have at once founded a University. An idea, a view, an indivisible object, which does not admit of more or less, a form, which cannot coalesce with any thing else, an intellectual principle, expanding into a consistent harmonious whole,—in short, Mind, in the true sense of the word,—they are, forsooth, too practi-cal to lose time in such reveries!" (*Idea*, 1852 Discourse V, 422–23).

11. Consider the striking characterization of the frame of mind of the defenders and imple-

Yet what exactly is this objective gold standard that the university's counterfeit seeks to imitate? It is the still tacitly accepted normative idea of what a university essentially is, a normative idea that encompasses all the essential features of the most advanced and rigorous kind of institution of higher learning and a curriculum characterized by a fundamental metaphysical and epistemological commitment to truth, the acquisition and communication of comprehensive knowledge—across centuries and across cultures. One of the most consistent and compelling articulations of this normative idea of what a university essentially is was formulated by John Henry Newman in what next to his *Apologia pro Vita Sua* is probably his most famous work, *The Idea of a University*. According to Newman, a university, properly conceived, is founded on the unity of all truth. The unity of truth in turn accounts for the unity of knowledge. And the unity of knowledge accounts for the unity of a university education. The discipline that inquires into the interrelationship of all sciences and hence into the unity of truth, Newman calls the "science of sciences," or "first science." The purpose of this "first science" is inquiring into and finding truth—comprehensive and ultimate truth. This "science of sciences" constitutes the keystone of the arch of sciences. This "first science" is the science of being *qua* being; it inquires into the first principles of being and thereby accounts for and advances the unity of knowledge and consequently facilitates the inner coherence of a university education. This "first science" is the unique characteristic of a university in the proper sense. Infused into any field of study, its comparative, analytic, and synthetic activity of reflection connects each field with all the other fields of study and research.[12] The acme of this "first science" is the study of the

---

menters of the university's counterfeit Newman offers in the 1852 Discourse V: "It is plain that such writers do not rise to the very idea of a University. They consider it a sort of bazaar, or pantechnicon, in which wares of all kinds are heaped together for sale in stalls independent of each other; and that, to save the purchasers the trouble of running about from shop to shop; or an hotel or lodging house, where all professions and classes are at liberty to congregate, varying, however, according to the season, each of them strange to each, and about its own work or pleasure" (ibid., 421).

12. In the original 1852 Discourse V, Newman does not hesitate to draw upon Scholastic terminology to characterize the "science of sciences": "Imagine a science of sciences, and you have attained the true notion of the scope of a University. We consider that all things mount up to a whole, that there is an order and precedence and harmony in the branches of knowledge one with another as well as one by one, and that to destroy that structure is as unphilosophical in a course of

first cause, the inquiry into the source and perfection of all being and truth. In short, its apex is natural theology. This "science of sciences" is intrinsically without use—that is, undetermined by ends extrinsic to its proper inquiry and the knowledge it yields—and therefore immune to all the typically modern efforts of instrumentalizing and thereby legitimizing philosophical inquiry. The "first science" is the most liberal of all liberal arts that carry their ends in their very exercise.

This "science of sciences" is indispensable for the integrity of the university precisely as university—for this reason. Liberal education carries its end in itself. Liberal education is a potentially universal education. While it is impossible to embrace all or even most fields of contemporary knowledge, liberal education fosters reflection upon one's knowledge in relation to other fields and in relation to the whole. This interrelatedness makes liberal education a potentially universal education. Such universal education requires a horizon of absolute, radical, and nonreductive transcendence, a horizon that affords a maximum of possible expansiveness, interconnectedness, and coherence. But such a horizon of transcendence can only be achieved and secured if the "first science," with natural theology as its acme, is an integral part of a university education. According to Newman, the greatest danger to the inner coherence of the university is a self-imposed normative naturalism or materialism with its foregone conclusion that God does not exist and that metaphysical inquiry is pointless because all knowledge humans can ever gain is ultimately pragmatic. Such a normative naturalism dramatically reduces the horizon of truth, changes its nature, and dissolves the inner unity of knowledge.

In order to protect the university from such a normative naturalism

---

education, as it is unscientific in the separate portions of it. We form and fix the Sciences in a circle and system, and give them a centre and an aim, instead of letting them wander up and down in a sort of hopeless confusion. In other words, to use scholastic language, we give the various pursuits and objects, on which the intellect is employed, a *form*" (ibid., 423–24). In the order of being, form accounts for the actuality of a thing; in the order of knowledge, form accounts for intelligibility of a thing realized in the act of understanding, and when reflected upon in the act of understanding for the nature of understanding, which is itself the form of the science of sciences. The most extensive modern inquiry into the nature of human understanding—an inquiry that requires the reader at each stage to come to a realization of the nature of understanding by way of understanding his or her own understanding—is Bernard Lonergan's *Insight: A Study of Human Understanding*, ed. Frederick Crowe and Robert M. Doran (Toronto: University of Toronto Press, 1992).

and to maintain the gold standard, Newman advances a claim that is as central to the very idea of a university as it is unacceptable for the university's counterfeit, the Baconian polytechnicum: "Religious Truth is not only a portion, but a condition of general knowledge. To blot it out is nothing short … of unravelling the web of University Teaching. It is, according to the Greek proverb, to take the Spring from out of the year, it is to imitate the preposterous proceeding of those tragedians who represented a drama with the omission of its principal part."[13] Examining Newman's controversial claim raises three questions: First, what does Newman mean by theology in the context of a university education? Second, why does he think theology is indispensable for university education? And third, what might it mean to take Newman's proposal seriously?

University Education and (Natural) Theology as a Science

Newman holds it as axiomatic that the idea and therefore also the term "university" is essentially related to "universe." Consequently, he argues, "as to the range of University teaching, certainly the very name of University is inconsistent with restrictions of any kind.… A University should teach universal knowledge."[14] "University" is first and foremost an institution of teaching universal knowledge. Hence, no subject matter that conveys knowledge is to be excluded from university teaching. Newman is quite insistent and explicit about this point:

If a University be, from the nature of the case, a place of instruction, where universal knowledge is professed, and if in a certain University, so called, the subject of Religion is excluded, one of two conclusions is inevitable,—either, on the one hand, that the province of Religion is very barren of real knowledge, or, on the other hand, that in such University one special and important branch of knowledge is omitted. I say, the advocate of such an institution must say *this*, or he must say *that*; he must own, either that little or nothing is known about the Supreme Being, or that his seat of learning calls itself what it is not.[15]

13. *Idea*, 70.
14. *Idea*, 20.
15. *Idea*, 21.

The secular university by and large—that is, when it is consistent with its self-understanding—insists upon the first alternative: little or nothing is known, or ever can be, about what Newman has called the "Supreme Being"—if such a supreme being exists at all. This does not mean that ideas and beliefs about such a supreme being cannot be studied. Indeed, many secular universities have departments of religion in which ideas pertaining to the anthropological phenomenon called "religion" are studied. Newman would not at all be opposed to such an empirical, historical, literary, and cultural study in the world's religions in university education, for he would regard such study and education as integral components of a liberal education.

But Newman has something categorically different in mind when he speaks of "theology." By "theology" he means "the Science of God, or the truths we know about God put into system; just as we have a science of the stars, and call it astronomy, or the crust of the earth, and call it geology."[16] It would be a mistake to assume that Newman regards the science of God as an exploration of a topic next to other topics. Rather, the science of God—if it indeed is science of God and not its counterfeit—must be taught as truth. In short, when Newman invokes "theology" in the context of his university lectures he has in mind first and foremost what Catholic theology has traditionally called the "preambles of faith," a properly scientific knowledge of God that is the intrinsic goal of the science of being *qua* being, of metaphysics, or first philosophy.[17] While this "first science" does not depend on divine revelation and is distinct from sacred theology, that is, the theology based on divine revelation, "the sci-

16. *Idea*, 61.

17. Thomas Aquinas puts the matter tersely in *ST* I, q. 2, a. 2, ad 1: "The existence of God and other like truths about God, which can be known by natural reason, are not articles of faith, but are preambles to the articles; for faith presupposes natural knowledge, even as grace presupposes nature, and perfection supposes something that can be perfected. Nevertheless, there is nothing to prevent a [person], who cannot grasp a proof, accepting, as a matter of faith, something which in itself is capable of being scientifically known and demonstrated." *Dei Filius* declares authoritatively as being *de fide* that the natural range of reason encompasses the following capacity: "The same holy mother church holds and teaches that God, the source and end of all things, can be known with certainty from the consideration of created things, by the natural power of human reason" (Eadem sancta mater ecclesia tenet et docet, Deum, rerum omnium principium et finem, naturali humanae rationis lumine e rebus creatis certo cognosci posse); in *Decrees* (ed. Tanner), 2:806.

ence of sciences" may receive, without compromising its integrity as "first science," insights from divine revelation that further its own proper inquiry. (See the appendix to this chapter for further explications.)

Newman is, of course, fully aware of materialism as a competing philosophical position, represented by the names of Epicurus and Hume: "If God is more than Nature, Theology claims a place among the sciences: but, on the other hand, if you are not sure of as much as this, how do you differ from Hume or Epicurus?"[18] While this rhetorical question would have had a considerable impact on the original, largely Catholic audience of Newman's university lectures, in relationship to an audience reflective of the modern research university, this question carries no force whatsoever. Hume and Epicurus would be placeholders of materialist beliefs widely shared in the modern research university. But then, Newman would observe, to the degree that the modern research university is committed to Epicurean and Humean materialism it is unable to realize itself as a *per se* unity pursuing intrinsically meaningful practices of education and inquiry. Such an institution has simply ceased to be a university in any meaningful sense of the term.[19]

Quite aware that his position was already controversial in the English-speaking university world (outside of Oxford and Cambridge) in the 1850s, Newman makes it most explicit that "University Teaching without Theology is simply unphilosophical. Theology has at least as good a right to claim a place there as Astronomy."[20] In this telling statement, Newman gives us a key for grasping his overall—and ever pertinent—understand-

18. *Idea*, 41.

19. If one wants, however, to move beyond a purely defensive strategy of argumentation of this kind, one would have to revisit Aristotle's proof in his *Physics* that the first mover is immaterial (*Physics* VIII.10) and the proof in his *De anima* that the intellect of the human soul is immaterial (*De anima* III.4 and 5). These proofs demonstrate that "being" extends beyond physical objects and that therefore materialism is untenable as a comprehensive philosophical theory. For a lucid presentation of Aristotle's arguments, see Ashley, *The Way toward Wisdom*, 92–124. For a compelling reformulation of the argument for the immateriality of the human intellect—an argument based on Aristotle but one that also draws on recent analytic philosophy (Kripke, Quine, Goodman)—see James F. Ross, *Thought and World: The Hidden Necessities* (Notre Dame, Ind.: University of Notre Dame Press, 2008), 115–27, and for its able defense against recent critics, see Edward Feser, "Kripke, Ross, and the Immaterial Aspect of Thought," in *American Catholic Philosophical Quarterly* 87, no. 1 (2013): 1–32.

20. *Idea*, 42.

ing of what the essential property of a university education is. As Newman explains in his sixth discourse: "The true and adequate end of intellectual training and of a University is not Learning or Acquirement, but rather, is Thought or Reason exercised upon Knowledge, or what may be called Philosophy."[21] What differentiates a proper university education for Newman from the "knowhow" training in a Baconian polytechnicum is thought exercised upon knowledge and upon the interrelationship of all the sciences. It is not unlike what Aristotle undertakes in his *Posterior Analytics*. Newman states as much quite explicitly:

The comprehension of the bearings of one science on another, and the use of each to each, and the location and limitation and adjustment and due appreciation of them all, one with another, this belongs, I conceive, to a sort of science distinct from all of them, and in some sense a science of sciences, which is my own conception of what is meant by Philosophy, in the true sense of the word, and of a philosophical habit of mind, and which in these Discourses I shall call by that name.[22]

According to Newman, philosophy is a "science of sciences" and a philosophical habit of mind is the acquired intellectual *habitus* that facilitates inquiry into the principles, the inner coherence, and the interconnectedness of all the sciences. In contemporary terminology, Newman understands philosophy to be first and foremost a "meta-science," that is, the architectonic science that reflects upon and thus in a certain way synthesizes all sciences. Yet its character as architectonic meta-science does not exhaust Newman's understanding of philosophy. Its implications go further. Because all sciences attend to certain aspects of being—what Newman calls facts and their relations to each other—this meta-science must also be "first philosophy," that is, the science that investigates not only the principles of all the other sciences but rather also the principles of being *qua* being. In order to fulfill the task Newman assigns to philosophy as meta-science it cannot be anything less than what has traditionally been called metaphysics or philosophy of being.[23] The end and culmination

21. *Idea*, 139.
22. *Idea*, 51.
23. For a remarkable introduction to metaphysics as meta-science and therefore as a philosophy of being, see Ashley, *The Way toward Wisdom*.

of such a philosophy of being is the inquiry into the first transcendent cause or the absolute. This end or culmination of this meta-science is natural theology. Historically revealed religious truth far surpasses the knowledge of God that natural theology affords and for this reason revealed truth about God affirms, corrects, and deepens natural theology. It is this knowledge of God—acquired by natural theology and affirmed, corrected, and deepened by revealed religion—that Newman holds to be an absolutely essential component, indeed the keystone, of an authentic university curriculum.

As soon as the modern research university imposes the criterion of naturalist secularism as the antecedent condition for admittance of sciences into its curriculum, Newman astutely observes, the institution decapitates itself philosophically and forfeits its ability to reflect critically on its operative naturalist commitments. By excluding the meta-science of philosophy in its full metaphysical scope on the basis of an unwarranted, dogmatic naturalist secularism, the modern university is morphing itself unbeknownst into its counterfeit, the Baconian polytechnicum. Plato, Aristotle, Aquinas, Scotus, and their modern disciples, as well as twentieth-century scientists like the physicist Carl Friedrich von Weizsäcker and the chemist Michael Polanyi knew that any truly philosophical form of critical reflection presupposes a horizon that genuinely transcends and thereby enables such critical reflection.[24] Indeed, excluding the theology that is the culmination of metaphysical inquiry and that is affirmed by revealed religion from the university can only be an unphilosophical decision. For such a decision to be a proper philosophical one it would require a metaphysical warrant. Such a warrant is, however, impossible, as first philosophy itself has become excluded together with natural theology.

Together with all still engaged in the inquiries of first philosophy,

24. See Carl Friedrich von Weizsäcker, *Unity of Nature* (New York: Farrar, Straus and Giroux, 1981) and *Der Garten des Menschlichen: Beiträge zur geschichtlichen Anthropologie* (Munich: Hanser, 1984), and Michael Polanyi, *Personal Knowledge: Toward a Post-Critical Philosophy* (Chicago: University of Chicago Press, 1974). For a trenchant critique of central aspects of modern science—the attempt at the comprehensive mathematization of nature, the bankruptcy of Hume's fictionist epistemology, and the preemptive constriction of what can be known to the absolutized norm of the scientific method—see Edmund Husserl, *The Crisis of European Sciences and Transcendental Phenomenology*, trans. David Carr (Evanston, Ill.: Northwestern University Press, 1970).

Newman knew perfectly well that there are significant and even profound ongoing disagreements about the precise nature of this science itself and about specific questions of substance and that it, furthermore, faces challenges and limitations of a kind no other science faces. For the apex of first philosophy, natural theology, deals, after all, with a subject matter that transcends all possible genera of scientific subject matters. But why should these circumstances, Newman would ask, disqualify first philosophy as a science? The fact that paleo-anthropology lives more by hypotheses than by evidences, that neuroscience—instead of investing into the labor of explaining human volition and free choice—is bent upon the strategy of simply dissolving that which it is meant to explain, that biochemistry so far has provided no cogent ontogenesis for the unique reality of "life," and that contemporary physics can neither reconcile quantum mechanics with the general theory of relativity nor move from postulating the existence of "dark matter" to an account of it, does not prove that these inquiries lack the characteristics of a proper science and must therefore be excluded from the secular university's curriculum and research program. Newman holds that the science of first philosophy is analogous to such sciences with one important difference: its subject matter is related to the whole cosmos and the totality of all facts and relations as cause to effect.

The speculative labor of first philosophy is arduous and time-consuming, and its proper scientific knowledge can be mastered by very few, after a long time of considerable intellectual effort, and with intermingling of error.[25] We would rightly expect nothing less from astrophysics or

25. This is at least what the fathers of the First Vatican Council seem to imply at the beginning of *Dei Filius*. Their teaching seems to correspond to the facts and simply points out that first philosophy is nothing but a proper science in the way Newman insists it is. They state the matter explicitly only the other way around: "It is indeed thanks to this divine revelation, that those matters concerning God which are not of themselves beyond the scope of human reason, can, even in the present state of the human race, be known by everyone without difficulty, with firm certitude and with no intermingling of error" (Huic divinae revelationi tribuendum quidem est, ut ea, quae in rebus divinis humanae rationi per se impervia non sunt, in praesenti quoque generis humani conditione ab omnibus expedite, firma certitudine et nullo admixto errore cognosci possint); in *Decrees* (ed. Tanner), 2:806. *Dei Verbum* explicitly affirms the teaching of Vatican I. In *Metaphysics* I.2 (982a23–25) Aristotle observes that philosophical knowledge that attains to truths about God is the most difficult for human beings. And Thomas Aquinas, in his commentary on the *Metaphysics*, states that the most difficult for human beings to know are those things entirely separate from matter in being, that is, immaterial substances. Consequently, "even though this science which is

biochemistry. These sciences are arduous and time-consuming, and that their proper scientific knowledge can be mastered by very few, after a long time of considerable research, and with an intermingling of error, that is, in openness to falsification and to the formation of new hypotheses and explanatory models.[26] What makes first philosophy, according to tacitly operative Baconian criteria, radically different from physics and biochemistry, is the following: even modest competency in physics and biochemistry creates expertise in the order of production and consumption and consequently leads to useful employment. According to the same Baconian criteria, not even advanced, let alone modest, competency in first philosophy creates expertise in the order of production and consumption. Consequently, it is a waste of time—time lost for production and consumption.

If Newmanian criteria of the university were to replace the Baconian criteria of its counterfeit, if there were a robust and visible presence of first philosophy in the core of the undergraduate curriculum of contemporary universities, it would complicate—to say the least—the rather uncritical reception of the overall remarkably superficial and in many ways ignorant claims advanced by the so-called new atheism.[27] Furthermore, first philosophy would be better equipped to investigate and account for miracles—a subject that since Hume has been left to medical historians to bring to our attention.[28] According to modern intellectual folklore,

---

called wisdom is the first in dignity, it is still the last to be learned." Thomas Aquinas, *Commentary on Aristotle's Metaphysics*, trans. John P. Rowan (Notre Dame, Ind.: Dumb Ox Books, 1995), 16.

26. First philosophy's unique character as science that is simultaneously meta-science in relation to all other sciences accounts for the fact that, unlike the natural sciences, it does not proceed by empirical falsification and the formation of new hypotheses and explanatory models. One way to think about development in first philosophy as a discursive tradition can be found in MacIntyre's *Three Rival Versions of Moral Enquiry: Encyclopaedia, Genealogy, and Tradition* (Notre Dame, Ind.: University of Notre Dame Press, 1990).

27. For a somewhat rhetorically heated, but lucid metaphysical reposte to the New Atheism, see Feser, *The Last Superstition*; for a brilliant theological deconstruction, see David Bentley Hart, *Atheist Delusions: The Christian Revolution and Its Fashionable Enemies* (New Haven, Conn.: Yale University Press, 2010), and for the precise clarification at which a logician is best, see Alvin Plantinga, *Where the Conflict Really Lies: Science, Religion, and Naturalism* (New York: Oxford University Press, 2011).

28. Jacalyn Duffin, *Medical Miracles: Doctors, Saints, and Healing in the Modern World* (New York: Oxford University Press, 2007).

the case against miracles has been made irrefutably by David Hume.[29] But miracles themselves do not seem to be all too impressed with Hume's argument for their putative impossibility. What is more, some contemporary philosophers have begun systematically to question Hume's case against miracles.[30] The discipline of first philosophy would be equipped to advance these initial and incipient discussions from the threshold of metaphysics into a fully-fledged metaphysical inquiry. Such an inquiry could demonstrate the compatibility between the *methodological* naturalism of the natural sciences in regard to the comprehensive order of secondary causality and the possibility of miracles that is entailed in the nature of the first cause's genuinely transcendent causality.[31]

29. David Hume, *An Enquiry Concerning Human Understanding* [1748], ed. Stephen Buckle (Cambridge: Cambridge University Press, 2007), section 10, "Of Miracles," 96–116. For a brief but lucid meta-critique of Hume's argument against miracles, see Gregory, *The Unintended Reformation*, 60–64: "Hume rightly asserted, in a manner consistent with traditional Christian beliefs, that 'it is a miracle, that a dead man should come to life,' but followed this by claiming that 'that has *never* been observed in any age or country.' This latter assertion begs the question about whether natural regularities *are* exceptionless, just as it implicitly begs the question about whether the God of traditional Christianity is real. It implies nothing more than that Hume did not believe the testimony in question. Standing squarely in the univocal metaphysical tradition and yet apparently oblivious of the tendentiousness of his beliefs, Hume did not base his argument against miracles on a careful, case-by-case evaluation of the evidentiary testimony pertaining to discrete, alleged miracles.... Hume, by contrast, dogmatically rejected all alleged miracles based on his own beliefs. His scornful repudiation of Christianity was a *premise* of his argument against miracles" (61).

30. J. Houston, *Reported Miracles: A Critique of Hume* (Cambridge: Cambridge University Press, 1994); David Johnson, *Hume, Holism, and Miracles* (Ithaca, N.Y.: Cornell University Press, 1999); and John Earman, *Hume's Abject Failure: The Argument against Miracles* (New York: Oxford University Press, 2000). For a most comprehensive recent study in two volumes by a New Testament scholar and former atheist who steps into the fray and exposes Hume's argumentation as operating in a nothing but "deductive circle," see Craig S. Keener, *Miracles: The Credibility of the New Testament Accounts* (Grand Rapids, Mich.: Baker Academic, 2011). For Benedict Ashley's critique of Hume's dismissal of the principle of causality, see *The Way toward Wisdom*, chap. 3, and on the testimony of miracles, where he discusses Hume and Newman, see 316–17.

31. It should not go unmentioned that Newman himself argued for most of his career explicitly and implicitly against the epistemological positions held by Locke and Hume on the matter of miracles. He did it less so as a metaphysician and more as a logician within a broadly empirical framework, thus anticipating argumentative strategies developed much later in somewhat similar ways by Alvin Plantinga and others. For Newman's early, Anglican work on miracles, see his *Two Essays on Biblical and on Ecclesiastical Miracles* and for his later, mature theoretical account of the logic of assent, see his *magnum opus, An Essay in Aid of a Grammar of Assent*.

The Indispensability of (Natural) Theology for University Education

With his argument for the indispensability of theology for a proper university education, Newman moves beyond his striking observation that by excluding theology from its curriculum the modern university betrays how unphilosophical it is. According to Newman, historically revealed religious truth far surpasses the comparatively limited and fragile knowledge of natural theology that metaphysics yields insofar as a natural theology that rightly considers all of the divine perfections or attributes will also have to consider divine personhood and agency, that is, divine providence and the governance of the universe. While natural theology is able to inquire into the principles of the perfections of divine personhood and agency, the knowledge it yields remains limited and, furthermore, completely notional, that is, conceptual. These perfections of divine personhood and agency become a concrete and living reality only in the theology implicit in the word "God" held as a historically revealed religious truth by all whom Newman calls "theists":

God is an Individual, Self-dependent, All-perfect, Unchangeable Being; intelligent, living, personal, and present; almighty, all-seeing, all-remembering; between whom and His creatures there is an infinite gulf; who has no origin, who is all-sufficient for Himself; who created and upholds the universe; who will judge every one of us, sooner or later, according to that Law of right and wrong which He has written on our hearts. He is One who is sovereign over, operative amidst, independent of, the appointments which He has made; One in whose hands are all things, who has a purpose in every event, and a standard for every deed, and thus has relations of His own towards the subject-matter of each particular science which the book of knowledge unfolds; who has with an adorable, never-ceasing energy implicated Himself in all the history of creation, the constitution of nature, the course of the world, the origin of society, the fortunes of nations, the action of the human mind; and who thereby necessarily becomes the subject-matter of a science, far wider and more noble than any of those which are included in the circle of secular Education.[32]

In this remarkable passage, Newman does not offer a summary of natural theology but rather a living image of the doctrine of God the creator, gov-

32. *Idea*, 36.

ernor, and judge, all-merciful and all-just, that is at play when Christians, Jews, and Muslims speak of God. Contemporaneously put, Newman summarizes here the religious truth that Christians, Jews, and Muslims hold together over against alternative beliefs, new and old: Epicurean and Humean atheist materialism, Spinozist pantheistic naturalism, and Buddhism. This doctrine of God is not only corroborated by natural theology but *de facto* alive as religious truth in the minds of Jews, Christians, and Muslims. Considered maximally, the philosophically established divine perfections of personhood and agency give rise to the question of revelation and revealed truth and call for a theology of history. In turn, the concrete facts of divine revelation in history demand the deepest speculative contemplation of divine personhood and agency—the task of speculative dogmatic theology. Arguably, the only form of Christian theology capable of elevating, complementing, and perfecting natural theology is the kind that Pope John Paul II prescribed in his 1998 encyclical letter *Fides et Ratio*, that is, speculative dogmatic theology:

Dogmatic theology must be able to articulate the universal meaning of the mystery of the One and Triune God and of the economy of salvation, both as a narrative and, above all, in the form of argument. It must do so, in other words, through concepts formulated in a critical and universally communicable way. Without philosophy's contribution, it would in fact be impossible to discuss theological issues such as, for example, the use of language to speak about God, the personal relations within the Trinity, God's creative activity in the world, the relationship between God and man, or Christ's identity as true God and true man. This is no less true of the different themes of moral theology, which employ concepts such as the moral law, conscience, freedom, personal responsibility and guilt, which are in part defined by philosophical ethics.... Speculative dogmatic theology thus presupposes and implies a philosophy of the human being, the world and, more radically, of being, which has objective truth as its foundation.[33]

Post-metaphysical or anti-metaphysical programs of Christian theology and programs reduced to exegetical and historical positivism, doctrinal traditionalism, pastoral pragmatism, sociopolitical or ecopolitical transformationism, or postmodern apocalypticism will be inherently unfit for

33. John Paul II, *Fides et Ratio*, par. 66.

this task. Such programs will rather intensify the intellectual self-isolation of Christian theology or—in a desperate attempt to break out of it and to gain immediate relevance in a secular age—will end up embracing sundry intellectual trends that happen to be momentarily *en courant*.

Sacred theology (with its acme, speculative dogmatic theology) differs in kind from the theology that is the acme of first philosophy.[34] In the following, I will distinguish between "natural theology" and "revealed theology," the latter being a condensation of "theology arising from and relying upon divine revelation." Newman has no interest in establishing or defending this distinction in his university discourses. He rather assumes this distinction as a given and as a presupposition that he and his audience share. He regards the former, the apex of first philosophy, natural theology, to be indispensable for the unity of knowledge characteristic of the university, and he regards—as every Catholic does or should do—the latter, the theology of sacred doctrine, with the exception of the *praeambula fidei*, as transcending all possible knowledge this side of the beatific vision. Consequently, the theology of sacred doctrine is the gratuitous *donum superadditum* that presupposes the gift of divine faith and crowns every Catholic university. It is of this divine science that St. Bonaventure rightly says: "All modes of knowledge serve theology."[35] It is this divine science that corrects, complements, perfects, and utterly transcends natural theology. It is the surpassing keystone of the arch of sciences in a Catholic university *qua* Catholic, while the "science of sciences" is the regular keystone of the arch of sciences in the Catholic university *qua* university. While Newman does not at all reject the former, in *The Idea of a University*, he focuses primarily on the latter.[36]

34. The difference in the formal character (*ratio*) of how something is known accounts for the difference between sciences. The "formal object" or "ratio" of sacred theology is whatever is revealable by God. Sec Thomas Aquinas, *ST* I, q. 1, a. 1, ad 2; a. 3, co., and a. 7, co.; see also his *Expositio super librum Boethii De trinitate*, q. 5, a. 4.

35. "Omnes cogitationes famulantur theologiae." St. Bonaventure, *De reductione artium ad theologiam*, c. 26, in *Seraphici Doctoris Sancti Bonaventurae Tria Opuscula ad Theologiam Spectantia Edita a PP Collegii S. Bonaventurae* (Ad Claras Aquas: Typis Collegii S. Bonaventurae, 1938), 384.

36. According to Newman's understanding, the Catholic University of Ireland was intended for the education of the Catholic laity and not for the formation of Catholic clergy. Newman was concerned that the persons with the greatest immediate influence upon the nascent university project in the audience of his lectures were the bishops. And the bishops would most likely want

To return to Newman's unfolding argument: Even if considered only minimally, this religious truth, alive in the minds of Jews, Christians, and Muslims, must have a significant impact upon any education that claims to be potentially universal:

Admit a God, and you introduce among the subjects of your knowledge, a fact encompassing, closing in upon, absorbing, every other fact conceivable. How can we investigate any part of any order of Knowledge, and stop short of that which enters into every order? All true principles run over with it, all phenomena converge to it; it is truly the First and the Last.... Granting that divine truth differs in kind from human, so do human truths differ in kind one from another. If the knowledge of the Creator is in a different order from knowledge of the creature, so, in like manner, metaphysical science is in a different order from physical, physics from history, history from ethics. You will soon break up into fragments the whole circle of secular knowledge, if you begin the mutilation with divine.[37]

Newman goes further still and makes the bold claim that "Religious Truth is not only a portion, but a condition of general knowledge. To blot it out is nothing short ... of unravelling the web of University Teaching."[38] Bracketing religious truth is suicidal for university teaching. Normative secularity is ultimately nothing but the university's undertaker.

How does Newman make good on this claim? He does so by constructing in three steps a *reductio ad absurdum* argument by way of an *a fortiori* analogy. Here are the steps of his argument. First, he asserts the fundamental relationship between objective truth and scientific inquiry. Based on the supposition of epistemological realism, he lays out in a second step the position that prepares the analogy he unfolds in the third step: as it would result in an radically false view of things to deny human volition as a proper cause, so it would be even more erroneous to dismiss God from one's account of reality. It will be instructive to consider Newman's argument in detail.

---

to conceive of the university as an expanded and glorified seminary. Arguing for the centrality of sacred theology for an undergraduate education would have meant, Newman feared, to encourage and even endorse tacitly a vision of the university fatal to the task of a universal education.

37. *Idea*, 26.
38. *Idea*, 70.

First, Newman asserts a version of epistemological realism that still informs much of contemporary natural science:

Truth is the object of Knowledge of whatever kind; and when we inquire what is meant by Truth, I suppose it is right to answer that Truth means facts and their relations.... All that exists, as contemplated by the human mind, forms one large system or complex fact.... Viewed altogether, [the sciences] approximate to a representation or subjective reflection of the objective truth, as nearly as possible to the human mind.[39]...

All knowledge forms one whole, because its subject-matter is one; for the universe in its length and breadth is so intimately knit together, that we cannot separate off portion from portion, and operation from operation, except by a mental abstraction; and then again, as to its Creator, though He of course in His own Being is infinitely separate from it, and Theology has its departments towards which human knowledge has no relations, yet He has so implicated Himself with it, and taken it into His very bosom, by His presence in it, His providence over it, His impressions upon it, and His influences through it, that we cannot truly or fully contemplate it without in some main aspects contemplating Him.[40]

The sole subject of natural theology, God, the transcendent first cause and final end, allows the understanding of the rest of reality as a contingent whole, as a universe, and consequently all knowledge that can be gained as essentially interrelated, and therefore as an integral component of universal knowledge.

In a second step, Newman sketches a scenario that anticipates in an uncanny way the current initiatives in contemporary research universities: to recast the curriculum in light of a normative evolutionary naturalism. Today, reason, volition, freedom, and spirit (*Geist*) must be studied as at best aspects of the phenomenon of "consciousness" that emerges from, or is a mere epiphenomenon of, physical and biochemical processes in light of which they must ultimately be accountable, and possibly predictable. In his own time, Newman observed a similar privileging of physical and mechanical causes: "Physical and mechanical causes are exclusively to be treated of; volition is a forbidden subject. A prospectus is put out, with a list of

39. *Idea*, 45 and 47.
40. *Idea*, 50–51.

sciences, we will say, Astronomy, Optics, Hydrostatics, Galvanism, Pneumatics, Statics, Dynamics, Pure Mathematics, Geology, Botany, Physiology, Anatomy, and so forth; but not a word about the mind and its powers, except what is said in explanation of the omission."[41] History, political science, economics, literature and language, art history, musical theory, and last but not least, philosophy (with the exception of logical positivism, formal logic, and the philosophy of mathematics and of the natural sciences) can happily be eliminated from the university curriculum.

In short, Newman observed, the human being was being eliminated as a subject worthy of study: "Henceforth man is to be as if he were not, in the general course of Education; the moral and mental sciences are to have no professional chairs, and the treatment of them is to be simply left as a matter of private judgment, which each individual may carry out as he will."[42] Replace the physical-mechanistic framework with a biological-evolutionary one in Newman's illustration and matters sound only all too familiar. At a well-known research university where I taught for almost twenty years, a materialist philosopher of science routinely argued that the humanities were an utter waste of time and that a future undergraduate training should focus exclusively on the natural sciences and on the methodological reflections of a materialist philosophy of science. Newman anticipates such a proposal in his own example:

Our professor ... after speaking with the highest admiration of the human intellect, limits its independent action to the region of speculation, and denies that it can be a motive principle, or can exercise a special interference, in the material world. He ascribes every work, every external act of man, to the innate force or soul of the physical universe.... Human exploits, human devices, human deeds, human productions, all that comes under the scholastic terms of "genius" and "art," and the metaphysical ideas of "duty," "right," and "heroism," it is his office to contemplate all these merely in their place in the eternal system of physical cause and effect. At length he undertakes to show how the whole fabric of material civilization has arisen from the constructive powers of physical elements and physical laws.[43]

41. *Idea*, 55.
42. *Idea*, 54.
43. *Idea*, 56–57.

Newman's prescience is impressive. Reductionism, whether that of a mechanistic physicalism or that of an evolutionary materialism, simply abolishes what it is supposed to explain.

In the third part of his *reductio ad absurdum* argument, Newman completes his analogy with an *a fortiori* conclusion. While not falsifying this professor's "definitions, principles, and laws," ignoring the reality of human reason and volition as proper motive causes would result in "a radically false view of the things which he discussed," namely, "his considering his own study to be the key of everything that takes place on the face of the earth." If this is true, *a fortiori*, the ignoring and consequent dismissal from the university of the study of a reality infinitely superior to human reason and volition as motive causes would have much graver distorting consequences. And finally Newman drives home the blade:

> If the creature is ever setting in motion an endless series of physical causes and effects, much more is the Creator; and as our excluding volition from our range of ideas is a denial of the soul, so our ignoring Divine Agency is a virtual denial of God. Moreover, supposing man can will and act of himself in spite of physics, to shut up this great truth, though one, is to put our whole encyclopaedia of knowledge out of joint; and supposing God can will and act of Himself in this world which He has made, and we deny or slur it over, then we are throwing the circle of universal science into a like, or a far worse confusion. Worse incomparably, for the idea of God, if there be a God, is infinitely higher than the idea of man, if there be man. If to blot out man's agency is to deface the book of knowledge, on the supposition of that agency existing, what must it be, supposing it exists, to blot out the agency of God?[44]

On the supposition that God exists, the exclusion of this all-important fact from the circle of universal science can only result in omission and distortion of truth. The supposition that God does not exist is a philosophical tenet that cannot be proven conclusively and hence can neither constitute a premise nor a conclusion of any of the academic disciplines that belong to the secular university's circle of sciences. Ideological atheism is as unphilosophical as it is unscientific.

How would Newman's *reductio ad absurdum* argument fare in the

44. *Idea*, 59.

present secular research university? It would hardly find a serious hearing and hence would fail in its rhetorical appeal. The argument nevertheless still carries objective force. For one can make a reasonably strong case that the faculties of the contemporary secular research universities are roughly but discernibly divided along the lines of the Kantian antinomy between determinism and freedom. Predictably, the defenders of determinism are by and large at home in the hard sciences, with the defenders of freedom in the humanities. The defenders of determinism are typically, though with noteworthy exceptions, embracing a posthumanist outlook, especially in the biosciences. They regard the human being as a highly developed animal bent on maximizing the success of its species—of which the natural sciences and their technical application are currently the most decisive instrument. The most articulate defenders of a radical notion of human freedom are increasingly, though with noteworthy exceptions, embracing a transhumanist outlook. They epitomize freedom in a new existentialist sense: the freedom of design, that is, the freedom of enhancing, or simply changing properties of one's own nature (intelligence, gender, emotions, body features, etc.) with the assistance of biotechnology.[45] Thus, human beings become the product of their own designer choices—or, worse, the result of designer choices made by others (parents, governments, lawmakers, silent majorities) who have gained the political power and legal legitimization to do so. And so the extremes meet. For transhumanism is nothing but the most consistent instantia-

45. One of the first to point out the transhumanist dynamic as an incipient cultural reality in Western late-modern societies was Peter Sloterdijk, *Regeln für den Menschenpark: Ein Antwortschreiben zu Heideggers Brief über den Humanismus* (Frankfurt: Suhrkamp, 1999). Since then, the transhumanist perspective has not only become explicit but also prescriptive. See, first and foremost, Simon Young, *Designer Evolution: A Transhumanist Manifesto* (New York: Prometheus, 2006), but also Gregory Stock, *Redesigning Humans: Our Inevitable Genetic Future* (Boston: Houghton Mifflin Harcourt, 2002); Ray Kurzweil, *The Singularity Is Near: When Humans Transcend Biology* (New York: Penguin, 2005); Ramez Naam, *More Than Human: Embracing the Promise of Biological Enhancement* (New York: Broadway, 2005); Joel Garreau, *Radical Evolution: The Promise and Peril of Enhancing Our Minds, Our Bodies—and What It Means to Be Human* (New York: Broadway Books, 2005); and Nikolas Rose, *The Politics of Life Itself: Biomedicine, Power, and Subjectivity in the Twenty-First Century* (Princeton, N.J.: Princeton University Press, 2007). For a striking account of the monstrous plans concocted in Silicon Valley and elsewhere to "decreate" the human person, see Bill McKibben, *Falter: Has the Human Game Begun to Play Itself Out?* (New York: Henry Holt and Co., 2019), 131–80.

tion of posthumanism, especially when the design will eventually be socially or politically enforced and collectively applied.[46] Welcomed at first as a liberation from the contingency, corruptibility, and fallibility of human nature, as an exercise of radical, Promethean freedom, and thus as the final flowering of the Enlightenment project, eugenic bioengineering will eventually result in a radical subjugation of human nature to *technē*, to willful production.

The proponents of a liberal eugenics are naïve enough to assume that the ensuing combination of biotechnological and sociopolitical dynamics can be "managed" by the benign intentions of enlightened individuals and an equally benign and enlightened political process in equally benign and enlightened democratic regimes. Despite their frequent rhetorical gestures to the contrary, they display a deplorable historical amnesia (among other things about the history of eugenics in the United States and Europe) and a conceited optimism grounded in the utterly unwarranted Enlightenment dogma that unencumbered technological application of scientific knowledge is identical with human progress. Inebriated by the vistas of new frontiers to be conquered and obsessed with the fear of being left behind by the dynamic of biotechnological research, the Baconian counterfeit rushes along and relegates to the margins of its liberal arts appendix what it most desperately needs—a critical examination of its own unexamined operative beliefs and a vision of the whole.[47]

But neither hyperspecialized research experts, nor university administrators, nor the board of trustees have the time or the intellectual preparation to engage in critical thought, let alone in the kind of philosophical inquiry that would lead to a vision of the whole. Where is the head that steers the body of the modern research university? Pointing to the numerous centers of ethics and especially bioethics all too quickly instituted by

46. Duke University, for example, calls no less than three genome centers its own, in addition to one institute, and the driving force behind them, including the financing, is not of a Platonic, but of a Baconian nature: the Duke Center for Humane Genome Variation, Duke Center for Genome Technology, Duke Center for Public Genomics, and Duke Institute for Genome Sciences and Policy.

47. The proponents of a liberal eugenics still have the lesson of the dialectic of the Enlightenment ahead of them spelled out in precise terms in a classic that deserves a careful rereading: Max Horkheimer and Theodor W. Adorno, *Dialectic of Enlightenment* (Palo Alto, Calif.: Stanford University Press, 2007).

the leading research universities will hardly be convincing. For the largely utilitarian and consistently post-metaphysical bent of most contemporary philosophical ethics offers these centers few if any conceptual tools to resist the powerful pressures to deliver strategies of legitimization for procedures that are individually and collectively willed on grounds that for much of contemporary philosophical ethics are arbitrary, that is, subject to preference. Where would such centers of bioethics find the intellectual resources that would offer a yardstick for critical thought and a vision of the whole? How would such centers of bioethics escape the logic of being simply part of managerial strategies meant to create a semblance of legitimacy and the required minimum of legality and to facilitate operative consensus?[48]

If there is only a grain of truth in this dire picture,[49] a picture which Aldous Huxley painted with great prescience in *A Brave New World* and C. S. Lewis satirized inimitably in *That Hideous Strength*, Newman's analogy is still pertinent. For in the case of the posthumanist program as well as in the case of the transhumanist program, university education loses its character as liberal education and turns into something completely different, into a training in the servile arts, that is, the kinds of expertise required for technical or managerial collective species optimization or for the optimization of individually desired design features.

In his very late notebooks, Friedrich Nietzsche seems to have anticipated both the posthumanist and the transhumanist implications of a purely secular utilitarian knowledge production:

48. For an approach to bioethics that escapes this problematic altogether and opens up a vista that transcends the theoretical as well as the political conundrum of contemporary secular bioethics, see Nicanor Pier Giorgio Austriaco, OP, *Biomedicine and Beatitude: An Introduction to Catholic Bioethics* (Washington, D.C.: The Catholic University of America Press, 2011).

49. Hans Jonas warned against this picture intensely in *The Imperative of Responsibility: In Search of an Ethics for the Technological Age* (Chicago: University of Chicago Press, 1984) as did, more recently, Jürgen Habermas in his *The Future of Human Nature* (Cambridge: Polity Press, 2003) and Leon R. Kass in his *Life, Liberty, and the Defense of Dignity: The Challenge for Bioethics* (San Francisco, Calif.: Encounter Books, 2002), not to forget, of course, Pope St. John Paul II in his 1995 encyclical letter *Evangelium Vitae*. For an instructive interpretation of Jonas's thought and for a helpful application of it to the pressing contemporary questions of bioengineering, see Stephan Kampowski, *A Greater Freedom: Biotechnology, Love, and Human Destiny* (Eugene, Ore.: Pickwick Publications, 2012).

There exists neither "spirit," nor reason, nor thinking, nor consciousness, nor soul, nor will, nor truth: all are fictions that are of no use. There is no question of "subject and the object," but of a particular species of animal that can prosper only through a certain relative rightness; above all, regularity of its perceptions (so that it can accumulate experience)—

Knowledge works as a tool of power. Hence it is plain that it increases with every increase of power—

The meaning of "knowledge": here, as in the case of "good" or "beautiful," the concept is to be regarded in a strict and narrow anthropocentric and biological sense. In order for a particular species to maintain itself and increase its power, its conception of reality must comprehend enough of the calculable and constant for it to base a scheme of behavior on it. The utility of preservation—not some abstract-theoretical need not to be deceived—stands as the motive behind the development of the organs of knowledge—they develop in such a way that their observations suffice for our preservation. In other words: the measure of the desire for knowledge depends upon the measure to which the will to power grows in a species: a species grasps a certain amount of reality in order to become master of it, in order to press it into service.[50]

If Nietzsche is right, the university as a humanist enterprise of education in universal knowledge is quite passé. What Nietzsche predicts is the species-relevant polytechnicum: "a species grasps a certain amount of reality in order to become master of it, in order to press it into service." This is the posthumanist program. And when we include human nature itself into the reality to be mastered, we have the transhumanist program. Consequently, Newman's analogy has lost nothing of its relevance. Rather, with uncanny prescience and precision, Newman perceived the radical implications hidden in the Baconian polytechnicum that Nietzsche eventually would lay bare. While we are busy ushering Newman, the all-too-uncomfortable visionary, out the front door of our modern research universities, assuring him in most cordial terms of the indubitable humanistic value of his *The Idea of a University*, which presently is—most regrettably—utterly unfeasible, Francis Bacon, a long-time university tenant, quietly opens the back door and beckons Friedrich Nietzsche to enter in.

50. Friedrich Nietzsche, *The Will to Power*, trans. Walter Kaufmann and R. J. Hollingdale (New York: Vintage Books, 1968), §480.

Newman's analogy indicates fundamental alternatives. Either the university is nothing but a species-relevant polytechnicum, whether it is a tool for mastering nature by pressing it more and more into the service of the human species, or the launch pad for mastering human nature itself with the technical and genetic optimization of the human being into some cyborg superhumanity or transhumanity. Or university education presupposes the possibility of universal knowledge and aspires to universal education as an end in itself that in its very exercise realizes a more perfect form of existence characteristic of that kind of living being about which Aristotle rightly observed: "All men by nature desire to know."[51] In this latter case, metaphysical and theological knowledge unavoidably bear upon other knowledge.

Might transhumanists not retort that genetic optimization brings about a more perfect form of existence and that the above alternative is therefore spurious? At first glance, it might seem plausible that transhumanism has a case. However, this case must rest either on an objective hierarchy of goods and an underlying order of proximate ends subordinated to a final end or it has to rest on subjective judgments antecedent to and consequent upon genetic optimization of those who wish to be themselves or to have their progeny subjected to such genetic optimization. The first alternative does not work, because for it to carry through and establish such an objective hierarchy of goods and of proximate ends ordered to a final end, it would require the kind of metaphysical inquiry and argumentation that transhumanism rejects. The second alternative does not work either, because antecedent subjective judgments about genetic optimization will be at variance with differing antecedent subjective judgments regarding kinds, scope, and extent of optimization, and might, in addition, be based on transient desires and specious hopes. (In short, the private judgments of individual consumers of genetic optimization will always diverge from each other regarding the kind, scope, and extent of optimization and hence about its nature.) The consequent judgments (post-optimization) might contradict the antecedent judgments in that

51. This famous opening line of Aristotle's *Metaphysics* is taken from *The Complete Works of Aristotle: The Revised Oxford Translation*, ed. Jonathan Barnes (Princeton, N.J.: Princeton University Press, 1984), 2:1552.

the recipients of optimization do not experience the optimization they hoped for, or more importantly, do not experience the happiness they hoped was integral to the genetic optimization, let alone the joy that accompanies genuine happiness. Consequently, the concept of "optimization" becomes vacuous. In short, the transhumanist claim that genetic optimization brings about a more perfect form of existence is spurious.

In conclusion, Newman's vision links the question of the nature of the university and of university education to the question of the nature and end of the human being, to the question of the nature of human flourishing, and to the ways of realizing a more perfect form of human existence. There is only one kind of university that can meaningfully inquire into these questions of a fundamentally philosophical and theological nature and regard them as integral to university education itself. This is Newman's university. The Baconian counterfeit in its most advanced state, the "polytechnic utiliversity," will brush questions of this kind aside as unscientific and as a waste of time. For an inquiry guided by such philosophical questions does not contribute to any tangible, that is, measurable knowledge-making. Such an answer will, of course, convict the modern research university only of its tacit Baconian ideological commitments. Newman would regard such a university as decapitated, as unable to reflect philosophically upon the ideology that drives its judgments and its operations, in short, as nothing but the university's counterfeit.

How to Take Newman's Prophetic Provocation Seriously

Newman's vision of a university education and of the unity of knowledge in *The Idea of a University* might best be received as an ideal, the criterion against which we might assess critically, that is, philosophically, the operative beliefs of modern research universities. If Newman is right, an all-too-facile dismissal of the ideal he proposes in *The Idea of a University* might come with a high price—having to live out the dystopian future of the comprehensive instrumentalization and commodification of the university and of university education.

If Newman is indeed right, the university disciplines resemble an arch: its keystone stabilizes the whole edifice; remove it and the arch collapses. All stones are still there in their distinct integrity, but now lie in an indistinct heap. On the undergraduate level, the current "multiversity" absent the center stone resembles such a heap, an ever-growing heap indeed. While each discipline has its integrity, the relationship between all of them is utterly unclear—excepting, of course, sub-coherences between mathematics and the natural sciences and among the natural sciences. In this situation of a curricular and disciplinary heterogeneity and even confusion, several disciplines are advancing themselves as keystones or as a multidisciplinary keystone configuration for the construction of a new arch. The strongest contender for such a multidisciplinary keystone configuration is presently an evolutionary naturalism. This emerging keystone configuration stretches from astrophysics via biochemistry to neuroscience, extends itself into the humanities, and even affords its own naturalist philosophy of science. With this keystone configuration, the size of the arch changes considerably. Indeed, many of the stones of the former arch can no longer be integrated, and the ones that are to be integrated have to change their form in order to accommodate the reduced scope imposed by evolutionary naturalism. Such a naturalist reconstitution of the remaining university disciplines for the sake of the new unity of knowledge would undoubtedly affect most deeply the remainder of the humanities, but would leave deep traces on the other remaining disciplines as well. In short, the ideological imposition of a naturalist immanence would force the sciences to accommodate themselves in the proverbial Procrustean bed. In this *novus ordo scientiarum*, the knowledge-making of the tool-using animal *homo sapiens sapiens* will turn out to be nothing but a most advanced form of tool-making and tool-using. And consequently, in light of the newly imposed horizon of naturalism the most advanced university training will be nothing but a training in the servile arts, in a highly advanced "tool-knowledge" of a technical or managerial sort in order to fix those kinds of things that can be fixed with the help of tools.[52]

52. With remarkable prescience, Newman concludes his original 1852 Discourse V, "General Knowledge Viewed as One Philosophy" thus: "A University, so called, which refuses to profess the Catholic Creed, is, from the nature of the case, hostile both to the Church and to Philosophy." The

And that would not be the end of the trouble. Rather, the new naturalist structure of the arch of university disciplines would be haunted by the specter of Nietzsche. For philosophical naturalism remains inherently vulnerable to the destructive acids of genealogical skepticism. Despite the realist intuitions at work in the natural sciences, the superimposed philosophical naturalism invites its own genealogical deconstruction: Among tool-making and tool-using animals of the species *homo sapiens sapiens*, "truth" is nothing but a cover for domination. Or, more radically and naturalistically conceived, the will to power is the only "truth" there is. Consequently, as Hobbes already understood, "homo homini lupus."[53] There is nothing more threatening than another's "truth" imposed upon us in order to subdue or crush our will of self-assertion. Such a genealogical deconstruction of the reigning philosophical naturalism would, of course, issue in the very termination of the university in any, even the remotest and most equivocal sense. Because they are historically oblivious, the proponents of philosophical naturalism are all too forgetful of a fact: the specter of Nietzsche has arisen with and in response to the ascendancy of modern philosophical naturalism and will continue to erode it from the inside out until it collapses or until it is abandoned as just another false image that held us captive for all too long.[54]

---

ideological imposition of a naturalist immanence characteristic of the late-modern Baconian polytechnicum exiles together with the horizon of transcendence the Catholic faith as well as philosophy in Newman's sense of "that large Philosophy, which embraces and locates truth of every kind, and every method of attaining it" (*Idea*, 434 and 428).

53. "The human being is a wolf to [his or her fellow] human being." Hobbes's famous saying is to be found in the *Epistola dedicatoria* of his treatise *De cive: On the Citizen*, ed. Richard Tuck and Michael Silverthorne (Cambridge: Cambridge University Press, 1998), 3.

54. For a winsomely written contemporary account of a scientifically based philosophical naturalism with a comprehensive scope and a universal claim of validity, see the latest work by the renowned Harvard entomologist E. O. Wilson, *The Meaning of Human Existence* (New York: W. W. Norton and Co., 2014). In this manifesto, Wilson advocates the search for universal knowledge, a search that would reunite all fields of inquiry into the fundamental nature of reality. The point of this unified inquiry is to find answers to questions about what kind of being the human being actually is. Because Wilson supposes that the answers to these questions and with it any form of meaning is found in human evolution, he takes evolutionary biology to be the keystone science for the new order of sciences. For Wilson it is a foregone conclusion that this project of research guided by evolutionary biology will yield true human self-understanding and liberation from the illusions of religion and "religion-like" political ideologies that hold the human imagination captive. Wilson regards human beings to be completely free (although free will is probably only a useful illusion) and well-equipped to build a genuinely good global society, even a paradise on earth. While widely

If nothing else, Newman's vision serves at least as a provocative reminder that the only thing that can save the university from the reductive and, in the end, detrimental distortions of *philosophical* naturalism—and from its Nietzschean genealogical deconstruction—is the discipline that allows for the widest possible scope of truth. Only with theology as the keystone of the arch of university disciplines will the arch achieve the widest possible scope, will the university remain open to a maximum of interrelated and complementary sciences, will a university education remain in all areas of knowledge essentially philosophical, and will universal knowledge as an end in and of itself be intelligible and desirable.

This most extensive scope of the arch is enabled by understanding the universe as creation. The difference between first being and participated being and the use of analogy allow for a surpassingly comprehensive vision of the whole of created reality without suppressing the unique kinds of knowledge to which its different parts give rise. Pope Benedict XVI, in his final address to the members of the Pontifical Academy of Sciences, put this crucial matter in broadly Thomistic terms:

It is precisely this inbuilt "logical" and "analogical" organization of nature that encourages scientific research and draws the human mind to discover the horizontal co-participation between beings and the transcendental participation by the First Being. The universe is not chaos or the result of chaos, rather, it appears ever more clearly as an ordered complexity which allows us to rise, through comparative analysis and analogy, from specialization towards a more universalizing viewpoint and vice versa. While the very first moments of the cosmos and life still elude scientific observation, science nonetheless finds itself pondering a vast set of processes which reveals an order of evident constants and correspondences and serves as essential components of permanent creation.[55]

---

popular in circles beholden by the quasi-religious form of scientistic humanism and utopianism Wilson propagates, his program has one decisive weakness—the absence of humanity in its *de facto* existential concreteness, transcendent orientation, and religious constitution. In Wilson's comprehensive evolutionary narrative, the human being becomes an anthropomorphism and his annunciation of complete freedom—echoing all too obviously Nietzsche's "death of God"—only invites its full Nietzschean realization and with it the complete destruction of Wilson's utopian *telos* of an earthly paradise.

55. Pope Benedict XVI, "Address of His Holiness Pope Benedict XVI to Members of the Pontifical Academy of Sciences on the Occasion of the Plenary Assembly," November 8, 2012; available at www.vatican.va.

The scope of the arch envisioned by Pope Benedict XVI allows the full, nonreductive integration of the natural sciences with all of the humanities in a universal horizon of maximal extension, complexity, and possible intelligibility. It is precisely the scope of such an arch of sciences that Newman envisioned in *The Idea of a University*.

Pace Nietzsche, human beings desire to know, not because they desire to master, but because knowledge is the proper perfection of the intellect which is a more perfect form of existence. It is an obvious fact that skepticism is unable to quench genuine philosophical inquiry that is teleologically ordered to the ultimate truth—the Sophists are superseded by Plato and Aristotle; Montaigne is superseded by Descartes; Hume is superseded by Kant, Fichte, Hegel, and Schelling; Nietzsche and Dilthey are superseded by Bergson and Husserl. But skepticism always seems to return, someone might rightly observe. Husserl offers a suggestive philosophical reason for the ongoing return of skepticism. According to Husserl, the philosophical inability definitively to overcome skepticism has its roots in a hitherto unacknowledged truth that skepticism again and again attests to—the dependence of all knowledge on subjective consciousness. Husserl's theory of transcendental, phenomenological, and apodictic reduction is his attempt to acknowledge this moment of truth in skepticism and thereby once and for all to overcome skepticism and thus definitively to establish a true and lasting first philosophy.[56] Alas, despite Husserl's most rigorous effort at re-establishing first philosophy in the post-skeptical form of a transcendental phenomenology, skepticism returned anyway in the form of Richard Rorty's pragmatism and Jacques Derrida's *différance*. *Pace* Husserl, it seems to be the case that what might be conceived as the moment of truth in skepticism—the dependence of knowledge on subjective consciousness—is consequent upon the preceding failure to recognize the principle of noncontradiction as a metaphysical first principle (that is, the principle of noncontradiction is true first and foremost of things themselves, without qualification, in short, of being in general, and therefore also true of things as they appear to us and

---

56. See Edmund Husserl, *Erste Philosophie*, vol. 1: *Kritische Ideengeschichte*, Husserliana 7, ed. R. Boehm (The Hague: M. Nijhoff, 1956); vol. 2: *Theorie der phänomenologischen Reduktion*, Husserliana 8, ed. R. Boehm (The Hague: M. Nijhoff, 1959).

as we conceive them). Hence, arguably, since Aristotle's successful defense of the principle of noncontradiction as a metaphysical principle in *Metaphysics* IV against the Sophists, the Aristotelian-Thomist instantiation of the perennial philosophy can be understood as the ongoing supersession of all forms of skepticism *a radice* up to and including the twentieth century. In short, the rock of realism on which all forms of skepticism shatter is the principle of noncontradiction as a metaphysical first principle. Instead of overcoming skepticism, all forms of transcendental idealism ever so subtly enshrine it by making the *res cogitans*, the transcendental ego, or the reflexive self the starting point of epistemic certitude. Skepticism does not return because of some hitherto unacknowledged moment of truth it points to, but because of the failure to recognize the principle of noncontradiction as a metaphysical first principle. Arguably, this recognition is so exceedingly difficult, not because the principle of noncontradiction as a *metaphysical* first principle might be so remote, but on the contrary, precisely because this principle obtains with such surpassing obviousness and because it is so utterly fundamental to the constitution of things and hence also to our thinking and speaking about them.

The science of being *qua* being, its apex in natural theology, and, *a fortiori*, revealed theology, affirm the intimation that the human intellect operates in a horizon of transcendent truth, indeed, of subsistent truth, first truth, and that the pursuit of knowledge is a created participation in the divine perfection of knowledge.[57] The science of being *qua* being—completed by natural theology and surpassingly perfected by sacred theology—as the keystone of the arch of sciences allows the university to understand, appreciate, and defend a university education as intrinsically meaningful, as a genuinely liberal education.

Newman's vision reminds us moderns that the sustained speculative contemplation at the very heart of a university education to which this "science of sciences" gives rise, is perhaps the only thing that can save the university from its total instrumentalization and commodification. This "science of sciences"—completed by natural theology and surpassingly perfected by sacred theology—constantly reminds all the other disciplines

---

57. See Thomas Aquinas, *De Veritate*, q. 1, aa. 7–8, and *ST* I, q. 16.

that the greatest freedom comes with the contemplation and communication of the transcendent truth of God. This "first science" might in the end also turn out to be about the only reliable guarantor of genuine academic freedom. For academic freedom has its origin in the "uselessness," the intrinsic value of an education in the liberal arts. Hence, academic freedom, in its core, is nothing but the freedom to inquire into, to contemplate, and to communicate the truth for its own sake—an activity that carries its *telos* in its very practice.[58]

In the end, we have to choose one of two prophets, one proposing an all too unlikely utopia, the other announcing an all too likely dystopia. We may either struggle with Newman upstream toward the "idea" of a university. Or we may drift with Nietzsche downstream, allowing ourselves to be carried away by the dominant jet stream, and eventually resign ourselves to the "polytechnic utiliversity," that is, to the tacit betrayal of the idea of the university. One thing is clear beyond doubt, however: wherever the science of being *qua* being, completed by natural theology and surpassingly perfected by sacred theology, is permitted to make its distinct contribution to universal education, it will without fail foster a keen awareness of the intrinsic value of the arduous journey upstream so that one may contemplate the source of all things. For, after all, "when God is forgotten the creature itself grows unintelligible."[59]

It is precisely the uselessness of contemplating the whole and its first cause that constitutes the very center of the education envisioned by Newman in *The Idea of a University*. And it is this useless contemplation of the whole and the first cause that is most vehemently denounced and most desperately needed in our late-modern, techno-capitalist societies. A lone but crucial voice among the moderns, Newman articulates the contemporary relevance of the classical wisdom, that contemplation is necessary for human flourishing. About a century later, another lone but crucial voice among the moderns, the Catholic philosopher Josef Pieper, reca-

58. See Josef Pieper, *Leisure, The Basis of Culture*, trans. Gerald Malsbary (South Bend, Ind.: St. Augustine's Press, 1998), for what is still the best account available of this crucial insight. The pertinent discourse from Newman's *The Idea of a University* to read and contemplate parallel to Pieper's book is "Knowledge Its Own End" (*Idea*, 99–123).

59. *Gaudium et Spes*, no. 36.

pitulates Newman's central insight that "'it is requisite for the good of the human community that there should be persons who devote themselves to the life of contemplation.' For it is contemplation which preserves in the midst of human society the truth which is at one and the same time useless and the yardstick of every possible use; so it is also contemplation which keeps the true end in sight, gives meaning to every practical act of life."[60]

Becoming a Master of the Twofold *Logos*, Thought and Word

There might be numerous academicians at home in the humanities departments of contemporary liberal arts colleges and even research universities who feel keenly the force of Newman's prophetic provocation but who find the prescribed medicine at the same time too bitter-tasting and the journey upstream too arduous for their students and possibly also for themselves. They might wonder whether there might not be a compromise, a solution that would allow one to stay in place midstream, resisting the university's crude counterfeit but despairing of the university's lofty idea. The proposed method for such a limited defense of a "status quo humanism" would most likely consist in an intensified education of the imagination by way of an increased "literacy," of a literary, cultural, historical, and artistic kind, a modern humanist program of the self-discovery of the sovereign subject, a soft *paideia* within the "immanent frame" closed to metaphysical and religious truths. Such an imagination-focused attempt at the recovery of humanities will, however, fail to produce sufficient energy to stem the pull downstream. First and foremost, there exist insurmountable disagreements between the proponents of classical, Enlightenment, and genealogical approaches over the exact scope and content of the canon of texts that is supposed to serve this purpose. But more importantly, even if such disagreements could be over-

60. Josef Pieper, *Happiness & Contemplation*, trans. Richard and Clara Winston (South Bend, Ind.: St. Augustine's Press, 1998). The internal citation is from Thomas Aquinas, *In Sent.* IV, d. 26, q. 1, a. 2: "Ad perfectionem humanae multitudinis sit necessarium aliquos contemplativae vitae inservire."

come, such a halfway solution will ultimately have to fail simply because of its exclusive or at least privileged focus on educating the imagination at the expense of the schooling in metaphysical inquiry and contemplation.

This is not to suggest that there is not a place for the imagination in the intellectual life. But it must be in its proper place. In 1946, Dom Eugene Boylan, an Irish contemplative of note—a person without any philosophical or academic agenda of his own—made a keen observation about an emerging problem in the intellectual life that has only escalated since then:

The source of all the evils and errors in the intellectual life today—the disease that makes much of its utterances, the mere wanderings of a feverish imagination—is the loss of metaphysics and of the ability for abstract thought.... The human intellect draws its food for thought from the working of the senses, and when it represents to itself the *idea* of any object, that internal sense which is called the imagination, tries to form some corresponding picture or phantasm of the same object in terms of sensation or sense experience.... Now, one of the first things one has to learn in metaphysical thought, is to think with *ideas* and not with *phantasms*.... Obviously failure to abstract completely from the particular accidents of the phantasm may lead to error, and when one argues from phantasms instead of ideas—doing one's thinking with the imagination instead of with the intellect—confusion and obscurity are inevitable. Metaphysics is the science of being—that is, of any thing that exists or can exist—as being, and is, therefore, at the root of all other sciences, which indeed presuppose it. It has been abandoned by the modern mind, which seems to be unable to think otherwise than with its imagination. What cannot be imagined is—according to it—impossible; what can be imagined is, therefore, capable of being and existence. From this disease of the mind, we get sentiment for principle in morals, the particular for the general in argument, metaphor in place of reality, opinion for certainty, prejudice for judgment, quantity for quality, matter for the ultimate reality, and all the whole host of false coins that are current in the intellectual commerce of today. Curiously enough, it is often the trained mind that shows the greatest tendency to errors of this sort. The mathematician tends to think in terms of symbols and graphs, or at least in terms of quantity; the scientist, when he is not a mathematician, tends to be a mechanic.[61]

61. Dom Eugene Boylan, OCSO, *This Tremendous Lover* (Allen, Tex.: Christian Classics, 1987 [1947]), 117–18. Frank J. Sheed puts the same insight quite straightforwardly thus in his *Theology and Sanity* (New York: Sheed and Ward, 1946): "Thinking is very hard and imagining is very

.

The Irish contemplative is right in denouncing the detrimental effects brought about by the loss of metaphysical inquiry and the confinement of thought to the limits of the imagination alone. At the same time, his somewhat unnuanced bemoaning of the "mere wanderings of a feverish imagination," though not inaccurate, makes his critique slightly lopsided. According to Boylan, it would seem that thought comes completely into its own only as abstract thought, that is, at the very moment when the intellect severs itself once and for all from the imagination. The perennial philosophy, however, has always acknowledged that for human beings due to our hylomorphic constitution, there obtains an intimate connection between the imagination (*phantasia*), the faculty of representation, and the intellect (*noûs*), the faculty of simple and complex thought.[62] As faculty of representation, the imagination remains the permanent foundation for the intellect's operation. Hence, while always depending on the imagination for representational content, the intellect's proper operation requires it to be essentially different from the imagination. Scientific knowledge, universal intelligibility, depends upon the ability of human thought to abstract degrees of intelligibility (*noemata*) from the deliveries of the senses and from the particular representations of the imagination (*phantasmata*).[63]

---

easy and we are very lazy. We have fallen into the habit of using imagination as a crutch, and our intellects have almost lost the habit of walking. They must learn to walk, and this must mean great pain for muscles so long unused. It is worth all the pain: not only for the intellect but for the imagination too. Once the intellect is doing its own work properly, it can use the imagination most fruitfully; and the imagination will find new joy in the service of a vital intellect" (17–18). For a more exacting formal consideration of the same issue as it pertains to the division of sciences, see Thomas Aquinas, *Expositio super librum Boethii De trinitate*, q. 5, a. 3, and q. 6, a. 2, in *The Divisions and Methods of the Sciences*, trans. Armand Maurer, 4th rev. ed. (Toronto: Pontifical Institute of Mediaeval Studies, 1986), 32–46 and 74–80.

62. See Aristotle, *De anima* III.7 and 8; Thomas Aquinas, *In Aristotelis Librum de Anima Commentarium*, liber III, lectio XII and XIII; and George P. Klubertanz, SJ, *The Philosophy of Human Nature* (New York: Appleton-Century-Crofts, Inc., 1953), 191–95. For a helpful elucidation of Aristotle's subtle and dense discussion in the *De anima*, see the extensive commentary by Ronald Polansky, *Aristotle's* De anima (Cambridge: Cambridge University Press, 2007), 489–93 and 497–500.

63. Aristotle establishes this absolutely crucial point in *De Anima* III.4. I will only offer the most pertinent section (430a2–9): "Thought is itself thinkable in exactly the same way as its objects are. For in the case of objects which involve no matter, what thinks and what is thought are identical; for speculative knowledge and its object are identical.... In the case of those which contain matter each of the objects of thought is only potentially present. It follows that while they will

It is crucial to realize that abstraction is not some automatic process of the human mind but rather an intentional achievement of intelligence realizing intelligibility in the act of understanding. The one philosopher and theologian of the twentieth century who, inspired early in his intellectual formation by Newman's *Essay in Aid of a Grammar of Assent*, thought most deeply about the reality of human understanding, was Bernard Lonergan, especially in his *magnum opus, Insight: A Study of Human Understanding*, a work uniquely intended to facilitate in the reader the very realization of the nature, dynamics, and levels of understanding.[64] In what is arguably the best introduction to Lonergan's philosophical and theological project, Jeremy Wilkins offers a lucid characterization of Lonergan's understanding of abstraction:

Abstraction is an intelligent and conscious disregard for whatever is irrelevant to understanding.... Thus "the very point of the celebrated three degrees of abstraction" is 'psychological': it is "the elimination by the understanding of the intellectually irrelevant because it is understood to be irrelevant."... According to Aquinas, the act of understanding is what properly distinguishes the intellect and perfectly demonstrates its power. The concept, the inner word, is derived from understanding; "conceptualization is the expression of an act of understanding; such self-expression is possible only because understanding is self-possessed, conscious of itself and its own conditions as understanding." There is a first degree of abstraction if those conscious conditions include reference to sense but not to 'here' and 'now' as such (physics, natural philosophy); a second degree if they include reference to the imaginable, but not to the sensible order (mathematics); and a third, finally, if the conditions are all in the intelligible order (metaphysics). The three degrees are not fundamentally a metaphysical theorem but a psychological fact: the intelligent disregard for what is irrelevant to the question.[65]

---

not have thought in them (for thought is a potentiality of them only in so far as they are capable of being disengaged from matter) thought may yet be thinkable." I have cited the translation from J. A. Smith that can be found in *Complete Works* (ed. Barnes), 1:683.

64. Lonergan, *Insight*.

65. Jeremy D. Wilkins, *Before Truth: Lonergan, Aquinas, and the Problem of Wisdom* (Washington, D.C.: The Catholic University of America Press, 2018), 109. The interior quotations refer to Bernard Lonergan, *Verbum: Word and Idea in Aquinas*, ed. Frederick E. Crowe and Robert M. Doran (Toronto: University of Toronto Press, 1997), 53–56, and the advertence to Thomas Aquinas refers to *ST* I, q. 88, a. 2, ad 3. For a more in-depth discussion of abstraction, see Lonergan, *Verbum*, 162–179.

To put this complex epistemological matter into the more proximate context of higher education and into the received idiom of the Aristotelian strand of the perennial philosophy: many college and university students are trained well to study objects of the first degree of abstraction, a process that abstracts physical, sensible nature from the accidental aspects and conditions of individual matter. The first degree of abstraction characterizes the objects of the natural sciences. Many students are also trained well to study objects of the second degree of abstraction, a process that attends to the intelligible matter of quantities, magnitudes, numbers, figures, and forms in separation from any accidental aspects of individual matter, from physical, sensible nature, and from essential configurations of things. The second degree of abstraction characterizes the objects of mathematics. Only few students are introduced, however, to study objects of the third degree of abstraction, a process that completely transcends the condition of what is sensible and quantifiable, and therefore characteristic of material objects. The third degree of abstraction characterizes the purely intelligible objects of logic and metaphysics—being, the one and the many, substance, accident, potency, act, existence, essence, etc.[66] What the Irish contemplative is rightly concerned with, if not alarmed about, is the almost comprehensive eclipse of the third degree of abstraction from higher education. What he does not emphasize sufficiently, however, is the indispensable role the imagination plays in preparing and accompanying intellectual inquiry and learning pertaining to all three degrees of abstraction. The imagination as the representational faculty can never be left behind like a ladder that one can dispense with after having reached the higher level. Furthermore, the productive associations of the

66. The three degrees of abstraction are not to be misunderstood as successive rungs of a ladder, one degree leading to the next, as if one had to master one degree of abstraction before one were able to move to the next. Rather, in the ordinary operations of the intellect all three degrees of abstraction are constantly actualized. Furthermore, it is the concepts of the third degree of abstraction by way of which the human intellect comes to understand what things are (see Aquinas, *De veritate*, q. 10, a. 6; q. 11, a. 1). Yet in the order of understanding, the grades of abstraction serve as classifications of the objects of study. The comprehension of the objects of the third degree of abstraction poses the greatest intellectual challenge and hence should, in the order of study not come first, but rather last. See Ashley, *The Way toward Wisdom*, 138; Thomas Aquinas, *Expositio super librum Boethii De trinitate*, q. 5, a. 3; and Thomas Aquinas, *Commentary on Aristotle's Metaphysics*, Marietti edition, *In duodecim libros Metaphysicorum Aristotelis expositio*, ed. M. R. Cathala, OP, and R. M. Spiazzi, OP (Rome: Marietti, 1964), nos. 1156, 1160–61, 1162–65.

imagination are central to narrative and symbolic thinking and hence crucial for the production, reception, and interpretation of poetry, literature, art, and music.

The humanities' halfway solution that proposes a privileged if not exclusive formation of the imagination (at the expense of thought and inquiry pertaining to the first, second, and especially third degree of abstraction) will undoubtedly increase textual, cultural, and historical literacy and will very likely contribute to formation of aesthetic sensibilities. If well done, it may even raise and consider so-called life questions: "'What should I live for, and why?' 'What should I believe, and why should I believe it?' 'What is morality, and where does it come from?' 'What kind of person should I be?' 'What is meaningful in life, and what should I do in order to lead a fulfilling life?'"[67] But if students are not introduced simultaneously or subsequently into the kind of philosophical inquiry that might enable them to pursue these questions in a rigorous and sustained metaphysical way, such an education of the imagination stands in danger of producing nothing but a vast array of ultimately incommensurable views that will have to be embraced or rejected on the basis of nothing else than the arbitrary predilections of the sovereign subject.

Neglecting inquiries into the first principles of the theoretical and practical intellect, inquiries that would entail discriminations between true and false, good and evil, students will find themselves unprepared, if not unable, to think on the level of principles. They will, consequently, rely on the transient deliveries of their imagination, emotions, and what they regard as personal experiences. The very lack of understanding first principles of reality, of knowledge, and of moral agency will give rise to a soft but persistent skepticism, to the embrace of the intellectually lazy and indifferent pluralism of the "Kingdom of Whatever,"[68] and eventually to the defiant or resigned journey downstream into the Nietzsche's nihilist dystopia. In short, when undertaken *without* the schooling in metaphysical inquiry and contemplation, the *per se* laudable education of the imagination will not generate sufficient energy to stem the pull downstream. When prepared and accompanied by a substantive education of

---

67. Gregory, *The Unintended Reformation*, 74.
68. Ibid., 112.

the imagination, a rigorous schooling in metaphysical inquiry and contemplation might develop the kind of intellectual energy and rigor necessary to resist the pull downstream and eventually even move upstream to the source. For a student with such a schooling of intellect and imagination will eventually become, as Newman felicitously put it, a "master of the two-fold Logos, the thought and the word, distinct, but inseparable from each other."[69]

A Pragmatic Postscript

On a very mundane, but very concrete level, it is all too obvious that the increasing use of technological tools in the college and university classroom—hailed as "aids of the imagination"—will only intensify the inability and the unwillingness of students to engage in thought and inquiry pertaining to the third degree of abstraction. Instead of liberating students from being tyrannized by the constant titillation of their imagination, and hence from "the wanderings of the feverish imagination," the use of these tools will only intensify the students' captivity to the imagination and will consequently make them unable and unwilling to sustain the arduous rigor, discipline, and indeed asceticism of genuinely abstract thought and, therefore, of intellectual contemplation. Within the limits of the imagination alone, thought becomes at best the transient acme of the productive imagination. Because the operation of the imagination depends on being fed (next to sense memory) by the senses, and especially the visual sense, students who think first and foremost, if not exclusively, within the limits of the imagination alone, depend for their thinking on the ongoing stimulation of their senses, especially of their visual sense. They tend to satisfy this need primarily by way of visual entertainment offered by a multitude of media outlets and electronic gadgets. The con-

---

69. Newman, *Idea*, 291. The schooling of the imagination does entail another dimension, one largely ignored or repressed in a modernity shaped by Protestant iconoclasm: the contemplation of the image and the central truth to which such contemplation gives rise, the antithesis of immanence and transcendence. For a philosophically and theologically instructive and historically saturated reflection on the centrality of the image/icon for the education of the imagination, see Thomas Pfau, "Rethinking the Image, With Some Reflections on G. M. Hopkins," *The Yearbook of Comparative Literature* 57 (2011): 30–60.

stant titillation of the imagination creates a state of perpetual mental dissipation, distraction, and disquiet, a state of mind contrary to the sustained attention, persistent concentration, and interior quiet requisite for intellectual contemplation.

It is, furthermore, not surprising at all that college and university students increasingly expect their education to appeal to their imagination and hence to take on the characteristics of the visual entertainment they rely on in order to keep their imagination in a way stimulated that is—fun. On the contemporary market of higher education in the United States, ruled by the consumer and consequently by a stiff competition between colleges and universities, the prospective student is lured with promises of existential excitement, physical comfort, visual entertainment, and comprehensively—fun (not to mention, of course, the promise of social and economic advancement, that is, utility). What chance of success would a program of universal education stand that promised to students, left largely unprepared by most American high schools to read competently texts of a mildly demanding nature and to write coherently structured and compellingly argued papers, neither entertainment nor utility—but rather the arduous inquiry into and the contemplation of truth and, indeed, the imperfect, albeit profound happiness that is a property of and the transient, albeit deep joy that is an accompaniment of such contemplation? If heeded today, would not Newman's vision fall victim to his own famous verdict of being "unreal," that is, while theoretically compelling, nevertheless being out of touch with the concrete exigencies of real life? The remedy needed most is often hated most by those who need it most desperately for their cure.[70] The remedy needed most entails a transvaluation of values such that the distinct community of teachers and students that originally constituted the Academy of Plato and the Lyceum of Aristotle and much later the medieval university would once again in some future, genuinely renewed or newly consti-

70. It was only after I had penned it that I became aware that this last sentence echoes a memorable phrase of Livy to be found in his preface to the first book of *The History of Rome from Its Foundation*, where he invites the reader to observe "the dark dawning of our modern day when we can neither endure our vices nor face the remedies needed to cure them." Livy, *The Early History of Rome*, trans. Aubrey de Sélingcourt (London: Penguin Classics, 2002), 30.

tuted university be able to affirm unequivocally the final end of what is truly "academic": "The least knowledge that one can attain of the highest things is more desirable than the most certain knowledge one can attain of the lowest things."[71] To affirm this insight into the final end of what is truly academic is to affirm the idea of a university; to invert this insight is to affirm the university's counterfeit, the Baconian polytechnicum.

Appendix: Metaphysics and Natural Theology

When Newman, in *The Idea of a University*, advances his prescriptive vision of the "science of sciences," he presupposes a certain way of un-

---

71. Aquinas, *ST* I, q. 1, a. 5, ad 1: "Minimum quod potest haberi de cognitione rerum altissimarum, desiderabilius est quam certissima cognitio quae habetur de minimis rebus." Thomas paraphrases here a thought from Aristotle's *Parts of Animals* I.5 (644b31). The considerations of the university and its counterfeit that make up this chapter are those of a long-term university citizen. Since 1979, I have in various ways been involved with a major university. I was a student of theology, philosophy, German philology, literature, and linguistics at a research university in Franconia, Germany, founded as a typical Enlightenment university in the middle of the eighteenth century by a Lutheran margrave (University of Erlangen). I continued my studies at a research university in the Catholic Rhineland, founded by Protestant Prussia in the early nineteenth century to check Catholic dominance in the area (University of Bonn). Subsequently, I studied at a private research university in the southern United States founded in the early twentieth century and named after a tobacco billionaire as an imitation of northern Ivy League universities (Duke University). In subsequent years, I taught theology and ethics in the "Windy City" at a large urban seminary (with its own PhD program) across the street from the most eminent Midwestern private research university (Lutheran School of Theology at Chicago). Later after having returned as a Divinity School professor to Duke University, I had a one-semester stint as a guest professor at a German university located in former Communist East Germany and founded soon after the Reformation, a university where Fichte, Schelling, and Hegel taught in the early years of the nineteenth century (University of Jena). During the 2012–13 academic year, I held a guest chair at a Catholic liberal arts college in the northeastern United States founded by the Dominican Order in 1917 (Providence College). In 2009, I was the finalist for the presidency of the only Catholic university in Germany, a university founded only in the 1980s (Catholic University of Eichstätt-Ingolstadt) and in 2016 I joined the theological faculty of the Catholic University of America in Washington, D.C., the one university I have been a part of that most closely embodies Newman's "idea of a university." I have lived longer in the institution of the university than I have lived in the United States. For all of my adult life, the academic rhythms and rituals of the university have been the water in which I swim and the air which I breathe. But only in the course of my preparation as a candidate for a university presidency, did I turn my attention directly to the idea of the university. I am deeply committed to the idea of the university, the gold standard by which every institution that claims the title "university" is to be measured and judged, and very grateful for the moments when extant universities strive to embody aspects of this idea. My commitment is simultaneously the source of my love for John Henry Newman's *The Idea of a University* and of my criticisms of the modern research university.

derstanding philosophy itself as a distinct scientific and simultaneously meta-scientific inquiry that allows the speculative contemplation of the whole in all its interconnections and in relationship to the transcendent first cause, God, a coherent inquiry that develops over generations and comprises various schools of thought. This understanding of philosophy has traditionally been called "perennial philosophy" (*philosophia perennis*). It is arguably the case that there do not exist many, if any, coherent traditions of philosophical inquiry other than the perennial philosophy that have the conceptual resources to envision, let alone to sustain, such an inquiry over a long period of time. Some would want to argue that phenomenology might be such an alternative philosophical tradition, or even, as Husserl would think, the very renewal of the perennial philosophy.[72] As my way of characterizing this "sciences of sciences" makes plain, I regard Aristotelian-Thomism to be the most successful instantiation of the perennial philosophy and, moreover, to be an instantiation that is fully compatible with Newman's prescriptive vision. In his *Three Rival Versions of Moral Enquiry*, Alasdair MacIntyre has offered what I take to be a compelling argument for the superiority of Aristotelian-Thomism as a tradition of inquiry in comparison with Enlightenment philosophy and with postmodern deconstruction.[73] His argument is not only fully congruent with Newman's, but indeed corroborates and strengthens Newman's case. Benedict Ashley, in his *The Way Toward Wisdom*, has advanced a profound vision of the whole—fully conversant with contemporary natural science and with the humanities and founded in the Aristotelian-Thomist tradition.[74] In his *Distinguish to Unite or The Degrees of Knowledge*, Jacques Maritain demonstrates how the Aristotelian-Thomist tradition can offer a coherent account of the whole of human knowing from the most basic act of intellectual cognition by way of scientific knowledge to infused mystical knowledge.[75] While Maritain's account stands in need of some

---

72. See Husserl, *Erste Philosophie*, vol. 1.

73. MacIntyre, *Three Rival Versions of Moral Enquiry*.

74. Ashley, *The Way toward Wisdom*.

75. Jacques Maritain, *Distinguish to Unite or The Degrees of Knowledge*, trans. Gerald B. Phelan (New York: Charles Scribner's Sons, 1959). A continuation of this tradition of inquiry can be found in two recent works of note: Paul A. MacDonald Jr., *Knowledge and the Transcendent: An Inquiry into the Mind's Relationship to God* (Washington, D.C.: The Catholic University of America Press,

updating in regard to the recent developments in the philosophy of mind and in neuroscience, the overall scope remains unsurpassed by any contemporary philosophical epistemology, possibly with one exception, Bernard Lonergan's extensive gnoseological inquiry *Insight: A Study in Human Understanding*.

The apex of this first science, natural theology, faces unique conceptual challenges and limitations. Its practitioners, metaphysicians, have to be on constant alert regarding the danger of ever so subtly turning God into an instantiation, albeit the most perfect one, of being (as modern "perfect being theology" does) or of identifying God with the world (as in Spinoza and Hegel) or placing God in a constitutive relationship with the world (as in process philosophy). The critique of such errors is integral to the metaphysical efforts of the perennial philosophy and, according to the principle *abusus non tollit usum* ("the misuse of something is no argument against its proper use"), distinct instantiations of falling into ontotheology, or worse, into pantheism, does not require the abandonment of the inquiry as such. Ironically, Newman's peculiar way of characterizing natural theology seems to make him vulnerable to the charge of ontotheology, as Martin Heidegger famously raised it against the metaphysics of being and as Jean-Luc Marion recently renewed it.[76]

For in Newman's way of putting the matter, God as infinite being seems to fall under a univocal reality of being, metaphysically understood, a view allegedly held by Scotus, Suárez, and their students. According to Scotus, properly understood, however, *ens inquantum ens*, being as such, is the primary object of the intellect and hence the simplest of all concepts, which consequently cannot be defined. Considered abstractly from the distinction between infinite and finite being (being signifying only opposition to nothing), Scotus arrives at a univocal concept of being. In line with his logico-semantic understanding of the univocity of

---

2009), and James D. Madden, *Mind, Matter, and Nature: A Thomistic Proposal for the Philosophy of Mind* (Washington, D.C.: The Catholic University of America Press, 2013).

76. See Martin Heidegger, *Identity and Difference*, trans. Joan Stambaugh (New York: Harper and Row, 1969), and Jean-Luc Marion, *God without Being: Hors-Texte*, trans. Thomas A. Carlson (Chicago: University of Chicago Press, 1991). These matters are discussed with great lucidity by Vittorio Possenti, *Nihilism and Metaphysics: The Third Voyage*, trans. Daniel B. Gallagher (Albany: State University of New York Press, 2014).

being, Scotus understands metaphysics as the science of being as such (*ens inquantum ens*), an inquiry into the transcendentals that comprises infinite being, God, as well as finite being. Thomas Aquinas, on the contrary, understands God to be the cause and principle of being in general (*ens commune*), and consequently regards the knowledge of the first cause as the goal of metaphysical inquiry and not as its subject.[77] In comparison with Scotus, Suárez, and their schools, Thomists are considerably more reserved about the scope and the conceptual precision that natural theory permits; for, according to the Thomist School, inquiry into the first cause has to proceed by causality, negation, and eminence, and is always expressed in analogical terms. Hence, Thomists are keenly aware that any natural knowledge of God that metaphysical inquiry does attain, is—even at its best—indirect, negative, and imperfect. The intricate issue under dispute (that forms the background for the question of the precise status of natural theology in relation to the proper subject matter of metaphysical inquiry) is the question of the analogy or univocity of being. By offering a pithy summary of the central thesis of Étienne Gilson's great opus on Duns Scotus,[78] Jean-François Courtine names the central problematic: "Thomist analogy and Scotist univocity do not treat of the same being, and it is therefore impossible, on the part of Scotus, in order to be at variance with or to refute the former, to pretend to retrieve the authentic thought of Aquinas."[79]

77. See Ashley, *The Way toward Wisdom*, 139–44, for a succinct presentation of this complex matter.

78. Étienne Gilson, *Duns Scot: Introduction à ses positions fondamentales* (Paris: Vrin, 1952).

79. Jean-François Courtine, *Inventio analogiae: Métaphysique et ontothéologie* (Paris: Vrin, 2005), 283n3 (author's translation). For presentations of the Scotist position, see Timotheus Barth, "Being, univocity, and analogy according to Duns Scotus," in *John Duns Scotus, 1265–1965*, ed. J. K. Ryan and B. M. Bonansea (Washington, D.C.: The Catholic University of America Press, 1965), 210–62, and Ludger Honnefelder, *Ens inquantum ens: Der Begriff des Seienden als solchen als Gegenstand der Metaphysik nach der Lehre des Johannes Duns Scotus* (Münster: Aschendorff, 1979). For a more accessible defense of Scotus's semantic (instead of metaphysical) claims about the concept of being as univocal for God and creatures and the misplaced charge of ontotheology against him (and by implication against Newman), see Richard Cross, "'Where Angels Fear to Tread:' Duns Scotus and Radical Orthodoxy," *Antonianum* 76 (2001): 7–41. For an instructive study of the development of the theory of analogy in the Thomist school up through the mid-sixteenth century in critical dialogue with Scotism, see Domenic D'Ettore, *Analogy after Aquinas: Logical Problems, Thomistic Answers* (Washington, D.C.: The Catholic University of America Press, 2019). For a presentation of the Thomist position as represented by John Capreolus and Sylvester of Ferrara,

see Lawrence Dewan, OP, *Form and Being: Studies in Thomistic Metaphysics* (Washington, D.C.: The Catholic University of America Press, 2006), 81–95, and Bernard Montagnes, OP, *The Doctrine of the Analogy of Being according to Thomas Aquinas*, trans. E. M. Macierowsky (Milwaukee, Wis.: Marquette University Press, 2004); for a presentation of the Thomist position as represented by Cajetan, see James F. Anderson, *The Bond of Being: An Essay on Analogy and Existence* (St. Louis, Mo.: Herder, 1949), Ralph McInerny, *Aquinas and Analogy* (Washington, D.C.: The Catholic University of America Press, 1996), and Long, *Analogia Entis*. For a brilliant reassessment along logical semantic lines of Cajetan's doctrine of analogy, see Joshua P. Hochschild, *The Semantics of Analogy: Rereading Cajetan's* De Nominum Analogia (Notre Dame, Ind.: University of Notre Dame Press, 2010) and for a comprehensive account—executed according to the exacting standard of analytic philosophy—of analogy as a pervasive feature of human language, see James F. Ross, *Portraying Analogy* (Cambridge: Cambridge University Press, 1981). For a Wittgenstein-inspired, apophaticist reconception of the analogical use of language, see Stephen Mulhall, *The Great Riddle: Wittgenstein and Nonsense, Theology and Philosophy* (Oxford: Oxford University Press, 2016). For a recent critical as well as constructive engagement of the Protestant theological dismissal of the analogy of being, see *The Analogy of Being: Invention of the Anti-Christ or the Wisdom of God?*, ed. Thomas Joseph White, OP (Grand Rapids, Mich.: Eerdmans, 2010).

EPILOGUE

A Newmanian Theological Journey into the Catholic Church

"I believe and profess all that the Holy Catholic Church believes, teaches, and proclaims to be revealed by God." On December 28, 2004, the Feast of the Holy Innocents, after the profession of the Nicene Creed, my wife and I spoke these words to the priest and the faithful gathered at what, moments afterwards, would be our first Eucharist. We were about to receive the sacrament of confirmation and thus enter into full communion with the Catholic church. I vividly remember the strong sense of joy, awe, and conviction with which I spoke these words: joy because after a long quest I had reached the goal; awe because I sensed that embracing the faith of the church was like embarking on a borderless ocean of truth with unfathomable depths; conviction because I made an act of assent about which I was certain after much theological searching, probing, and reflecting. And it was precisely this long theological journey that made me keenly aware on this Feast of the Holy Innocents of the two essential features that constitute this profession: "I believe and profess all that the holy Catholic church believes, teaches, and proclaims to be revealed by God."

The first essential feature is an act of intentional assent to the church's teachings and a simultaneous surrender to the church's judgment in matters of divine truth. The second feature, enclosed in the first, is an act of equally intentional renunciation. By assenting to the divine truth as believed, taught, and proclaimed by the Catholic church, I renounced myself as the supreme and final arbiter of divine truth. In short, I renounced the supreme privilege to which the modern sovereign subject takes itself to be entitled: the right, as Justice Anthony Kennedy put it in *Planned Parenthood v. Casey*, "to define one's own concept of existence, of meaning, of the universe, and of the mystery of human life." In these pages I have called this act of deciding, this individual arbitration and adjudication of matters of divine truth, the *principle of private judgment*.[1]

Yet there is no renunciation without a prior affirmation. As the thunderclap follows upon the flash of lightning, renouncing the principle of private judgment in matters of divine truth follows upon the act of surrendering to the judgment of the church. It follows upon accepting all that the church proposes and teaches to be revealed by God, explicitly and implicitly. And it follows, last but not least, upon accepting the magisterium of the Catholic church as the infallible, divinely created and ordained instrument of communicating, expounding, defining, and defending the divine truth.

It took me almost seven years more as a Catholic-theologian-in-the-making to understand that this intentional assent and surrender are properties of the fullness of the one divine faith that is a gift of grace.[2] Believ-

---

1. *Nota bene*: it is not only legitimate but necessary/obligatory to use private judgment in *penultimate* matters that involve the use of the virtue of prudence in choosing particular means in order to achieve specific ends. In *ultimate* matters of divinely revealed truth, to apply the principle of private judgment across the board of all proposed beliefs is simply to reject the authority of the divine truth in its fullness and the authority of the divinely instituted infallible instrument that proclaims, defines, and defends this truth. There is, however, one specific region of legitimate private judgment in religion. This region comprises possible acts of assent motivated by credulity, superstition, and other moral faults that, due to considered private judgment, are withheld. In his *Apologia pro Vita Sua*, Newman states: "This was the region of Private Judgment in religion; that is, of a Private Judgement, not formed arbitrarily and according to one's fancy or liking, but conscientiously, and under a sense of duty" (21). Proper judgments in this region are always guided by a well-formed conscience and by right reason. For an extensive discussion of this complex matter, see chapter 1.

2. "And so faith in itself, even though it may not work through charity, is a gift of God, and its operation is a work belonging to the order of salvation, in that a person yields true obedience to God himself when he accepts and collaborates with his grace which he could have rejected. Wherefore, by divine and catholic faith all those things are to be believed which are contained in the word

ing the one, holy, Catholic, and apostolic church to be God's infallible instrument of conveying divine truth, "the Church of the living God, the pillar and bulwark of the truth" (1 Tm 3:15; RSV), and surrendering to her judgment in matters of divine truth are intrinsic and indispensable features of the fullness of the one divine faith, that is, the Catholic faith.

What stood at the beginning of this quest for the fullness of the Catholic faith was the slow but sure realization that the principle of private judgment in matters of divine truth is a burden and a bane inescapably embedded in all versions of Protestantism. And what sent me eventually on the road to the Catholic church was my increasing realization that as a Protestant theologian I could not escape from abiding by the principle of private judgment in matters of divine truth.[3]

For me, then a Lutheran theologian, the crisis that sent me on my theological quest came from the very heart of Protestant theology itself. Three theological areas turned out to come together to form the critical mass of the catalyst that propelled me forward: first, moral theology; second, justification, church, and Eucharist; and third, the question of an incontrovertibly authoritative and, indeed, infallible magisterium. In each of these areas I came to understand the principle of private judgment in matters of divine truth to be a reality as inescapable as it was detrimental for me as a Protestant theologian, a principle that made it impossible to entrust myself fully to the guidance of the light of divine faith.

---

of God as found in scripture and tradition, and which are proposed by the church as matters to be believed as divinely revealed, whether by her solemn judgment or in her ordinary and universal magisterium." *Dei Filius*, no. 3, in *Decrees* (ed. Tanner), 2:807.

3. Many other factors undoubtedly contributed to my entering into full communion with the Catholic church, but none of them was sufficient reason on its own. I could speak about growing up in Germany as part of a sizable Lutheran minority in a largely Catholic area graced by a beautiful countryside that is still suffused with the signs of Catholic piety. I could speak about my youth in a valley framed by the most gorgeous Baroque churches, with the Benedictines, who long ago brought the faith to the area, on one side and, on the other, the Cistercians who cultivated the wilderness. I could speak about an important journey to Rome after graduating from high school; about an even more important visit to the ecumenical community of Taizé as a college student; and about two memorable week-long visits to a famous Benedictine monastery as a university student. I could speak about regular encounters with Catholic theologians during my years of teaching ethics in Chicago; of my encounter with the thought of Thomas Aquinas; and of attending the Easter vigils at a most remarkable Catholic parish church in Hyde Park, Chicago, three minutes' walking distance from our apartment. All of this contributed somehow to my journey, but in retrospect none of this was on its own sufficient or decisive.

Moral Theology

My first teaching position was at a Lutheran seminary in one of the largest urban centers of the United States. My primary task was to teach Christian ethics in a Lutheran key to future Lutheran ministers. After only a short while of teaching, I realized that I was in serious trouble. I felt as if on a small boat without rudder, sail, or compass, tossed about on a rough sea by strong winds and high waves. I had expected rudder, sail, and compass to be provided by the three normative points of reference on which I thought a proper teaching of Christian ethics had to rest: scripture, God's law (natural and revealed), and conscience. I quickly discovered that most, if not all, of these three normative points of reference had been more or less eroded for my students by the time they reached my class. The required ethics course that I was to teach was scheduled for the third and final year of the Master of Divinity program required for Lutheran ordination, and by the time the students enrolled in this course, they were profoundly shaped by the ways they had been taught biblical exegesis and Lutheran church history and theology. After the students had been thoroughly trained to deconstrue and reconstrue the meaning of biblical texts according to the latest trends and fashions of historical-critical exegesis, there was not much left that could serve as one of the normative pillars for a Lutheran ethics that was grounded in the witness of scripture. Scripture itself had become the victim of a mode of hyper-critical historical exegesis that resulted in an understanding supposedly guided by the objectivity of historical science but *de facto* governed by the principle of private judgment. Having been encaged in their respective historical, social, and political contexts—that is, having been reduced to products of and responses to these contexts—biblical texts could only in the widest sense, if at all, bear upon contemporary moral matters. It was left to the students to adjudicate between the multiple, variant, and often contradicting interpretations they encountered in their courses on the Old and the New Testaments and to determine whatever significance they might have for the Christian life.

What then about conscience as a normative point of reference? Conscience exists in Lutheran faith and theology, but not as an internal guide in matters of good and evil. Traditional Lutheran theology regards conscience as part of a human nature that after the Fall is irretrievably damaged. Lutheran theologians, therefore, usually take conscience to be inherently troubled, to be constantly accusing the person, and hence to be in continual need of assurance and peace. For this reason, the more traditional Lutheran students did not seek guidance from their conscience, and the students who regarded themselves as progressive and "with it" unsurprisingly followed the secular culture at large—after having embraced the Enlightenment notion of the inherent goodness of human nature—in simply identifying conscience with the principle of private judgment.

What then about God's law, natural and revealed? As just mentioned, according to traditional Lutheran theology, human reason and will, as part of human nature, are also ravaged by the effects of the Fall. Because of the devastation of human nature consequent to the Fall, the natural law, reason's original participation in God's eternal law and original source of understanding of the created order and destiny of human life, has now, under the condition of original sin, ceased to provide any reliable guidance. But what about the revealed law granted after the Fall in the course of salvation history? According to traditional Lutheran teaching the primary and proper function of God's revealed law is to convict humanity of its sinfulness and to drive it to the Gospel promise of forgiveness and justification by faith alone. Therefore, unsurprisingly, most of my students understood Christian freedom predominantly as a freedom *from* God's law, a spiritual freedom, purportedly enabled and guided by the Holy Spirit alone, but, again unsurprisingly, *de facto* guided primarily if not exclusively by the principle of private judgment.

In sum, the dominant default position I found solidly in place in the minds of most of my students by the time they took my ethics course was one of private judgment or arbitration that was ultimately guided by individual sentiments and desires, self-constructed identities, and the utilitarian principle of the greatest good for the greatest number. The more traditional students embraced this or that aspect of Martin Luther's own teaching as a normative guide for their lives. But the particular selection and combination of aspects of Luther's teaching was at best the result of their own exercise of the principle of private judgment.

Scripture, God's law (natural and revealed), and conscience—according to my best understanding at that time, the three-legged stool on which a proper teaching of Christian ethics had to rest—found hardly any traction with most of my students. They had experienced the dissolution of scripture's authority by the acids of hypercritical exegesis; they had imbibed the teaching that natural law had to be rejected on Lutheran dogmatic grounds and that on the same grounds conscience was either to be rejected as treacherous or to be embraced as a barely camouflaged celebration of moral autarky of the sovereign subject.

In this situation I found myself confronted with an exceedingly ironic alternative. The one alternative was to embrace the principle of private judgment in matters of divine truth as tragic but unavoidable. Was I not myself constantly forced to exercise it in my teaching of ethics and then to impose upon the students by way of my personal teaching authority the deliverances of my own exercise of private judgment as received and established truth? The other alternative was to encourage the students to cultivate the exercise of their own private judgment so that through my action as a "midwife" they would develop their own, authentic, considered, and hence what some would call "theologically mature" arbitrations of faith and morals. I regarded the second alternative to be nothing but a subtle capitulation to the increasingly dominant cultural forces of moral relativism. Hence, I chose the first alternative and decided to swim upstream on my own by reasserting the three-legged stool on which I thought the teaching of Christian ethics had to rest—scripture, God's law (natural and revealed), and conscience—but it was a matter of my own private judgment to do so. And what I offered to the students, of course, was my own personal construal of an ethics in a Lutheran key. The goal of the ethics I taught according to my own best lights, as supported and sustained by the three-legged stool, was to battle the enemy whose name was "antinomianism," the widespread tendency in Lutheranism, ever-recurring since the Lutheran Reformation, to denigrate the ongoing constructive role of God's law in the Christian life. For especially in the area of what we now call the "ethics of life," this Lutheran antinomianism was beginning to take on rather dramatic forms.

In the early 1990s, the ecclesiastical leadership of my Lutheran body, the Evangelical Lutheran Church of America (ELCA), had begun to soften, and eventually it abandoned, the once rather strict Lutheran opposition to abortion. Abortion was increasingly regarded by the ecclesiastical leadership as a privilege of private judgment exercised by the pregnant woman (of course, as it was put, a "responsibly informed" and therefore purportedly "ethical" and hence inherently justified private judgment). While she was encouraged to listen to God's Word, seek advice, and search her conscience, in the end her choice, an act of the sovereign subject, was the legitimate and hence final and decisive authority. What happened in the 1990s in regard to the ELCA's teaching on abortion—namely, exchanging properly formed conscience for the principle of private judgment in matters of divine truth, and thereby foregoing the objective natural and received revealed norms—had already happened decades earlier in regard to contraception and divorce and remarriage. The same was eventually to happen regarding matters of sexual relationships between consenting adults, whether of the opposite or the same sex. Neither divine truth as witnessed in scripture, nor right reason, nor natural law, nor the tradition that has informed Christian thinking about these matters for almost two millennia, guided the ELCA in these matters. The guiding norm was the principle of private judgment exercised individually under the culturally dominant counterfeit of conscience, the entitlement to subjective sovereignty in matters of faith and morals, extended managerially by way of strategic church-political processes initiated by the church headquarters legitimized by way of the instrument of assembly voting.

It was into this desolate and at points desperate situation that in August 1993, at the end of my third year of teaching Christian ethics in a Lutheran key, Pope John Paul II promulgated his encyclical letter *Veritatis Splendor*. I still vividly remember my first reading of it. I was struck as by lightning. Here the church spoke in her authoritative voice, interpreting scripture in a way that was as powerful as it was beautiful, affirming the reality of conscience and simultaneously instructing it in view of God's law, natural and revealed. And in the very core of the encyclical, I encountered a rich account of the ontology and teleology of moral action that was as illuminating as it was profound. I suddenly saw the three-legged stool fully at work and unequivocally affirmed by the church's magisterium. I found myself in vehement agreement with the teaching of *Veritatis Splendor*. At the same time I was greatly confused: for all this splendid teaching was obviously Roman Catholic and not Lutheran—but I was a Lutheran ethicist. Was my vehement agreement leading me into the traps of legalism and works-righteousness, that is, into what Lutherans would see as exchanging the freedom of the Gospel for ecclesially imposed laws and as exchanging salvation by faith alone for meriting salvation by way of religious works? I was unable to discover any of these traps in *Veritatis Splendor*—but how could this be?

For the first time in my life I committed myself to a serious study of Catholic moral theology and immersed myself especially into the thought of Thomas Aquinas, for his voice and vision seemed to me to inform what was most centrally at stake in *Veritatis Splendor*. When, two years later, the encyclical letter *Evangelium Vitae* came along, it only affirmed the initial and overwhelming impression I had when I read *Veritatis Splendor* for the first time: here the church was teaching authoritatively and truthfully, and in such a way that it became possible to teach Christian ethics in accord with scripture, God's law (natural and revealed), and the voice of conscience—and if need be, against the spirit of the age, and the winds of the times, and most importantly, in a way that avoided making private judgment the final arbiter of truth in matters of faith and morals. Embracing this teaching meant freedom from the seemingly interminable necessity of individual theological wrestling over the truths and norms of the Christian life. In light of the teaching of *Veritatis Splendor* and *Evangelium Vitae*, the task for all Christians seemed to be exercising fidelity and prudence in the faithful application of the church's teaching to one's own life of discipleship. And for the moral theologian, the specific task became teaching—not inventing—moral theology. Instead of constantly changing the rules of the game according to one's own best liking or latest whims, it had become a matter of finally playing the game on a clearly circumscribed playing field with explicit rules. And the fact that an authoritative magisterial encyclical letter opened my eyes to these truths, taught me for the first time that there indeed is a referee on the playing field of moral theology and that his presence is indeed indispensable for moral theology to remain accountable to the truth of the faith.

To the degree that *Veritatis Splendor* became a decisive point of reference for my thinking and writing, I became estranged from the project of a Christian ethics in a Lutheran key. And—needless to say—my estrangement did not go unnoticed. Less than well-meaning colleagues, especially in Germany, began to characterize me as "crypto-catholic" and "Rome-friendly"—synonyms for "unreliable" and "deviant." But this did not matter much to me, as other parts of my research and writing had carried me increasingly from ethics to dogmatics and fundamental theology. I had begun to become preoccupied with the question of what theology itself is and how "to do theology" accountable to and in fidelity to the church. By asking this question, I had to pursue the question of the nature of the church and of the church's doctrinal tradition and teaching authority. Unsurprisingly, but at that time unforeseen by me, it was here that the Catholic question caught up with me most forcefully.

It was during the time of researching and writing my *Habilitationsschrift* in dogmatic theology—what was to become eventually *Suffering Divine Things: Theology as Church Practice*—that I immersed myself for the first time in John Henry Newman's intellectual and religious autobiography, his *Apologia pro Vita Sua*. I was profoundly struck by the account of his journey of faith from Calvinistic Evangelicalism, High Church Anglicanism, and the *via media* of the Oxford Movement to the Roman Catholic church. The problems that Newman was wrestling with—especially the most vexing one, the Protestant inescapability of the principle of private judgment in matters of faith and morals—were all too familiar to me. Unsurprisingly, therefore, Newman's spiritual and theological sojourn struck a deep chord with me. I was, however, not quite ready yet to fully absorb the lesson Newman was conveying in his *Apologia* and to draw the obvious consequence from this lesson. I still faced what I regarded at that time considerable theological impediments that first needed to be removed. These impediments were located, as one might expect, in themes Lutheran theologians would tend to be most concerned about— justification, church, Eucharist, and magisterium.

Justification, Church, and Eucharist

Six years after the promulgation of *Veritatis Splendor*, the president of the Council for Christian Unity of the Roman Catholic Church and the general secretary of the Lutheran World Federation signed the *Joint Declaration on the Doctrine of Justification*. The vast majority of German Lutheran theologians hotly debated and contested earlier drafts and—in open defiance of their own ecclesial authorities—rejected the final draft. Again I found myself in a position of profound estrangement, especially from my German Lutheran colleagues in theology. Unlike most of them, I warmly welcomed this declaration, for it officially removed the one central theological and doctrinal obstacle that kept me from even beginning to contemplate full communion with the Catholic church. Now I heard it officially from both sides of the Reformation divide: in the core of their understanding of justification by faith through grace, there is substantial agreement between the current teaching of the Catholic church and the current teaching of the Lutheran bodies that are part of the Lutheran World Federation.[4]

For most of the Lutheran theologians who supported the *Joint Declaration on the Doctrine of Justification*, this agreement meant that irrespective of all remaining differences one could and should move to immediate Eucharistic communion that would celebrate and acknowledge a state of reconciled difference. In a nutshell, because we agree in the one point that truly matters, we are free to differ in everything else; we simply cease to regard these other differences as church-dividing. Again at odds with most of my German Lutheran peers—this time the small group of supporters of the *Joint Declaration*—I drew quite a different conclusion from the document. I was not only entitled but now indeed mandated to explore and consider the fullness of the teachings of the Catholic church. While others mainly inferred that now, for sure, there was no need to consider the Catholic faith more closely, because the Catholic church seemed to have come around to the Lutheran position on the one issue that from the Lutheran point of view really matters, I inferred the opposite: if there ever was a mandate upon the Lutheran theologian to con-

---

4. In recent years, the World Methodist Council also adopted and affirmed this declaration.

sider most carefully and attentively the teaching of the Catholic church in its full scope, it was now, after the *Joint Declaration on the Doctrine of Justification* had been signed, and the one obstacle had been removed that might have stood in the way of such a consideration.

This conviction became deeper and deeper in the years after the *Joint Declaration* and formed the silent background of most of my theological work. The foreground, however, was not that silent. I found myself increasingly troubled, if not annoyed, by the context of the life of faith most central to me: the kinds of treatment that the remaining consecrated elements suffer after the completion of the celebration of what Lutherans usually call the Lord's Supper.

During the years of my childhood and youth in a liturgically rather conservative German Lutheran body, hosts, wine, and kneelers had been in regular use; now in my adopted U.S. Lutheran communion, not only were the kneelers gone in most places, but in many places grape juice had replaced the wine, and in all places a loaf of bread had replaced the communion hosts. These matters were irritating, but not detrimental. What I came to regard as increasingly disturbing and eventually detrimental to the authenticity of the faith in Christ's real presence, however, was a most troubling lack of respect, let alone reverence, for the remaining elements after communion. It was a common practice to throw out the remaining bread as food for the birds and to pour the remaining wine into the ground outside the church building. There was no consumption, let alone reservation, in any shape or form. I do not even want to mention what the carpets around the communion rails looked like when too often the bread turned out to be too dry and crumbled or when the distribution had been careless. All that was left of Luther's own intense personal reverence for Christ's real presence in the elements was the aroma of an empty bottle. And where the sacramental piety was gone, the practice seemed to go awry, too.

Being greatly disturbed about this practice, I began to investigate more closely what various Protestant bodies, primarily Lutheran, Anglican, Methodist, and Reformed, taught about Christ's presence in the blessed bread and wine. For I rather naïvely thought that in this way a greater clarity might be gained about how to treat the elements with reverence, not only during but also after communion. The findings were thoroughly sobering. Anglicans allow for at least three ways to conceive of Christ's presence in the elements, and these three views entail considerably different attitudes about the practice of treating the remaining elements. Lutherans and Reformed have disagreed about these matters fiercely since the Reformation; and only after the Second World War did they reach an ecumenical agreement in Germany, the *Leuenberg Concord*. This concord, so-called, amounted essentially to agree not to disagree anymore on questions pertaining to the mode of Christ's presence or absence during the Lord's Supper celebration and to abstain in the future from precise dogmatic teachings about it, but rather to commune together and acknowledge each other's differing (and possibly contradictory) theological construals of the event as not church-dividing, but as matters of reconciled difference.

The various construals, of course, unavoidably become a matter of one's spiritual and theological predilection, or taste—in short, a matter to be submitted to the principle of private judgment. And, of course, the question as to how the remaining elements are to be treated after communion also become a matter of one's theological predilection, that is, a matter subjected to the selfsame principle of private judgment. And even inside the older Lutheran tradition there did not seem to be unanimity about so central a question. The dominant doctrinal notion seemed to be that Christ's real presence in, with, and under the elements ceases to obtain with the end of communion, a notion that had no clear warrants from scripture or the theological tradition. Treating the elements that remained after communion in the way I have described seemed to be driven largely by the rejection of the Catholic doctrine of transubstantiation. As a justification for the post-liturgical vacuuming of the remaining elements from the carpet around the altar rail, I was once told by a Lutheran pastor: "If He can get Himself in, He surely can get Himself out." This is, *in nuce*, the Lutheran doctrine of "consubstantiation," and the practice of vacuuming seems to be quite consistent with it.[5] In short, there simply was no authoritative doctrinal teaching and disciplinary rul-

5. I should emphasize explicitly, though, that by no means all Lutheran pastors followed this practice. Some are eager to treat the remaining elements in reverent ways.

ing on it that is normative for all Lutheran pastors. Luther's own position was invoked by some, if not many, but it is expressed in texts of his that are not regarded as authoritative by all Lutheran communions. In short, the matter was left to the individual private judgment of each pastor, or the collective private judgment of a congregational council, or of some synod, the authority of which is ambiguous at best. Because the Lutheran ecclesial teaching of Christ's real presence lacked clarity and definition, the practice of treating the elements remaining after communion is left to the arbitration of various groups of individuals, an inescapable mode of exercising private judgment in a matter at the core of the faith.

Where to turn in such a situation? Thanks to God's good providence, I was not tortured for too long by this question. On April 17, 2003, Pope John Paul II promulgated what was to be his last encyclical letter: *Ecclesia de Eucharistia*. Again I encountered a teaching as consistent as it was convincing. It answered all of my questions and troubles definitively and so freed me from the need to submit this most central mystery of the faith, Christ's Eucharistic presence, to the lights of my own or my pastor's private judgment. Moreover, I encountered more in *Ecclesia de Eucharistia* than I had bargained for—an account of the Eucharistic sacrifice that most satisfyingly addressed all lingering misconceptions, concerns, and reservations Lutherans had entertained since the Protestant Reformation. What had seemed to be intractable problems on Protestant dogmatic, liturgical, and practical terms suddenly received surpassingly beautiful solutions in an authoritative teaching of the Catholic church, answers that opened a path to the very heart of the mystery of Christ and his church.[6]

---

6. There was furthermore a striking fittingness between the doctrinal teaching of the encyclical letter on the Eucharist and the church and the normative practical guidelines given in great detail and care in *Redemptionis Sacramentum*, issued on March 25, 2004, by the Congregation for Divine Worship and the Discipline of the Sacraments. The instruction *Redemptionis Sacramentum* expresses explicit concern about the phenomenon closely connected with private judgment in matters of divine truth: "Not infrequently, abuses are rooted in a false understanding of liberty. Yet God has not granted us in Christ an illusory liberty by which we may do what we wish, but a liberty by which we may do that which is fitting and right. This is true not only of precepts coming directly from God, but also of laws promulgated by the Church, with appropriate regard for the nature of each norm. For this reason, all should conform to the ordinances set forth by legitimate ecclesiastical authority" (no. 7). This document is available at www.vatican.va.

Magisterium

Things were obviously coming to a head. In my own teaching and writing as a Lutheran theologian I increasingly realized the burden hidden deep in the identity of the Lutheran theologian: a tangible vacuum of magisterial authority and guidance. I came to understand this vacuum as caused by a systemic lack of clarity about the question as to whether a proper magisterium—an authoritative teaching office—exists at all in the various Lutheran, or other Protestant, bodies; and if such a teaching office exists, what it is, how far it extends, and with what kind of authority it is equipped. The individual theologian was to fill this vacuum of magisterial authority with his or her own best theological judgments. But the particular selections of normative sources on which the individual theologian's most considered theological judgments rested were unavoidably the result of his own private judgment: sundry passages from scripture (judged to be most in accordance with Luther's teaching and forming the truly normative canon in the wider canon of scripture), combined with the Trinitarian and Christological doctrines of the first ecumenical councils (Luther happened to affirm these doctrines as ultimately biblical and to emphasize at the same time that the councils could and did err in matters of doctrine and morals), and finally a selection of what were regarded as the normative writings of the Reformation period. There was no unanimity as to how these sources related to one another, nor was there an authoritative office to clarify definitively how they were to be ordered and ranked; and there was no authoritative, let alone infallible, instrument that was in a position to adjudicate between variant theological and quasi-magisterial construals. I slowly realized that, in order to ease this quandary somewhat, many if not most Lutheran theologians tended to take what Luther regarded as the most central theological tenets (that were supposedly directly received from scripture) as an infallibly normative point of reference. The ironic result of this pervasive tendency was the fully operative but completely unacknowledged infallibility that granted *de facto* veracity and authority to Luther's teaching and to the unique capability accorded to him by his followers to open up the true theological meaning of scripture. The tacit assumption was that by faithfully following the central tenets of his theology, under no circumstances could one wander from the truth of the faith and fall into error.

Once I became fully aware of the operative infallibility *de facto* supporting the central tenets of Luther's theological teaching, a most serious theological question arose. Whence should such a gift of infallibility come? The only even remotely conceivable theological explanation would have to be to claim the special gift of an extraordinary prophetic inspiration, analogous to that of an Old Testament prophet, that would enable Luther to become the one and only authoritative interpreter of St. Paul's theology and thereby of the Gospel of Christ and through it all of scripture. Yet upon closer inspection, such a theological account would be utterly unsustainable, for neither did Luther himself claim to have received such a gift of prophecy, nor was this view widely shared among his immediate followers, let alone was it an emerging and eventually accepted tradition in Lutheranism. But if, bereft of such an alleged divine gift, Luther was just one theologian among many; and even if we were to grant him to have been a unique genius of religious intuition and imagination, gifted with the most exceptional rhetorical powers and zealous for the truth as he understood it, he was indeed as fallible a theologian as I was and still am. Hence he had no superior claim upon my allegiance to his teaching. My allegiance or non-allegiance to his teaching, rather, was again a matter of my private theological judgment. For what other criterion integral to the faith and superior to the principle of private judgment could lay a claim upon my allegiance and fidelity to Luther's theological tenets? The Protestant canon of scripture as interpreted in light of Luther's own fallible theological tenets? Hardly so. A contingent consensus of Lutherans gathering in one place at one time and agreeing upon a particular expression of the faith based on a reading of scripture in light of Luther's theological tenets? Hardly so. A Lutheran selection of the ecumenical councils—whose doctrinal decisions, according to Luther and Lutheran teaching, are not infallible—and a Lutheran selection of patristic teachings meant to corroborate Luther's teaching? Hardly so. Individual Lutheran theologians of great standing? Hardly so. An accumulative combination of all the above? Hardly so.

I had finally reached the end of a road that turned out to be a cul-desac. Short of some subtle mode of self-deception or foregoing the quest for truth in this crucial matter, there was no way forward in the direction taken by the Reformation theologians. I was faced by a simple alternative internal to Lutheranism, as plain as it was painful. Either I had to bite the bullet and posit—based on my private judgment—the tacit functional infallibility of Luther as the authoritative magisterium in identifying the normative canon in the canon of scripture and in the most central matters of faith and morals, or I had to accept the reality of a fallible, collective magisterium made up of sundry Lutheran church leaders, synods, and theologians from whose fallible teachings I would accept what I, according to my own fallible lights, would regard as right. In either alternative, what stared back at me was the ugly face of the seemingly inescapable principle of private judgment in matters of divine truth.

In light of these equally unacceptable alternatives internal to Lutheranism, I became increasingly aware that I was in a theological and spiritual position impossible to sustain over time. Contemplating the theological contours of the quandary I faced, it dawned on me slowly but surely that I was confronted with a much deeper and more fundamental problem than the one internal to Lutheranism: It seemed that I had to embrace the principle of private judgment in matters of divine truth as a tragic, but unavoidable, last resort. This seemingly inescapable consequence entailed that the truth of the faith in its cognitive content as well as its amissible certitude is only eschatologically attainable. What is available and attainable in the present state under the condition of original sin and eschatological nonfulfillment is at best some sort of historically received and interpreted divine promise that takes shape in variegated, fallible, and hence conditional creedal expressions affirmed by my own private judgment in an act of belief that, due to the lack of certitude, has a constant companion—doubt. This seemingly unavoidable consequence would furthermore entail that the Christ, who called himself the way, the truth, and the life, was himself nothing but an eschatological promise without any inchoate present fulfillment in the form of the divine Paraclete who leads the church into all truth and hence without an infallible aid that would protect the church from error in all the central truths of faith and morals.

What looked first like a tragic last resort turned out to entail a disconcerting reduction of the most central tenets of the faith to a promise qualified by a radical eschatological reservation referring everything pertaining to the faith to a future fulfillment. The consequent vacating of faith's cognitive content and the concomitant removal of faith's certitude would indeed void not only the present pledge of Christ's promise but eventually also Christ's identity as the incarnate Lord. Traveling further down this road of cancelling faith's cognitive content and eradicating its certainty would unavoidably lead to the embrace of an ever-less-subtle skepticism about the truth of the faith itself and an increasing personal tentativeness about holding it. One would inescapably become at first vulnerable and eventually subject to unequivocal unbelief, an unbelief that often masks itself with the pretension to reinterpret and thereby "update" the Christian faith such that it finally accords with the rationalistic or naturalistic framework of post-Enlightenment modernity. Such an "update" would finally acknowledge as a sheer fact that all that is left of "traditional Christianity" is nothing but the aroma of an empty bottle, an aroma just strong enough to sustain a post-metaphysical, post-dogmatic, and post-ecclesial spirituality of universal acceptance, affirmation, and compassion after the "death of God." One might, of course, stop somewhere on this road to uninhibited infidelity and settle for some of the purportedly "updated" reconstructions of Christ and corresponding reinterpretations of Christianity, but such a "settlement" would only be the consequence of an act of private judgment and the pusillanimous unwillingness to face what is waiting at the end of the road taken.

Was there an alternative, an "or" to the stark "either" of this ever accelerating interior self-secularization of Protestant Christianity first into some soft agnosticism, then into a complacent indifferentism, and finally into confident unbelief? If so, what was it? Well, obviously the relinquishment of the principle of private judgment in matters of divine truth! But how was this to be done? Had I not been guided to this very impasse and hence to this insight by my own private judgments? How could one relinquish private judgment in matters of divine truth on the basis of one's private judgment in matters of divine truth? Could one pull oneself by one's own hair from sinking ever deeper into the quicksand?

Encountering Mother Church

In the summer of 2004 I taught as a visiting professor at a German university in a traditionally Protestant area. There were no Catholic theological faculty in this university, and the Catholics in town were a tiny minority. The theological faculty on which I served for this semester was thoroughly and decidedly Protestant. Interestingly, the oldest part of the university—its heart, so to speak—was the remnant of a Dominican convent, dissolved during the Protestant Reformation, shortly after which the university was founded as an intentionally Lutheran bulwark of higher learning.

On the Solemnity of the Ascension of our Lord, a state holiday in Germany, I planned to attend the Lutheran worship service in the main medieval church downtown. When I arrived, to my great surprise I found the church doors locked and a note informing me that the worship service was taking place somewhere in the woods. It was, after all, a beautiful spring day, and worshiping outdoors was a customary practice, especially on this holiday, among German Protestants. I did not have a car and in addition had no familiarity with the geography of the surrounding area. After a brief moment of being lost about what to do, I realized that the Catholics must have Mass on this feast day, and I happened to know that a Catholic parish church was less than fifteen minutes' walking distance away. Upon arriving, I learned that Mass would start in half an hour. So I put myself onto the outer edge of the last pew and waited in the peaceful silence of the sanctuary. Slowly the church filled with the faithful, young and old, rich and poor, and with a surprising number of children. Eventually the sanctuary was packed, standing room only. And then I forgot everything, including myself. For from the first moments of the liturgy, I was overwhelmed with the most powerful sense of having simply arrived home. Here was mother church, ever so gently embracing me in a liturgy that was virtually identical with what I had grown up with more than thirty years earlier as a Bavarian Lutheran; with a homily that illuminated Christ's ascension in a simple but profound way; and with a most reverent and at the same time joyful celebration of the Eucharist. Here was the Catholic church in all its humility and glory, in all its poverty and richness, in all its simplicity and beauty, a heavenly treasure in earthen vessels.

I wept from the beginning to the end of Mass—tears of joy and gratitude. I had come upon the one pearl, and suddenly I understood what Augustine might have felt when he exclaimed in his *Confessions*: "Late have I loved you, Beauty so ancient and so new, late have I loved you!"[7] I had been so close to mother church all these years without realizing it and without heeding the gentle but persistent beckoning of her teaching. Now I had arrived in the place that disclosed fully the teaching of *Ecclesia de Eucharistia*. And it was here, in the gentle embrace of the liturgy of the Mass that I was able, peacefully and joyfully, to relinquish the principle of private judgment in matters of divine truth and to let myself be guided by mother church into the fullness of divine faith. When I left this Ascension Day Mass, I had become a Catholic without yet fully realizing it. While I had not received explicit answers to all the questions lingering in my still largely Lutheran mind, I had encountered mother church in the core of her life as described so beautifully in *Ecclesia de Eucharistia*; in this celebration of the Mass, I had been able to relinquish the principle of private judgment in matters of divine truth in an existential act of assent, which was as fundamental as it was comprehensive, an act of assent simply to receive the whole as it was explicitly and implicitly present in the celebration of the Eucharistic liturgy, as proposed to me by the Catholic church.

Clarity

It took me the remainder of my time in this German university town to digest this dramatic, life-changing experience. I was not able to speak to anyone about it, because I was still dazed and dazzled by the weight of the encounter, and in need of God's guidance regarding how to move forward. It will hardly come as a surprise that from this Ascension Day onward I sought God's guidance primarily in prayer in front of the tabernacle in this particular Catholic church. I did not wish to return again to the principle of private judgment and simply follow my own best lights in matters of faith and morals, and so I asked God for the grace of an incon-

7. St. Augustine, *The Confessions*, trans. Maria Boulding, OSB (Hyde Park, N.Y.: New City Press, 1997), 10.26 (262).

trovertible sign that would signal to me God's approval to move forward; and after my return to the United States, several weeks into the fall semester at Duke University, during one memorable night, I received the grace of such an incontrovertible sign. From this moment on I was in a state of great inner clarity and peace, and things began to unfold almost by themselves. And on December 28 of the same year, on the Feast of Holy Innocents, with a strong sense of joy, awe, and conviction my wife and I were able to say: "I believe and profess all that the holy Catholic church believes, teaches, and proclaims to be revealed by God."[8]

Recall the central conundrum I faced on my theological sojourn into full communion with the Catholic church: how could I relinquish the principle of private judgment in matters of divine truth on the very basis and by way of my own private judgment? It was not long after I became a Catholic that I came across a text by John Henry Newman in which he offers a striking description of the conundrum I faced and a solution to it that helped me to understand retrospectively how it was indeed resolved for me. To the objection that converts must use their own private judgment in the act of conversion, Newman responds that

they use it in order ultimately to supersede it; as a man out of doors uses a lamp in a dark night, and puts it out when he gets home. What would be thought of his bringing it into his drawing room? … if he came in with a great-coat on his back, a hat on his head, an umbrella under his arm, and a large stable-lantern in his hand?[9]

Newman assumes that after a long search in the darkness of the night relying on the only light one has available, one might indeed find one's way back home. But upon the house, one, of course, puts out one's own light, for inside the house one obviously relies on the light already lit there at

---

8. My wife, a trained theologian but not working in an academic institution and therefore not burdened with the particular challenges of the academic theologian, was less, if at all, infected by the principle of private judgment in matters of divine truth. In fact, gifted with a deep faith and very strong spiritual instinct, she was ready a number of years before me to enter into full communion with the Catholic church, but patiently waited for me to be granted the theologian's way of relinquishing the principle of private judgment in matters of divine truth. After this had finally happened in a place far away, we were able to move forward again together upon my return to the United States from my guest semester at the German university.

9. Ker, *John Henry Newman: A Biography*, 335.

one's arrival. The convert uses private judgment right up to the act of assent. Yet by assenting to the divine truth as believed, taught, and proclaimed by the Catholic church, the convert simultaneously relinquishes the principle of private judgment in matters of divine truth. It was only upon encountering this particular text of Newman's that I realized how deeply the reading of his *Apologia pro Vita Sua* had influenced and shaped my own spiritual and theological sojourn. In retrospect, I can only understand and appreciate it as a quintessentially Newmanian journey into full communion with the Catholic church.

More than a century and a half before I made my profession of faith on the Feast of the Holy Innocents in 2004, the Anglican priest and theologian, John Henry Newman, made the same profession of faith on October 9, 1845. Newman understood his spiritual journey as a providentially guided sojourn from shadows and images into the truth, a sojourn that would find its fulfillment only in the beatific vision.

SELECTED BIBLIOGRAPHY

Works by John Henry Newman

[1826; 1843 (date of first publication); 1870 (date of uniform edition)]. *Two Essays on Biblical and on Ecclesiastical Miracles*. London: Longmans, Green, and Co., 1907.

[1828; 1871]. "Poetry with Reference to Aristotle's Poetics." In John Henry Cardinal Newman, *Essays Critical and Historical*, 1:1–29. London: Longman, Greens, and Co., 1907.

[1833; 1871]. *The Arians of the Fourth Century*. London: Longmans, Green, and Co., 1908.

[1833; 1841]. *Tracts for the Times*. Introduction and notes by James Tolhurst. Notre Dame, Ind.: University of Notre Dame Press, 2013.

[1834–1843; 1869]. *Parochial and Plain Sermons*. 8 vols. London: Longmans, Green, and Co., 1907.

[1837; 1877]. *Lectures on the Prophetical Office of the Church: viewed relatively to Romanism and Popular Protestantism*. In John Henry Cardinal Newman, *The Via Media of the Anglican Church Illustrated in Lectures, Letters and Tracts Written Between 1830 and 1841*, vol. 1. London: Longmans, Green, and Co., 1901.

[1838; 1874]. *Lectures on the Doctrine of Justification*. London: Longmans, Green, and Co., 1908.

All works of Newman are available for free perusal at an outstanding website of the National Institute of Newman Studies (NINS), a nonprofit organization dedicated to promoting the study and knowledge of Newman's life, work, and influence. All readers and scholars of John Henry Newman are greatly indebted to the vision and the hard work that went into the creation of this precious resource. For all persons interested in entering deeper into Newman's sprawling *oeuvre*, this website is the place to begin: www.newmanreader.org.

Those readers who desire a deeper scholarly engagement of Newman's thought in its intellectual, ecclesiastical, historical, cultural, and political context might want to turn to the premier journal of Newman scholarship, the *Newman Studies Journal: The Journal of the National Institute for Newman Studies*. This journal is published by National Institute for Newman Studies and distributed by the Catholic University of America Press.

[1842; 1844]. *Select Treatises of St. Athanasius in Controversy with the Arians Translated with Notes and Indices.* 2 vols. London: James Parker and Co. and Rivingtons, 1877.

[1843; 1870]. *Fifteen Sermons Preached before the University of Oxford between A.D. 1826 and 1843.* London: Longmans, Green, and Co., 1909.

[1843; 1869]. *Sermons Bearing on Subjects of the Day.* London: Longmans, Green, and Co., 1902.

[1845; 1878]. *An Essay on the Development of Christian Doctrine* [1845]. Edited by Stanley L. Jaki. Pinckney, Mich.: Real View Books, 2003; *An Essay on the Development of Christian Doctrine* [1878]. London: Longmans, Green, and Co., 1909.

[1848; 1874]. *Loss and Gain: The Story of a Convert.* London: Longmans, Green, and Co. 1906.

[1849; 1870]. *Discourses Addressed to Mixed Congregations.* London: Longmans, Green, and Co., 1906.

[1851]. *Lectures on the Present Position of Catholics in England Addressed to the Brothers of the Oratory in the Summer of 1851.* London: Longmans, Green, and Co., 1908.

[1852; 1858; 1873]. *The Idea of a University Defined and Illustrated.* London: Longmans, Green, and Co., 1907.

[1852]. "1852 Discourse V." In John Henry Newman, *The Idea of a University Defined and Illustrated. I. In Nine Discourses Delivered to the Catholics of Dublin. II. In Occasional Lectures and Essays Addressed to the Members of the Catholic Church.* Edited with introduction and notes by I. T. Ker, 419–34. Oxford: Clarendon Press, 1976.

[1852]. "1852 Appendix." In John Henry Newman, *The Idea of a University Defined and Illustrated. I. In Nine Discourses Delivered to the Catholics of Dublin. II. In Occasional Lectures and Essays Addressed to the Members of the Catholic Church.* Edited with introduction and notes by I. T. Ker, 435–92. Oxford: Clarendon Press, 1976.

[1855; 1888]. *Callista: A Tale of the Third Century.* London: Longmans, Green, and Co., 1901.

[1859]. *On Consulting the Faithful in Matters of Doctrine.* Edited by John Coulson. New York: Sheed and Ward, 1961.

[1865]. *Apologia pro Vita Sua Being a History of His Religious Opinions.* London: Longmans, Green, and Co., 1908.

[1865]. "A Letter Addressed to the Rev. E. B. Pusey, D.D., on Occasion of His Eirenicon of 1864." In John Henry Cardinal Newman, *Certain Difficulties Felt by Anglicans in Catholic Teaching*, 2:1–170. London: Longmans, Green, and Co., 1900.

[1865]. *The Dream of Gerontius.* In John Henry Cardinal Newman, *Verses on Various Occasions*, 323–70. London: Longmans, Green, and Co., 1903.

[1867; various]. *Verses on Various Occasions.* London: Longmans, Green, and Co., 1903.

[1870]. *An Essay in Aid of a Grammar of Assent.* London: Longmans, Green, and Co., 1903.

[1871]. "The Orthodoxy of the Body of the Faithful during the Supremacy of Arianism," appendix V to the third edition of *The Arians of the Fourth Century.* London:

Longmans, Green, and Co., 1908. Also in *On Consulting the Faithful in Matters of Doctrine*, edited by John Coulson, 109–18. New York: Sheed and Ward, 1961.

[**1871; various**]. *Essays Critical and Historical*. 2 vols. London: Longmans, Green, and Co., 1907.

[**1871; various**]. *Tracts Theological and Ecclesiastical*. London: Longmans, Green, and Co., 1899.

[**1873; 1956**]. "The Infidelity of the Future: Sermon on the Occasion of the Opening of St. Bernard's Seminary, 2nd October 1873." In John Henry Newman, *Faith and Prejudice and Other Sermons*, edited by The Birmingham Oratory, 113–28. New York: Sheed and Ward, 1956.

[**1874; various**]. *Sermons Preached on Various Occasions*. London: Longmans, Green, and Co., 1908.

[**1875**]. *Letter to the Duke of Norfolk*. In John Henry Cardinal Newman, *Certain Difficulties Felt By Anglicans in Catholic Teaching*, 2:175–378. London: Longmans, Green, and Co., 1900.

[**1879**]. *Speech of His Eminence Cardinal Newman on the reception of the "Biglietto": at Cardinal Howard's palace in Rome on the 12th of May 1879, with the address of the English-speaking Catholics in Rome and His Eminence's reply to it, at the English College on the 14th of May 1879*. Rome: Libreria Spithöver, 1879. In Wilfrid Ward, *The Life of John Henry Cardinal Newman Based on His Private Journals and Correspondence*, 2:459–62. London: Longmans, Green, and Co., 1912.

[**1884**]. "On the Inspiration of Scripture." *The Nineteenth Century* 15, no. 84 (February 1884): 185–99.

[**1885**]. "The Development of Religious Error." *The Contemporary Review* (October 1885): 457–69.

[**1890**]. *Stray Essays on Controversial Points, Variously Illustrated* by Cardinal Newman. Privately printed, 1890.

[**1935**]. *The Newman-Perrone Paper on Development*. Introduced and edited by T. Lynch. *Gregorianum* 16 (1935): 402–47.

[**1937**]. *Cardinal Newman's Theses de fide and His Proposed Introduction to the French Translation of the University Sermons*. Introduced and edited by Henry Tristram. *Gregorianum* 18 (1937): 219–60.

[**1956**]. *Autobiographical Writings*. Edited by Henry Tristram. New York: Sheed and Ward, 1956.

[**1956**]. *Faith and Prejudice and Other Unpublished Sermons of Cardinal Newman*. Edited by The Birmingham Oratory. New York: Sheed and Ward, 1956.

[**1958**]. *An Unpublished Paper by Cardinal Newman on the Development of Doctrine*. Edited by Hugo M. de Achával, SJ. *Gregorianum* 39 (1958): 585–96.

[**1969; 1970**]. *The Philosophical Notebook of John Henry Newman*. Edited at the Birmingham Oratory by Edward Sillem. *Vol. I: General Introduction to the Study of Newman's Philosophy*. Louvain: Nauwelaerts Publishing House, 1969; *The Philosophical Notebook of John Henry Newman*. Edited at the Birmingham Oratory by Edward Sillem and Revised by A. J. Boekraad. *Vol. II: The Text.* Louvain: Nauwelaerts Publishing House, 1970.

[1976]. *The Theological Papers of John Henry Newman on Faith and Certainty.* Edited by Hugo M. de Achaval and J. Derek Holmes. Oxford: Clarendon Press, 1976.

[1979]. *The Theological Papers of John Henry Newman on Biblical Inspiration and on Infallibility.* Edited by J. Derek Holmes. Oxford: Clarendon Press, 1979.

Biographies of Newman

Bouyer, Louis, CO. *Newman, His Life and Spirituality.* London: Burnes, Oates, and Washbourne Ltd., 1958.

Dessain, Charles Stephen. *John Henry Newman.* London: Nelson Co., 1967.

Ker, Ian. *John Henry Newman: A Biography.* Oxford: Oxford University Press, 1988 (second edition, 2009).

Short, Edward. *Newman and His Contemporaries.* New York: T and T Clark International, 2011.

Tristram, Henry. *Newman and His Friends.* London: John Lane, 1933.

Ward, Maisie. *Young Mr. Newman.* London: Sheed and Ward, 1948.

Ward, Wilfrid. *Ten Personal Studies.* New York: Longmans, Green, and Co., 1908.

———. *The Life of John Henry Cardinal Newman Based on His Private Journals and Correspondence.* 2 vols. London: Longmans, Green, and Co., 1912.

Zeno, Dr., OFM Cap. *John Henry Newman. His Inner Life.* San Francisco, Calif.: Ignatius Press, 1987.

Works on John Henry Newman

Aquino, Frederick D. *Communities of Informed Judgment: Newman's Illative Sense and Accounts of Rationality.* Washington, D.C.: The Catholic University of America Press, 2004.

———. *An Integrative Habit of Mind: John Henry Newman on the Path to Wisdom.* DeKalb: Northern Illinois University Press, 2012.

Aquino, Frederick D., and Benjamin J. King, eds. *Receptions of Newman.* Oxford: Oxford University Press, 2015.

———, eds. *The Oxford Handbook of John Henry Newman.* Oxford: Oxford University Press, 2018.

Barr, Colin. *Paul Cullen, John Henry Newman, and the Catholic University of Ireland, 1854–1864.* Notre Dame, Ind.: University of Notre Dame Press, 2011.

Bastable, James D., ed. *Newman and Gladstone: Centennial Essays.* Dublin: Veritas Publications, 1978.

Benard, Edmond Darvil. *A Preface to Newman's Theology.* St. Louis, Mo.: Herder, 1945.

Biemer, Günther. *Newman on Tradition.* Translated and edited by Kevin Smyth. London: Burns and Oates, 1967.

Bilotta, Salvatore. *Sapienza e teologia. Tommaso d'Aquino e J. H. Newman a confrontato.* Assisi: Cittadella Editrice, 2016.

Blum, Christopher O. "The Historian and His Tools in the Workshop of Wisdom." *Logos* 13, no. 4 (2010): 15–34.

Boekraad, Adrian J. *The Personal Conquest of Truth According to J. H. Newman.* Louvain: Éditions Nauwelaerts, 1955.

Boekraad, Adrian J., and Henry Tristram. *The Argument from Conscience to the Existence of God according to J. H. Newman.* Louvain: Éditions Nauwelaerts, 1961.

Bouyer, Louis, CO. *Newman's Vision of Faith: A Theology for Times of General Apostasy.* San Francisco, Calif.: Ignatius Press, 1986.

Brickel, A. G., SJ. "Cardinal Newman's Theory of Knowledge." *American Catholic Quarterly Review* 43 (1918): 507–18 and 645–53.

Briel, Don J. *The University and the Church: Don J. Briel's Essays on Education.* Edited with an introduction by R. Jared Staudt. Providence, R.I.: Cluny Media, 2019.

Chadwick, Owen. *From Bossuet to Newman: The Idea of Doctrinal Development.* Cambridge: Cambridge University Press, 1957.

Chadwick, Owen, ed. *The Mind of the Oxford Movement.* London: A and C Black, 1960.

Church, R. W. *The Oxford Movement: Twelve Years 1833–1845.* London: Macmillan and Co., 1892.

Connolly, John R. "Newman on Human Faith and Divine Faith: Clarifying Some Ambiguities." *Horizons* 23, no. 2 (1996): 261–80.

———. *John Henry Newman: A View of Catholic Faith for the New Millennium.* New York: Sheed and Ward, 2005.

Connolly, John R., and Brian W. Hughes. *Newman and Life in the Spirit: Theological Reflections on Spirituality for Today.* Minneapolis, Minn.: Fortress Press, 2014.

Cronin, John Francis. *Cardinal Newman: His Theory of Knowledge.* Washington, D.C.: The Catholic University of America Press, 1935.

Crosby, John F. "A 'Primer of Infidelity' Based on Newman? A Study of Newman's Rhetorical Strategy." *Newman Studies Journal* 8, no. 1 (2011): 6–19.

———. *The Personalism of John Henry Newman.* Washington, D.C.: The Catholic University of America Press, 2014.

Culler, A. Dwight. *The Imperial Intellect: A Study of Cardinal Newman's Educational Ideal.* New Haven, Conn.: Yale University Press, 1955.

D'Arcy, M. C., SJ. *The Nature of Belief.* Dublin / London: Clonmore and Reynolds / Burns, Oates, and Washbourne, 1958.

Davis, H. Francis. "Newman and Thomism." In *Newman-Studien: Dritte Folge,* edited by Heinrich Fries and Werner Becker, 157–69. Nürnberg: Glock und Lutz, 1957.

Delio, David P. *'An Aristocracy of Exalted Spirits:' The Idea of the Church in Newman's Tamworth Reading Room.* Leominster: Gracewing, 2016.

Duffy, Eamon. *John Henry Newman: A Very Brief History.* London: SPCK, 2019.

Dulles, Avery Cardinal, SJ. *John Henry Newman.* London: Continuum, 2002.

Evans, G. R. "Newman and Aquinas on Assent." *The Journal of Religious Studies, New Series* 30, no. 1 (1979): 202–11.

Fey, William R., OFM Cap. *Faith and Doubt: The Unfolding of Newman's Thought on Certainty*. Preface by Charles Stephen Dessain. Shepherdstown, W.Va.: Patmos Press, 1976.

Flanagan, Philip. *Newman, Faith and the Believer*. London: Sands and Co., 1946.

Gilley, Sheridan. *Newman and His Age*. London: Darton, Longman and Todd, 1990 (revised edition, 2003).

Gilson, Etienne. "Introduction." In John Henry Cardinal Newman, *An Essay in Aid of a Grammar of Assent*, 9–21. New York: Image Books, 1955.

Gladen, Karl. *Die Erkenntnisphilosophie J. H. Newmans im Lichte der thomistischen Erkenntnislehre beurteilt*. Paderborn: Jungfermannsche Buchdruckerei, 1933.

Harrold, Charles Frederick. *John Henry Newman: An Exposition and Critical Study of His Mind, Thought, and Art*. London: Longmans, Green, and Co., 1945.

Hughes, Gerard J. "Conscience." In *The Cambridge Companion to John Henry Newman*, edited by Ian Ker and Terrence Merrigan, 189–220. Cambridge: Cambridge University Press, 2009.

Jaki, Stanley, L. *Newman's Challenge*. Grand Rapids, Mich.: Eerdmans, 2000.

Juergens, Sylvester P. *Newman on the Psychology of Faith in the Individual*. New York: Macmillan, 1928.

Karl, Alfons. *Die Glaubensphilosophie Newmans. Ein Beitrag zur Geschichte und Methodologie der modernen Glaubensbegründung*. Bonn: Peter Hanstein Verlagsbuchhandlung, 1941.

Ker, Ian. "Editor's Introduction." In John Henry Newman, *The Idea of a University Defined and Illustrated. I. In Nine Discourses Delivered to the Catholics of Dublin. II. In Occasional Lectures and Essays Addressed to the Members of the Catholic Church*. Edited with introduction and notes by I. T. Ker, xi–lxxxv. Oxford: Clarendon Press, 1976.

———. *The Achievement of John Henry Newman*. Notre Dame, Ind.: University of Notre Dame Press, 1990.

———. *Newman and the Fullness of Christianity*. Edinburgh: T and T Clark, 1993.

———. *Newman on Vatican II*. Oxford: Oxford University Press, 2014.

Ker, Ian, and Terrence Merrigan, eds. *The Cambridge Companion to John Henry Newman*. Cambridge: Cambridge University Press, 2009.

Koritensky, Andreas. *John Henry Newmans Theorie der religiösen Erkenntnis*. Stuttgart: Kohlhammer, 2011.

Lyons, James W. *Newman's Dialogues on Certitude*. Rome: Officium Libri Catholici, 1978.

Marr, Ryan J. *To Be Perfect Is to Have Changed Often: The Development of John Henry Newman's Ecclesiological Outlook, 1845–1877*. Lanham, Md.: Rowman and Littlefield, 2018.

McGrath, Fergal, SJ. *Newman's University: Idea and Reality*. London: Longmans, Green, and Co., 1951.

———. *The Consecration of Learning: Lectures on Newman's "Idea of a University."* New York: Fordham University Press, 1962.

McGrath, Francis. *John Henry Newman: Universal Revelation*. Macon, Ga.: Mercer University Press, 1997.

Merrigan, Terrence. *Clear Heads and Holy Hearts: The Religious and Theological Ideal of John Henry Newman*. Louvain: Peeters Press, 1991.

———. "Revelation." In *The Cambridge Companion to John Henry Newman*, edited by Ian Ker and Terrence Merrigan, 47–72. Cambridge: Cambridge University Press, 2009.

———. "Conscience and Selfhood: Thomas More, John Henry Newman, and the Crisis of the Postmodern Subject." *Theological Studies* 73 (2012): 841–69.

Meszaros, Andrew. "The Influence of Aristotelian Rhetoric on J. H. Newman's Epistemology." *Journal for the History of Modern Theology* 21, no. 1 (2014): 192–225.

———. *The Prophetic Church: History and Doctrinal Development in John Henry Newman and Yves Congar*. Oxford: Oxford University Press, 2016.

———. "Some Neo-Scholastic Receptions of Newman on Doctrinal Development." *Gregorianum* 97, no. 1 (2016): 123–50.

———. "Newman and First Principles: The Noetic Dimension of the Illative Sense." *Heythrop Journal* 59 (2018): 770–82.

Middleton, Robert D. *Newman at Oxford: His Religious Development*. Oxford: Oxford University Press, 1950.

Morerod, Charles, OP. "Conscience according to John Henry Newman." *Nova et Vetera* (English edition) 11, no. 4 (2013): 1057–79.

Nichols, Aidan, OP. "John Henry Newman and the Illative Sense: A Re-Consideration." *Scottish Journal of Theology* 38, no. 3 (1985): 347–68.

———. *From Newman to Congar: The Idea of Doctrinal Development from the Victorians to the Second Vatican Council*. Edinburgh: T and T Clark, 1990.

Norris, Thomas J. *Newman and His Theological Method*. Leiden: E. J. Brill, 1977.

O'Dwyer, Edward Thomas. *Cardinal Newman and the Encyclical "Pascendi Dominici Gregis."* London: Longmans, Green, and Co., 1908.

O'Reilly, Kevin E., OP. "God, the University, and Human Flourishing." *Nova et Vetera* (English edition) 14, no. 4 (2016): 1213–38.

Ondrako, Edward J., OFM Conv., ed. *The Newman-Scotus Reader: Contexts and Commonalities*. New Bedford, Mass.: Academy of the Immaculate, 2015.

Pattison, Robert. *The Great Dissent: John Henry Newman and the Liberal Heresy*. New York: Oxford University Press, 1991.

Przywara, Erich, SJ. *Einführung im Newmans Wesen und Werk*. Freiburg im Breisgau: Herder, 1922.

———. "Newman—Möglicher Heiliger und Kirchenlehrer der Neuen Zeit?" In *Newman-Studien: Dritte Folge,* edited by Heinrich Fries and Werner Becker,

28–36. Nürnberg: Glock und Lutz, 1957. English translation by Christopher M. Wojtulewicz. "Newman: Saint and Modern Doctor of the Church?" *Church Life Journal: A Journal of the McGrath Institute of Church Life*, October 11, 2019; https://churchlifejournal.nd.edu/articles/newman-possible-saint-and-modern-doctor-of-the-church/

Richardson, Laurence. *Newman's Approach to Knowledge*. Leominster: Gracewing, 2007.

Rickaby, Joseph, SJ. *Index to the Works of John Henry Cardinal Newman*. London: Longmans, Green, and Co., 1914.

Shea, C. Michael. C. "From Implicit and Explicit Reason to Inference and Assent: The Significance of John Henry Newman's Seminary Studies in Rome." *The Journal of Theological Studies* 67, no. 1 (2016): 143–71.

———. *Newman's Early Roman Catholic Legacy 1845–1854*. Oxford: Oxford University Press, 2017.

Shea, C. Michael, and Robert J. Porwoll. "Newman's *Theses de Fide*: A New Edition, Translation, and Commentary." *Newman Studies Journal* 14, no. 1 (2017): 16–45.

Shrimpton, Paul. *The 'Making of Men': The Idea and Reality of Newman's University in Oxford and Dublin*. Leominster: Gracewing, 2014.

Tillman, Mary Katherine. *John Henry Newman: Man of Letters*. Milwaukee, Wis.: Marquette University Press, 2015.

Tolksdorf, Wilhelm. *Analysis fidei: John Henry Newmans Beitrag zur Entdeckung des Subjektes beim Glaubensakt im theologiegeschichtlichen Kontext*. New York: Peter Lang, 2000.

Tristram, Henry, ed. *John Henry Newman: Centenary Essays*. London: Burns, Oates, and Washbourne, 1945.

———, ed. *The Living Thoughts of Cardinal Newman*. London: Cassell, 1948.

Walgrave, Jan H., OP. *Newman the Theologian: The Nature of Belief and Doctrine as Exemplified in His Life and Works*. Translated by A. V. Littledale. New York: Sheed and Ward, 1960.

———. *Unfolding Revelation: The Nature of Doctrinal Development*. London / Philadelphia: Hutchinson / Westminster, 1972.

———. *Selected Writings—Thematische Geschriften: Thomas Aquinas, J. H. Newman, Theologia Fundamentalis*. Edited by G. de Schrijver and J. Kelly. Leuven: Leuven University Press, 1982.

Willam, Franz Michel. "Die philosophischen Grundpositionen Newmans." In *Newman-Studien: Dritte Folge*, edited by Heinrich Fries and Werner Becker, 111–56. Nürnberg: Glock und Lutz, 1957.

———. "Aristotelische Bausteine der Entwicklungstheorie Newmans." In *Newman-Studien. Sechste Folge*, edited by Heinrich Fries and Werner Becker, 193–226. Nürnberg: Glock und Lutz, 1960.

———. *Aristotelische Erkenntnislehre bei Whately und Newman und ihre Bezüge zur Gegenwart*. Freiburg: Herder, 1960.

———. *Die Erkenntnislehre Kardinal Newmans. Systematische Darlegung und Doku-mentation.* Bergen-Enkheim: Kaffke, 1969.

Zeno, Dr., OFM Cap. *John Henry Newman, Our Way to Certitude: An Introduction to Newman's Psychological Discovery, the Illative Sense, and his Grammar of Assent.* Leiden: E. J. Brill, 1957.

Zuijtwegt, Geertjan. "Richard Whately's Influence on John Henry Newman's Oxford University Sermons on Faith and Reason (1839–1840)." *Newman Studies Journal* 10, no. 1 (2013): 82–95.

Other Works Cited

Anderson, James F. *The Bond of Being: An Essay on Analogy and Existence.* St. Louis, Mo.: Herder, 1949.

André-Vincent, Philippe-Ignace, OP. *La Liberté religieuse: Droit fondamental.* Paris: Téqui, 1976.

Aquinas, Thomas. *De veritate.* In *Sancti Thomae Aquinatis opera omnia*, vol. 22. Leoni-ne Edition. Rome: Editori di San Tommaso, 1975–76. English translation: *Truth*, vol. 1, *Questions 1–9.* Translated by Robert W. Mulligan, SJ. Indianapolis, Ind.: Hackett, 1994. *Truth*, vol. 2: *Questions 10–20.* Translated by James V. McGlynn, SJ. Indianapolis, Ind.: Hackett, 1994. *Truth*, vol. 3: *Questions 21–29.* Translated by Robert W. Schmidt, SJ. Indianapolis, Ind.: Hackett, 1994.

———. *In decem libros Ethicorum Aristotelis ad Nicomachum expositio.* Third edition. Edited by Raymund M. Spiazzi, OP. Rome: Marietti, 1964. English translation: *Commentary on Aristotle's* Nicomachean Ethics. Translated by C. J. Litzinger, OP. South Bend, Ind.: Dumb Ox Books, 1993.

———. *In duodecim libros Metaphysicorum Aristotelis expositio.* Edited by M. R. Cathala, OP, and R. M. Spiazzi, OP. Rome: Marietti, 1964. English translation: *Commentary on Aristotle's* Metaphysics. Translated by John P. Rowan. Notre Dame, Ind.: Dumb Ox Books, 1995.

———. *In librum Boetii de Trinitate expositio.* In *Opuscula Theologica*, edited by Ray-mund M. Spiazzi, OP, 2:313–89. Rome: Marietti, 1954. English translation: *Faith, Reason, and Theology: Questions I–IV of his Commentary on the* De Trinitate *of Boethius.* Translated by Armand Maurer. Toronto: Pontifical Institute of Mediaeval Studies, 1987. *The Divisions and Methods of the Sciences.* Translated by Armand Maurer. Fourth revised edition. Toronto: Pontifical Institute of Mediaeval Studies, 1986.

———. *In quattuor libros Sententiarum.* In *S. Thomae Aquinatis Opera Omnia*, vol. 1, edited by R. Busa, SJ. Stuttgart-Bad Cannstatt: Frommann, 1980.

———. *Quaestiones quodlibetales.* Edited by Raymund M. Spiazzi, OP. Rome: Mari-etti, 1949.

———. *Sentencia libri De Anima.* In *Sancti Thomae Aquinatis opera omnia*, vol. 45.1. Leonine Edition. Paris: Vrin, 1984. English translation: *Commentary on Aristotle's*

De Anima. Translated by Kenelm Foster, OP, and Sylvester Humphries, OP. New Haven, Conn.: Yale University Press, 1951.

—————. *Summa theologiae*. Third edition. Turin: Edizioni San Paolo, 1999.

—————. *Summa Theologiae*. Translated by the Fathers of the English Dominican Province. New York: Benziger Bros., 1948.

—————. *Summa theologiae*, vol. 26 *(1a2ae 81–85): Original Sin*. Translated by T. C. O'Brien, OP. Cambridge: Cambridge University Press, 2006.

—————. *Summa theologiae*, vol. 31 *(2a2ae 1–7): Faith*. Translated by T. C. O'Brien, OP. Cambridge: Cambridge University Press, 2006.

—————. *Summa theologiae*, vol. 33 *(2a2ae 17–22): Hope*. Translated by W. J. Hill, OP. Cambridge: Cambridge University Press, 2006.

Arendt, Hannah. *Eichmann in Jerusalem: A Report on the Banality of Evil*. Revised and enlarged edition. New York: Penguin, 1977.

Aristotle. *The Complete Works of Aristotle: The Revised Oxford Translation*. Edited by Jonathan Barnes. 2 vols. Princeton, N.J.: Princeton University Press, 1984.

—————. *Metaphysics. Vol. I: Books I–IX*. Translated by Hugh Tredennick. Loeb Classical Library 271. Cambridge, Mass.: Harvard University Press, 1933.

—————. *Metaphysics. Vol. II: Books X–XIV. Oeconomica. Magna Moralia*. Translated by Hugh Tredennick and C. Cyril Armstrong. Loeb Classical Library 28. Cambridge, Mass.: Harvard University Press, 1935.

—————. *Aristotelis Ethicorum Nicomacheorum libri decem*. Edited by William Wilkinson. Fourth edition. Oxford: Clarendon, 1818.

—————. *The Nicomachean Ethics of Aristotle: A New Translation, Mainly from the Text of Bekker. With Explanatory Notes*. Translated by Drummond Percy Chase. Oxford: William Graham, 1847.

—————. *Nicomachean Ethics*. Translated by H. Rackham. Loeb Classical Library 73. New York: G. P. Putnam's Sons, 1926.

Ashley, Benedict M., OP. *The Way toward Wisdom: An Interdisciplinary and Intercultural Introduction to Metaphysics*. Notre Dame, Ind.: University of Notre Dame Press, 2009.

Augustine. *The Confessions*. Translated by Maria Boulding, OSB. Hyde Park, N.Y.: New City Press, 1997.

Austriaco, Nicanor Pier Giorgio, OP. *Biomedicine and Beatitude: An Introduction to Catholic Bioethics*. Washington, D.C.: The Catholic University of America Press, 2011.

Barth, Timotheus. "Being, Univocity, and Analogy according to Duns Scotus," in *John Duns Scotus, 1265–1965*. Edited by J. K. Ryan and B. M. Bonansea, 210–62. Washington, D.C.: The Catholic University of America Press, 1965.

Beiner, Ronald. *Philosophy in a Time of Lost Spirit*. Toronto: University of Toronto Press, 1997.

Belmans, Théo G., O. Praem. "Le paradoxe de la conscience erronée d'Abélard à Karl Rahner." *Revue Thomiste* 90 (1990): 570–86.

Berger, Peter. *The Heretical Imperative: Contemporary Possibilities of Religious Affirmation*. New York: Anchor Press, 1979.

Billy, Dennis J., CSSR. "Aquinas on the Content of Synderesis," *Studia Moralia* 29 (1991): 61–83.

Bloom, Allan. *The Closing of the American Mind*. New York: Simon and Schuster, 1987.

Bonaventure. "*De reductione artium ad theologiam*." In *Seraphi Doctoris Sancti Bonaventurae Tria Opuscula ad Theologiam Spectantia Edita a PP Collegii S. Bonaventurae*, 365–85. Fifth edition. Ad Claras Aquas: Typis Collegii S. Bonaventurae, 1938.

Bourke, Vernon J. "The Background of Aquinas's Synderesis Principle." In *Graceful Reason: Essays in Ancient and Medieval Philosophy Presented to Joseph Owens, C.Ss.R.*, edited by Lloyd P. Gerson, 345–60. Toronto: Pontifical Institute of Mediaeval Studies, 1983.

Boylan, Dom Eugene, OCSO. *This Tremendous Lover*. Allen, Tex.: Christian Classics, 1987 [1947].

Butler, Joseph. *The Analogy of Religion to the Constitution and Course of Nature. Also Fifteen Sermons*. Edited by Joseph Angus. London: The Religious Tract Society, 1855.

Calvin, John. *Institutes of the Christian Religion*. Edited by John T. McNeill. Translated by Ford Lewis Battles. Louisville, Ky.: Westminster John Knox Press, 1960.

Cano, Melchor, OP. *De locis theologicis*. Translated by Juan Belda Plans. Madrid: Biblioteca de Autores Cristianos, 2006.

Cessario, Romanus, OP. *Christian Faith and the Theological Life*. Washington, D.C.: The Catholic University of America Press, 1996.

Chenu, Marie-Dominique, OP. "Pro supernaturalitate fidei illustrando." In *Xenia Thomistica*, edited by Sadoc Szabo, 3:297–307. Rome: Polyglottis Vaticanis, 1925.

Cleve, Thomas Curtis van. *The Emperor Frederick II von Hohenstaufen: Immutator Mundi*. Oxford: Oxford University Press, 1972.

Cross, Richard. "'Where Angels Fear to Tread:' Duns Scotus and Radical Orthodoxy." *Antonianum* 76 (2001): 7–41.

Crowe, Michael Bertram. "Synderesis and the Notion of Law in Saint Thomas." In *L'homme et son destin d'après les penseurs du moyen âge*, Actes du Premier Congrès International de Philosophie Médiévale 1958, 601–9. Louvain: Éditions Nauwelaerts, 1960.

Curran, Charles. *Catholic Moral Theology in Dialogue*. Notre Dame, Ind.: Fides Publications, 1972.

Davies, Michael. *The Second Vatican Council and Religious Liberty*. Long Prairie, Minn.: Neumann Press, 1992.

Dawkins, Richard. *The God Delusion*. New York: Houghton, 2006.

———. *The Selfish Gene*. Oxford: Oxford University Press, 2006 [1976].

D'Costa, Gavin. *Vatican II: Catholic Doctrines on Jews and Muslims*. Oxford: Oxford University Press, 2014.

D'Ettore, Domenic. *Analogy after Aquinas: Logical Problems, Thomistic Answers*. Washington, D.C.: The Catholic University of America Press, 2019.

Dennett, Daniel C. *Breaking the Spell: Religion as a Natural Phenomenon*. New York: Viking, 2006.

Dewan, Lawrence, OP. *Form and Being: Studies in Thomistic Metaphysics*. Washington, D.C.: The Catholic University of America Press, 2006.

———. "'Objectum': Notes on the Invention of a Word." In Lawrence Dewan, OP, *Wisdom, Law, and Virtue: Essays in Thomistic Ethics*, 403–43. New York: Fordham University Press, 2007.

Dostoevsky, Fyodor. *Demons*. Translated by Robert A. Maguire. New York: Penguin Classics, 2008.

Duffin, Jacalyn. *Medical Miracles: Doctors, Saints, and Healing in the Modern World*. New York: Oxford University Press, 2007.

Dulles, Avery Cardinal, SJ. *The Assurance of Things Hoped For: A Theology of Faith*. New York: Oxford University Press, 1997.

———. "Development or Reversal?" *First Things* (October 2005): 53–61.

———. "*Dignitatis Humanae* and the Development of Catholic Doctrine." In *Catholicism and Religious Freedom: Contemporary Reflections on Vatican II's Declaration on Religious Liberty*, edited by Kenneth L. Grasso and Robert P. Hunt, 43–67. Lanham, Md.: Rowman and Littlefield, 2006.

Earman, John. *Hume's Abject Failure: The Argument Against Miracles*. New York: Oxford University Press, 2000.

Fabro, Cornelio. *God in Exile: Modern Atheism from Its Roots in the Cartesian Cogito to the Present Day*. Edited and translated by Arthur Gibson. Westminster, Md.: Newman Press, 1968.

Feser, Edward. *The Last Superstition: A Refutation of the New Atheism*. South Bend, Ind.: St. Augustine's Press, 2008.

———. "Kripke, Ross, and the Immaterial Aspect of Thought," *American Catholic Philosophical Quarterly* 87, no. 1 (2013): 1–32.

Fichte, Johann G. *The Purpose of Higher Education: Also Known as the Vocation of the Scholar* [1794]. Translated by John K. Bramann. Mt. Savage, Md.: Nightsun Books, 1988.

———. *System der Sittenlehre* [1798]. In his *Werke* IV. Berlin: de Gruyter, 1971.

Gardeil, Ambroise, OP. *Le Donné revélé et la théologie*. Second edition. Paris: Cerf, 1932.

Garreau, Joel. *Radical Evolution: The Promise and Peril of Enhancing Our Minds, Our Bodies—and What It Means to Be Human*. New York: Broadway Books, 2005.

Garrigou-Lagrange, Reginald, OP. *The Theological Virtues. Volume One: On Faith. A Commentary on St. Thomas' Theological Summa I^{a}II^{ae}, qq. 62, 65, 68: II^{a}II^{ae}, qq. 1–16*. Translated by Thomas a Kempis Reilly, OP. St. Louis, Mo.: Herder, 1965.

Garvey, John. "Intellect and Virtue: The Idea of a Catholic University." *Catholic University Law Review* 60, no. 3 (2011): 563–73.

Gillespie, Michael Allen. *Nihilism before Nietzsche*. Chicago: University of Chicago Press, 1995.

Gladstone, William Ewart. *The Vatican Decrees in Their Bearing on Civil Allegiance: A Political Expostulation*. London: John Murray, 1874.

Gloede, Günter. *Theologia naturalis bei Calvin*. Stuttgart: Kohlhammer, 1935.

Gregory, Brad S. *The Unintended Reformation: How a Religious Revolution Secularized Society*. Cambridge, Mass.: The Belknap Press of Harvard University Press, 2012.

Habermas, Jürgen. *The Future of Human Nature*. Translated by William Rehg, Max Pensky, and Hella Beister. Cambridge: Polity Press, 2003.

Hain, Raymond F., IV. "Practical Virtues: Instrumental Practical Reason and the Virtues." PhD diss., University of Notre Dame, 2009.

———. "Consilium and the Foundations of Ethics." *The Thomist* 79, no. 1 (2015): 43–74.

Harris, Sam. *The End of Faith: Religion, Terror, and the Future of Reason*. New York: Norton, 2004.

Hart, David Bentley. *Atheist Delusions: The Christian Revolution and Its Fashionable Enemies*. New Haven, Conn.: Yale University Press, 2010.

Healy, Nicholas J., Jr. "Dignitatis Humanae." In *The Reception of Vatican II*, edited by Matthew L. Lamb and Matthew Levering, 367–92. New York: Oxford University Press, 2017.

Hegel, Georg Wilhelm Friedrich. *Hegel's Philosophy of Right*. Translated by T. M. Knox. Oxford: Clarendon Press, 1942.

Heidegger, Martin. *Identity and Difference*. Translated by Joan Stambaugh. New York: Harper and Row, 1969.

———. "The Self-Assertion of the German University" [1933]. Translated by Karsten Harries. *Review of Metaphysics* 38 (1985): 467–502.

Hitchens, Christopher. *God Is Not Great: How Religion Poisons Everything*. New York: Twelve, 2007.

Hittinger, F. Russell. "The Declaration on Religious Freedom, *Dignitatis Humanae*." In *Vatican II: Renewal Within Tradition*, edited by Matthew L. Lamb and Matthew Levering, 359–82. New York: Oxford University Press, 2008.

Hobbes, Thomas. *De cive: On the Citizen*. Edited by Richard Tuck and Michael Silverthorne. Cambridge: Cambridge University Press, 1998.

Hochschild, Joshua P. *The Semantics of Analogy: Rereading Cajetan's* De Nominum Analogia. Notre Dame, Ind.: University of Notre Dame Press, 2010.

Honnefelder, Ludger. *Ens inquantum ens: Der Begriff des Seienden als solchen als Gegenstand der Metaphysik nach der Lehre des Johannes Duns Scotus*. Münster: Aschendorff, 1979.

Horkheimer, Max, and Theodor W. Adorno. *Dialectic of Enlightenment: Philosophical Fragments*. Edited by Gunzelin Schmid Noerr. Translated by Edmund Jephcott. Palo Alto, Calif.: Stanford University Press, 2007.

Houston, Joseph. *Reported Miracles: A Critique of Hume*. Cambridge: Cambridge University Press, 1994.

Howard, Thomas Albert. *Protestant Theology and the Making of the Modern German University*. New York: Oxford University Press, 2006.

Hudson, William Donald, ed. *The Is-Ought Question*. London: Macmillan, 1969.

Hume, David. *A Treatise of Human Nature* [1738–40]. Edited by David Fate Norton and Mary J. Norton. Oxford: Oxford University Press, 2000.

———. *An Enquiry Concerning Human Understanding* [1748]. Edited by Stephen Buckle. Cambridge: Cambridge University Press, 2007.

Husserl, Edmund. *Erste Philosophie,* vol. 1: *Kritische Ideengeschichte*. Husserliana 7. Edited by R. Boehm. The Hague: M. Nijhoff, 1956.

———. *Erste Philosophie*, vol. 2: *Theorie der phänomenologischen Reduktion*. Husserliana 8. Edited by R. Boehm. The Hague: M. Nijhoff, 1959.

———. *The Crisis of European Sciences and Transcendental Phenomenology*. Translated by David Carr. Evanston, Ill.: Northwestern University Press, 1970.

Hütter, Reinhard. *Dust Bound for Heaven: Explorations in the Theology of Thomas Aquinas*. Grand Rapids, Mich.: Eerdmans, 2012.

———. *Bound for Beatitude: A Thomistic Study in Eschatology and Ethics*. Washington, D.C.: The Catholic University of America Press, 2019.

———. *Aquinas on Transubstantiation: The Real Presence of Christ in the Eucharist*. Washington, D.C.: The Catholic University of America Press, 2019.

John of Damascus. *An Exact Exposition of the Orthodox Faith* (*De fide orthodoxa*). In his *Writings*, translated by Frederick H. Chase, Jr., 165–406. New York: Fathers of the Church, Inc., 1958.

Johnson, David. *Hume, Holism, and Miracles*. Ithaca, N.Y.: Cornell University Press, 1999.

Jonas, Hans. *The Imperative of Responsibility: In Search of an Ethics for the Technological Age*. Chicago: University of Chicago Press, 1984.

Journet, Charles. *What Is Dogma?* Translated by Dom Mark Pontifex. London: Burns and Oates, 1964.

Kampowski, Stephan. *A Greater Freedom: Biotechnology, Love, and Human Destiny*. Eugene, Ore.: Pickwick Publications, 2012.

Kant, Immanuel. "An Answer to the Question: 'What Is Enlightenment?'" [1784]. In his *Political Writings*, edited by Hans Reiss, translated by H. B. Nisbet, 54–60. Second edition. Cambridge: Cambridge University Press, 1991.

———. *The Metaphysics of Morals* [1785]. Edited and translated by Mary Gregory. Cambridge: Cambridge University Press, 1996.

———. *Religion within the Boundaries of Mere Reason* [1793]. In his *Religion within the Boundaries of Mere Reason and Other Writings*, translated and edited by Allen Wood and George di Giovanni, 31–192. Cambridge: Cambridge University Press, 1998.

———. *The Conflict of the Faculties* [1798]. Translated by Mary J. Gregor. New York: Abaris Books, 1979.

———. *Opus postumum*. Edited by Eckart Förster. Translated by Eckart Förster and Michael Rosen. Cambridge: Cambridge University Press, 1993.

Kass, Leon R. *Life, Liberty, and the Defense of Dignity: The Challenge for Bioethics.* San Francisco, Calif.: Encounter Books, 2002.

Keener, Craig S. *Miracles: The Credibility of the New Testament Accounts.* Grand Rapids, Mich.: Baker Academic, 2011.

Klempa, William. "John Calvin on Natural Law." In *John Calvin and the Church: A Prism of Reform*, edited by Timothy George, 72–95. Louisville, Ky.: Westminster/ John Knox, 1990.

Kleutgen, Joseph, SJ. *Die Theologie der Vorzeit.* 4 vols. Münster: Theissigsche Buch- handlung, 1853–70 (second edition, 1867–74).

———. *Die Philosophie der Vorzeit.* 2 vols. First edition. Münster: Theissigsche Buch- handlung, 1860–63 (second edition, 1878).

———. *Pre-Modern Philosophy Defended.* Translated by William H. Marshner. South Bend, Ind.: St. Augustine's Press, 2019.

Klubertanz, George P., SJ. *The Philosophy of Human Nature.* New York: Appleton- Century-Crofts, Inc., 1953.

Körner, Bernhard. *Melchior Cano, De locis theologicis: Ein Beitrag zur theologischen Erkenntnislehre.* Graz: Styria-Medienservice, 1994.

———. *Orte des Glaubens—loci theologici: Studien zur theologischen Erkenntnislehre.* Würzburg: Echter, 2014.

Kretzmann, Norman. "LEX INIUSTA NON EST LEX: Laws on Trial in Aquinas' 'Court of Conscience.'" *American Journal of Jurisprudence* 33 (1988): 99–122.

Kurzweil, Ray. *The Singularity Is Near: When Humans Transcend Biology.* New York: Penguin, 2005.

Legaspi, Michael. *The Death of Scripture and the Rise of Biblical Studies.* New York: Oxford University Press, 2010.

Lefebvre, Marcel. *Religious Liberty Questioned.* Kansas City, Mo.: Angelus Press, 2002.

Lichacz, Piotr. "Did St. Thomas Aquinas Justify the Transition from 'Is' to 'Ought'?" STD diss., University of Fribourg (Switzerland), 2008.

Livius, Titus (Livy). *The Early History of Rome.* Translated by Aubrey de Sélingcourt. London: Penguin Classics, 2002.

Locke, John. *An Essay Concerning Human Understanding.* Edited with an introduction by Peter H. Niddich. Oxford: Clarendon Press, 1975.

Lonergan, Bernard. *Verbum: Word and Idea in Aquinas.* Edited by Frederick E. Crowe and Robert M. Doran (Collected Works of Bernard Lonergan 2). Toronto: Uni- versity of Toronto Press, 1997.

———. *Insight: A Study of Human Understanding.* Edited by Frederick E. Crowe and Robert M. Doran (Collected Works of Bernard Lonergan 3). Toronto: University of Toronto Press, 1992.

Long, Steven A. *Analogia Entis, Metaphysics, and the Act of Faith*. Notre Dame, Ind.: University of Notre Dame Press, 2011.

———. "The Gifts of the Holy Spirit and Their Indispensability for the Christian Moral Life: Grace as *Motus*." *Nova et Vetera* (English edition) 11, no. 2 (2013): 357–73.

Lottin, Odon D. "Syndérèse et conscience aux xiie et xiiie siècles." In *Problèmes de morale*, 2.1:101–349. Louvain: Abbaye de Mont César, 1948.

Luther, Martin. "Disputatio contram scholasticam theologiam (Disputation against Scholastic Theology)" [1517]. In his *D. Martin Luthers Werke. Kritische Gesamtausgabe*, 7:224–28. Weimar: Hermann Böhlau und Nachfolger, 1883–2009.

———. "Großer Katechismus (Large Catechism)" [1529]. In his *D. Martin Luthers Werke: Kritische Gesamtausgabe*, 30.1:125–238. Weimar: Hermann Böhlau und Nachfolger, 1883–2009.

———. *In epistolam S. Pauli ad Galatas Commentarius* (*Lectures on Galatians*) [1535]. In his *D. Martin Luthers Werke: Kritische Gesamtausgabe*, vol. 40. Weimar: Hermann Böhlau und Nachfolger, 1883–2009.

MacDonald, Paul A., Jr. *Knowledge and the Transcendent: An Inquiry into the Mind's Relationship to God*. Washington, D.C.: The Catholic University of America Press, 2009.

MacIntyre, Alasdair. "The Intelligibility of Action." In *Rationality, Relativism, and Human Sciences*, edited by J. Margolis, M. Krausz, and R. M. Burian, 63–80. Dordrecht: Nijhoff, 1986.

———. *Three Rival Versions of Moral Enquiry: Encyclopaedia, Genealogy, and Tradition*. Notre Dame, Ind.: University of Notre Dame Press, 1990.

———. "The End of Education: The Fragmentation of the American University." *Commonweal* 133, no. 18 (October 20, 2006): 10–14.

———. *God, Philosophy, Universities: A Selective History of the Catholic Philosophical Tradition*. Lanham, Md.: Rowman and Littlefield, 2009.

———. "The Very Idea of a University: Aristotle, Newman, and Us." *British Journal of Educational Studies* 57, no. 4 (2009): 347–62.

Madden, James D. *Mind, Matter, and Nature: A Thomistic Proposal for the Philosophy of Mind*. Washington, D.C.: The Catholic University of America Press, 2013.

Mahoney, John, SJ. *The Making of Moral Theology: A Study of the Roman Catholic Tradition*. Oxford: Oxford University Press, 1987.

Marín-Sola, Francisco, OP. *The Homogeneous Evolution of Catholic Dogma*. Translated by Antonio T. Piñon. Manila: Santo Tomas University Press, 1988. French version: *L'Évolution homogène du dogme catholique*. 2 vols. Fribourg: Saint-Paul, 1924. Spanish edition: *La evolución homogénea del dogma católico*. Madrid: Biblioteca de Autores Cristianos, 1952 (second edition, 1963).

Marion, Jean-Luc. *God without Being: Hors-Texte*. Translated by Thomas A. Carlson. Chicago: University of Chicago Press, 1991.

Maritain, Jacques. *Distinguish to Unite or The Degrees of Knowledge*. Translated by
Gerald B. Phelan. New York: Charles Scribner's Sons, 1959.

———. *On the Church of Christ: The Person of the Church and Her Personnel*. Translated by Joseph W. Evans. Notre Dame, Ind.: University of Notre Dame Press, 1973.

McCormick, Richard A. *The Critical Calling*. Washington, D.C.: Georgetown University Press, 1989.

McDowell, John. *Mind and World*. Cambridge, Mass.: Harvard University Press, 1994.

———. "Knowledge by Hearsay." In *Meaning, Knowledge, and Reality*, 414–44. Cambridge, Mass.: Harvard University Press, 1998.

McInerny, Ralph. "Prudence and Conscience." *The Thomist* 38 (1974): 291–305.

———. *Aquinas and Analogy*. Washington, D.C.: The Catholic University of America
Press, 1996.

———. "Conscience and the Object of the Moral Act." In *Crisis of Conscience: Philosophers and Theologians Analyze Our Growing Inability to Discern Right from Wrong*,
edited by John M. Haas, 93–110. New York: Crossroad, 1996.

McKibben, Bill. *Falter: Has the Human Game Begun to Play Itself Out?* New York:
Henry Holt and Co., 2019.

Melanchthon, Philip. *Commentarius de anima*. Wittenberg, 1540.

Meyer, Harding. "Ecumenical Consensus: Our Quest For and the Emerging Structures
of Consensus." *Gregorianum* 77 (1996): 213–25.

———. "Die Prägung einer Formel: Ursprung und Intention." In *Einheit - Aber Wie?
Zur Tragfähigkeit der ökumenischen Formel vom "differenzierten Konsens,"* edited by
Harald Wagner, 36–58. Freiburg: Herder, 2000.

Michaelis, Johann David. *Raisonnement über die protestantischen Universitäten in
Deutschland*. 4 vols. Frankfurt, 1768–76.

Mill, John Stuart. *On Liberty and Other Essays*. Edited by Jonathan Gray. Oxford:
Oxford University Press, 1991.

Montagnes, Bernard, OP. *The Doctrine of the Analogy of Being according to Thomas
Aquinas*. Translated by E. M. Macierowsky. Milwaukee, Wis.: Marquette University Press, 2004.

Moore, G. E. *Principia Ethica*. Cambridge: Cambridge University Press, 1903.

Mulhall, Stephen. *The Great Riddle: Wittgenstein and Nonsense, Theology and Philosophy*. Oxford: Oxford University Press, 2016.

Naam, Ramez. *More Than Human: Embracing the Promise of Biological Enhancement*.
New York: Broadway, 2005.

Nietzsche, Friedrich. *The Anti-Christ, Ecce Homo, Twilight of the Idols and Other Writings*. Edited by Aaron Ridley and Judith Norman. Translated by Judith Norman.
Cambridge: Cambridge University Press, 2005.

———. *Ecce Homo*. Edited and translated by Walter Kaufmann. New York: Vintage
Books, 1989.

———. *On the Future of Our Educational Institutions*. Translated by J. M. Kennedy.
Edinburgh: T. N. Foulis, 1910.

————. *On the Genealogy of Morals*. Translated by Walter Kaufmann and R. J. Hollingdale. New York: Vintage Books, 1989.

————. *The Will to Power*. Translated by Walter Kaufmann and R. J. Hollingdale. New York: Vintage Books, 1968.

Noonan, John T. *A Church That Can and Cannot Change: The Development of Catholic Moral Teaching*. Notre Dame, Ind.: University of Notre Dame Press, 2005.

O'Brien, T. C., OP. "Appendix 1: Objects and Virtues." In St. Thomas Aquinas, *Summa theologiae*, vol. 31: *Faith (2a2ae 1–7)*, translated by T. C. O'Brien, 178–85. Cambridge: Cambridge University Press, 2006.

O'Reilly, Kevin E., OP. "The Church as the Defender of Conscience in Our Age." *Nova et Vetera* (English edition) 12, no. 1 (2014): 193–215.

Page, Carl. *Philosophical Historicism and the Betrayal of First Philosophy*. University Park: Pennsylvania State University Press, 1995.

Patrologiae Cursus Completus: Series Latina. Edited by J.-P. Migne. Paris: Garnier Frères, 1958.

Pfau, Thomas. "Rethinking the Image, With Some Reflections on G. M. Hopkins." *The Yearbook of Comparative Literature* 57 (2011): 30–60.

————. *Minding the Modern: Human Agency, Intellectual Traditions, and Responsible Knowledge*. Notre Dame, Ind.: University of Notre Dame Press, 2015.

Pieper, Josef. *Happiness and Contemplation*. Translated by Richard and Clara Winston. South Bend, Ind.: St. Augustine's Press, 1998.

————. *Leisure, The Basis of Culture*. Translated by Gerald Malsbary. South Bend, Ind.: St. Augustine's Press, 1998.

Pinckaers, Servais, OP. *The Sources of Christian Ethics*. Translated by Sr. Mary Thomas Noble, OP. Washington, D.C.: The Catholic University of America Press, 1995.

————. "Conscience, Truth, and Prudence." In *Crisis of Conscience: Philosophers and Theologians Analyze Our Growing Inability to Discern Right from Wrong*, edited by John M. Haas, 79–92. New York: Crossroad, 1996.

————. *Morality: The Catholic View*. Translated by Michael Sherwin, OP. South Bend, Ind.: St. Augustine's Press, 2001.

Pink, Thomas. "Conscience and Coercion," *First Things* (August/September 2012): 45–51.

Plantinga, Alvin. *Where the Conflict Really Lies: Science, Religion, and Naturalism*. New York: Oxford University Press, 2011.

Polansky, Ronald. *Aristotle's "De anima."* Cambridge: Cambridge University Press, 2007.

Polanyi, Michael. *Personal Knowledge: Toward a Post-Critical Philosophy*. Chicago: University of Chicago Press, 1974.

Possenti, Vittorio. *Nihilism and Metaphysics: The Third Voyage*. Translated by Daniel B. Gallagher. Albany: State University of New York Press, 2014.

Postman, Neil. *Amusing Ourselves to Death: Public Discourse in the Age of Show Business*. New York: Penguin, 1985.

Rahner, Karl. "Anonymous and Explicit Faith." In his *Theological Investigations*, vol. 16: *Experience of the Spirit, Source of Theology*, translated by David Moreland, 52–59. New York: Seabury/Crossroad, 1979.

———. "Faith between Rationality and Emotion." In his *Theological Investigations*, vol. 16: *Experience of the Spirit, Source of Theology*, translated by David Moreland, 60–78. New York: Crossroad, 1979.

———. "Vom irrenden Gewissen." *Orientierung* 48 (1983): 246B–250A.

———. "The Act of Faith and the Content of Faith." In his *Theological Investigations*, vol. 21: *Science and Christian Faith*, translated by Hugh M. Riley, 151–61. New York: Crossroad, 1988.

Ratzinger, Joseph Cardinal (Pope Benedict XVI). *On Conscience: Two Essays by Joseph Ratzinger*. San Francisco, Calif.: Ignatius Press, 2007.

Reichenbach, Hans. *Experience and Prediction: An Analysis of the Foundations and the Structure of Knowledge*. Chicago: University of Chicago Press, 1938.

Reiner, H. "Gewissen." In *Historisches Wörterbuch der Philosophie*, vol. 3: *G–H*, edited by Joachim Ritter, K. Gründer, and G. Gabriel, 574–92. Stuttgart: Schwabe and Co., 1974.

Renz, Oskar. *Die Synteresis nach dem Hl. Thomas von Aquin*. Münster: Aschendorff, 1911.

Rhonheimer, Martin. "Benedict XVI's 'Hermeneutic of Reform' and Religious Freedom." In his *The Common Good of Constitutional Democracy: Essays in Political Philosophy and on Catholic Social Teaching*, edited by William F. Murphy, 429–54. Washington, D.C.: The Catholic University of America Press, 2013.

Richards, David A. J. *Tolerance and the Constitution*. New York: Oxford University Press, 1986.

Rose, Nikolas. *The Politics of Life Itself: Biomedicine, Power, and Subjectivity in the Twenty-First Century*. Princeton, N.J.: Princeton University Press, 2007.

Ross, James F. *Portraying Analogy*. Cambridge: Cambridge University Press, 1981.

———. *Thought and World: The Hidden Necessities*. Notre Dame, Ind.: University of Notre Dame Press, 2008.

Rziha, John. *Perfecting Human Actions: St. Thomas Aquinas on Human Participation in Eternal Law*. Washington, D.C.: The Catholic University of America Press, 2009.

Sander, Hans-Joachim. "Theologischer Kommentar zur Pastoralkonstitution über die Kirche in der Welt von heute." In *Herders theologischer Kommentar zum Zweiten Vatikanischen Konzil*, edited by Bernd Jochen Hilberath and Peter Hünermann, 5:581–886. Freiburg i.B.: Herder, 2005.

Sartre, Jean-Paul. *Being and Nothingness: An Essay on Phenomenological Ontology*. Translated by Hazel Barnes. New York: Philosophical Library, 1956.

Sauter, Gerhard, et al. *Wissenschaftstheoretische Kritik der Theologie: Die Theologie und die neuere wissenschaftstheoretische Diskussion*. Munich: Kaiser, 1973.

Schelling, F. W. J. von. *On University Studies* [1803]. Translated by E. S. Morgan. Edited by Norbert Guterman. Athens: Ohio University Press, 1966.

Schenk, Richard, OP. "*Perplexus supposito quodam*: Notizen zu einem vergessenen Schlüsselbegriff thomanischer Gewissenslehre." *Recherches de théologie ancienne et médiévale* 57 (1990): 62–95.

Schindler, David L., and Nicholas J. Healy, Jr. *Freedom, Truth, and Human Dignity: The Second Vatican Council's Declaration on Religious Freedom. A New Translation, Redaction History, and Interpretation of "Dignitatis Humanae."* Grand Rapids, Mich.: Eerdmans, 2015.

Schleiermacher, Friedrich. *Occasional Thoughts on Universities in the German Sense. With an Appendix Regarding a University Soon to Be Established* [1808]. Translated by Terrence N. Tice and Edwina G. Lawler. Lewiston, N.Y.: Edwin Mellen Press, 1991.

Schneewind, J. B. *The Invention of Autonomy: A History of Modern Moral Philosophy.* Cambridge: Cambridge University Press, 1998.

Schockenhoff, Eberhard. *Wie gewiss ist das Gewissen? Eine ethische Orientierung.* Freiburg: Herder, 2003.

Schultes, Reginald-Maria, OP. *Introductio in historiam dogmatum.* Paris: Lethielleux, 1922.

———. "Circa dogmatum homogeneam evolutionem." *Divus Thomas* (1925): 83–89 and 554–64.

———. "Éclaircissements sur l'évolution du dogme." *Revue des sciences philosophiques et théologiques* 14 (1925): 286–302.

Sheed, Frank J. *Theology and Sanity.* New York: Sheed and Ward, 1946.

Sherwin, Michael S., OP. *By Knowledge and By Love: Charity and Knowledge in the Moral Theology of St. Thomas Aquinas.* Washington, D.C.: The Catholic University of America Press, 2005.

Sloterdijk, Peter. *Regeln für den Menschenpark: Ein Antwortschreiben zu Heideggers Brief über den Humanismus.* Frankfurt: Suhrkamp, 1999.

Sokolowski, Robert. *Introduction to Phenomenology.* Cambridge: Cambridge University Press, 2000.

Spaemann, Robert. *Philosophische Essays.* Second edition. Stuttgart: Reclam, 1994.

Stock, Gregory. *Redesigning Humans: Our Inevitable Genetic Future.* Boston: Houghton Mifflin Harcourt, 2002.

Taylor, Charles. *The Ethics of Authenticity.* Cambridge, Mass.: Harvard University Press, 1991.

———. *A Secular Age.* Cambridge, Mass.: Belknap Press of Harvard University Press, 2007.

Valuet, Basile. *La liberté religieuse et la tradition catholique: Un cas de développement doctrinal homogène dans le magistère authentique.* 3 vols. Le Barroux: Abbaye Sainte-Madeleine, 1998.

Wahlberg, Mats. *Revelation as Testimony: A Philosophical-Theological Study.* Grand Rapids, Mich.: Eerdmans, 2014.

Wannenwetsch, Bernd. "Owning Our Bodies? The Politics of Self-Possession and the

Body of Christ (Hobbes, Locke and Paul)." *Studies in Christian Ethics* 26, no. 1 (2013): 50–65.

Weber, Max. "Science as Vocation" [1919]. In his *From Max Weber: Essays in Sociology*, edited and translated by H. H. Gerth and C. Wright Mills, 129–56. New York: Oxford University Press, 1946.

Weizsäcker, Carl Friedrich Freiherr von. *Der Garten des Menschlichen: Beiträge zur geschichtlichen Anthropologie*. Munich: Hanser, 1984.

———. *The Unity of Nature*. Translated by Francis J. Zucker. New York: Farrar, Straus and Giroux, 1980.

Westberg, Daniel. *Right Practical Reason: Aristotle, Action, and Prudence in Aquinas*. Oxford: Clarendon Press, 1994.

White, Thomas Joseph, OP, ed. *The Analogy of Being: Invention of the Anti-Christ or the Wisdom of God?* Grand Rapids, Mich.: Eerdmans, 2010.

Wiegler, Paul. *The Infidel Emperor and His Struggle against the Pope*. London: Routledge, 1930.

Wilkins, Jeremy D. *Before Truth: Lonergan, Aquinas, and the Problem of Wisdom*. Washington, D.C.: The Catholic University of America Press, 2018.

Wilson, E. O. *The Meaning of Human Existence*. New York: W. W. Norton, 2014.

Young, Simon. *Designer Evolution: A Transhumanist Manifesto*. New York: Prometheus, 2006.

Zagzebski, Linda. *Epistemic Authority: A Theory of Trust, Authority, and Autonomy in Belief*. Oxford: Oxford University Press, 2012.

Magisterial Documents

Catechism of the Catholic Church. Second Edition Revised in Accordance with the Official Latin Text Promulgated by Pope John Paul II. Vatican City: Libreria Editrice Vaticana, 1997.

Congregation for Divine Worship and the Discipline of the Sacraments. "Instruction *Redemptionis Sacramentum*." March 25, 2004. Available at www.vatican.va.

Congregation for the Doctrine of the Faith. "Notification on the book *Church: Charism and Power* by Fr. Leonardo Boff." *Acta Apostolicae Sedis* 77 (1985): 756–62.

———. "Declaration *Dominus Iesus* on the Unicity and Salvific Universality of Jesus Christ and the Church." August 6, 2000. Available at www.vatican.va.

Decrees of the Ecumenical Councils. 2 vols. Edited by Norman P. Tanner, SJ. London / Washington, D.C.: Sheed and Ward / Georgetown University Press, 1990.

Denzinger, Heinrich. *Compendium of Creeds, Definitions, and Declarations on Matters of Faith and Morals. Latin-English*. Revised, enlarged, and, in collaboration with Helmut Hoping, edited by Peter Hünermann and edited by Robert Fastiggi and Anne Englund Nash for the English edition. Forty-third edition. San Francisco, Calif.: Ignatius Press, 2012.

The Documents of Vatican II. Edited by Walter M. Abbott, SJ. London: Geoffrey Chapman, 1966.

Pope St. Pius X. *Sacrorum Antistitum.* Motu Proprio. September 1, 1910. Available at www.vatican.va.

Pope St. John Paul II. "Common Declaration of Pope John Paul II and his Holiness Mar Ignatius Zakka I Iwas." June 23, 1984. Available at www.vatican.va.

———. *Centesimus Annus.* Encyclical Letter. May 1, 1991. Available at www.vatican.va.

———. *Veritatis Splendor.* Encyclical Letter. August 6, 1993. Available at www.vatican.va.

———. "Common Christological Declaration between the Catholic Church and the Assyrian Church of the East." November 11, 1994. Available at www.vatican.va.

———. *Evangelium Vitae.* Encyclical Letter. March 25, 1995. Available at www.vatican.va.

———. *Fides et Ratio.* Encyclical Letter. September 14, 1998. Available at www.vatican.va.

Pope Benedict XVI. "Address to Members of the Pontifical Academy of Sciences on the Occasion of the Plenary Assembly." November 8, 2012. Available at www.vatican.va.

———. *A Reason Open to God: On Universities, Education, and Culture.* Edited by J. Steven Brown. Washington, D.C.: The Catholic University of America Press, 2013.

INDEX OF NAMES

GENERAL INDEX

abstraction, 35n41, 205–8

Aeterni Patris (Leo XIII), 16–17, 54

agnosticism, 30, 68n127, 231

analogy of being, 198, 200, 213

analysis fidei, 122

anamnesis, 86–88

angelism-animalism polarity, 91

apostolic succession, 98, 132

appetition, power of, 109

apprehension, power of, 38–39, 58–59, 109

Arian crisis, 119n58

articles of faith, 9, 106–7, 111, 116, 159, 176n17

asceticism, 140, 208

assent: concept of, 2, 72n140, 97, 104, 106, 111–17, 122–27; real vs. notional, 125–27

atheism, 2, 27n18, 30, 41, 74, 95n8, 101, 128, 181–82, 184, 189

baptism, 101–2, 104–6, 118n57, 128

beatific vision, 44

categorical imperative (Kant), 39, 81, 95n8

Catholic Church, magisterium of: and conscience, 22–23, 26, 52, 59–65, 72, 88; and development of doctrine, 120–21, 132–33, 135–38, 155; infallibility of, 60, 120–21, 125, 128–29, 136, 155, 159–60, 216–17. *See also* conscience; doctrinal development; papal infallibility

certitude: and change in religious affiliation, 127–129; of conviction, 106, 125–29; of

faith, 97, 100, 106–7, 129, 230–31; and truth, 125–27, 180, 199–200

charity, 44, 101–2, 105n31, 108, 112–14, 121, 162, 216n2

conscience: as "aboriginal Vicar of Christ," 26, 55, 61–62; Aquinas on, 33–50, 52–59, 61, 63–64, 71–72, 77–78, 84, 86, 88, 148, 151; Augustine on, 33–34, 71, 86, 88; authority of, 22, 25–26, 41, 45–49, 51–52, 61–65, 74–75, 147–48, 150–51, 218–22; Calvin on, 77–78; counterfeit of, 14, 21–33, 37, 41–42, 45–46, 51–53, 59, 61–62, 64–67, 71, 73, 82, 85, 88–89; erroneous, 37, 45–53, 82, 85, 88, 147; examination of, 48, 52, 59; experience as demonstrating existence of, 32, 37, 74–77; Fichte on, 82–83; first principles of, 32–41, 47, 53, 55–59, 61, 63–64, 67, 82, 84, 87; formation of, 43–44, 52–53, 59–60, 65, 69; freedom of, 22–24, 30, 40–41, 60, 65–73, 84, 147, 149–50, 154; judgment of, 33–37, 41–48, 50–53, 55, 58, 63, 66–67, 69, 85, 87, 147; Kant on, 79–82; Luther on, 78–79; Newman's toast to, 22, 64; Rahner on, 83–85; Ratzinger on, 86–88; relation to magisterium, 22–23, 26, 52, 59–65, 72, 88, 149–51; rights of, 29–30; theonomic nature of, 24–27, 32–33, 37–41, 49–50, 53–55, 60–70, 73, 80, 84, 89, 148

consumerism, 3, 14, 30, 90–91, 95, 99, 169, 194, 209

as One, 141, 183–84; in relation to conscience, 24–29, 49, 55, 61–62, 64–66, 71,
73–78, 81–82, 84–86, 148, 151; as Trinity,
65, 141, 184. *See also* conscience; faith;
grace

grace: and infused virtues, 42–44, 95n8,
97, 101–2, 105n31, 106–7, 122–24, 216;
and nature, 24–25, 122–24, 162, 176n17;
sanctifying, 108, 117, 162; state of, 48. *See
also* faith

heresy, 114, 117–18, 121, 146
historicism, 5, 139, 157, 163, 165
hope, 43, 101, 105n31, 108, 162
human action: nature of, 38–39, 50n88, 56,
106
human being: as created in God's image and
likeness, 33, 41, 65–66, 73, 86; final end,
38, 40–41, 44, 48, 65–66, 71, 80–81, 121,
187, 194, 197
human mind, 32–33, 58–59, 80, 91, 106n34,
109–10, 125–27, 173n12, 187, 198, 204–7,
212. *See also* conscience
human nature, 5, 14, 25, 27–35, 38–41, 44,
48, 63, 65–66, 68, 71, 78, 82–84, 86–88,
110–12, 144, 150–51, 162, 177n19, 184,
187–91, 193–97, 199–202. *See also* conscience; freedom
hyperpluralism, 169–170

icons, 208n69
imaginary, social, 92, 99, 116n54, 117, 119
infallibility. *See* papal infallibility
inference, 45, 58–59, 106n34, 114, 159–61
invincible ignorance, 46, 49–50, 119n58
invocation of the saints, 9–10, 141

*Joint Declaration on the Doctrine of
Justification,* 224–25
justice, virtue of, 38, 43
justification, doctrine of, 6, 217, 219,
223–26

law: eternal, 25, 33, 37–38, 40, 44n69, 46,
55, 57, 63–64, 66n124, 71, 83, 219; human,
70–72, 78; natural, 33, 35, 37–41, 46,

56, 63–64, 66n124, 69–73, 78, 219–21;
revealed, 52, 219; unjust, 70–71, 88
Lefebvrist schism, 145, 153–54
liberal education, 172, 174, 176, 191–92,
200–202. *See also* university
liberalism, 1, 3–4, 6–8, 30
liberal principle of harm, 29
Lumen Gentium (Vatican II), 105, 119,
120n61, 121, 131n3, 133
Lutheran Christianity, 78–80, 94, 103–4,
217–30

martyrdom, 73
Mary, the Blessed Virgin, 9–10, 133, 141,
143n28
materialism, 174, 177, 184, 187–90. *See also*
naturalism
metaphysics, 55n101, 76–77, 80, 126–27,
160, 173–74, 176–84, 186, 194, 199–200,
202–8, 210–13, 231
miracles, 181–82
modernism, 117, 146, 157, 159, 163
monasticism, 132, 140
motives of credibility, 97, 100, 106–8,
111–18, 120–25

natural law. *See* law
naturalism, 91–92, 168, 174, 182, 184,
187–90, 196–98
naturalistic fallacy, 40
natural theology, 174–76, 178–80, 183–87,
200–201, 210–13. *See also* metaphysics;
university
neo-Scholasticism, 54, 158
new atheism, 2, 27n18, 181
nihilism, 41, 207
noncontradiction, principle of, 32,
199–200
Nostra Aetate (Vatican II), 143n29
notes of doctrinal development, 139–43;
application to test case, 143–53
noûs, faculty of, 58–59, 204

obiectum formale quod vs. *quo,* 113, 115
ontotheology, 212–13
opinion, 4, 32, 68, 106, 115–16, 126–28, 203

papal authority: infallibility, 13, 21, 60–62, 119n58; jurisdiction of, 23–24; magisterium, 23–24, 52, 60, 62–63, 65, 72, 88. *See also* Catholic Church

phenomenology, 54, 76, 199, 211

phronesis. See prudence

posthumanism, 91, 190–95

practical reason, 34–45, 46, 47, 49n84, 55–59, 65, 73, 80–82, 84, 88, 123, 207

praeambula fidei. See faith

private judgment in matters of religion: as characteristic of modern world, 1, 14, 92, 99, 117, 188, 194, 216–23; as counterfeit of faith, 14, 92–93, 95–96, 98–100, 117–21, 216–23; proper role of, 11, 108, 216n1, 234–35; as substitute for authority, 11, 98–100, 102–4, 106–8, 114, 116, 119–21, 127–28, 216–17, 225–27, 229–31, 233–35

process philosophy, 212

proof for God's existence. *See* God

Protestantism: Liberal, 104; mainline, 94; principled vs. accidental, 103–6, 118, 127–129. *See also* private judgment in matters of religion; *and specific denominations by name*

prudence, virtue of, 37, 42–46, 48, 55–59, 65, 87–88, 122–23, 147, 216n1

relativism, 3, 26, 51–53, 68n127, 69, 99, 139, 163, 165, 207, 220

relic veneration, 141

religion, revealed: vs. natural religion, 26n10, 64n120, 176–77, 179, 183–85; and private judgment, 92, 95–96, 98–100, 102–4, 108, 114–21, 129

religious freedom. *See Dignitatis Humanae*; freedom, human

revelation: as comprising first principles of theology, 45, 176–77, 185; as given to the church, 26n10, 102–3, 108, 124–25, 132–33, 135, 154, 159–60, 216n2; as having cognitive content, 122–24, 159–65; nature of, 26n10, 97n12, 108, 122–25, 132–33, 159–65, 184; propositional character of, 159–65; relation to conscience,

27, 32. *See also* Catholic Church; religion, revealed; theology

rupture, doctrinal, 134–36, 145–46, 152n61, 153–54

sacrifice of the Mass. *See* Eucharist

sacrificium intellectus, 120

Scholasticism, 17–18, 163, 165n76, 173n12

scripture: and private judgment, 102–4, 127, 218, 220–22, 228–30; relation to magisterium, 102–4, 105n31, 115–16, 127–29, 132–33, 135, 165n76, 216n2; spiritual senses of, 140; and tradition, 26n10, 112, 132, 135, 159, 165n76, 216n2. *See also* revelation; *sola scriptura*

Second Vatican Council. *See* Vatican II

secularism, 60, 68, 73, 168–69, 179

secularist democratic regimes, 28, 29n23, 60, 66n125, 67n126, 68–73, 89

self-proprietorship, 29, 90

sin, 46, 48, 50, 61, 67n126, 73, 114

skepticism, philosophical, 58n105, 61, 126, 197, 199–200, 207

sola scriptura, 102–5

soul, immortality of, 81

sovereign self-determination, 25, 27, 29–31, 41, 45, 53, 65–66, 83–85, 88–89. *See also* freedom, human

sovereign subject, 3, 5, 14, 83–85, 90–92, 99, 109, 116n54, 117, 119–20, 170, 202, 207, 216, 221. *See also* freedom, human

synderesis, 33–42, 44, 46–47, 49–50, 52–53, 55–57, 59, 61, 63, 65, 67, 73, 78–80, 83–88. *See also* conscience

temperance, virtue of, 43

theology: post-metaphysical programs for, 184–85, 212, 231; sapiential moral, 37n48, 44n70, 45, 54, 56–57; as science of conclusions, 159–62, 184–85, 200–201; speculative dogmatic, 19, 159–62, 184–85, 201. *See also* natural theology; revelation; scripture

thoughtlessness (*inconsideratio*), sin of, 43n68, 45, 52, 59, 67n126

totalitarianism, 67n126, 68

transcendental idealism, 50, 83–85, 200
transhumanism, 27n18, 91, 190, 192–95
transubstantiation, 9, 226
Trinity. *See* God

Unitatis Redintegratio (Vatican II), 105, 119,
　131n3
university: accommodation to immanent
　frame, 168n3, 202, 207; Baconian
　university paradigm, 168n3, 171–72,
　174–75, 178–79, 181, 191–96, 210; com-
　modification of, 170–72, 181, 188, 195,
　200; counterfeit of, 14, 171–75, 178–81,
　193–97, 209–10; formative quality of, 14,
　173, 178; as founded on unity of truth,
　171–81, 186–202; German univer-
　sity paradigm, 168n3; modern research
　university, 168n3, 170–72, 177, 179–81,
　187–91, 193–97, 210n71; natural theology
　in, 174, 176–81, 183–95, 198, 200–201;
　reductionist naturalism in, 174, 179–80,
　186–90, 193–98; revealed theology in,
　176–77, 179, 183–85, 200–201
univocity of being, 212–13

Vatican I, 13, 21, 95n8, 97n12, 136–38, 152n61,
　159–160, 180n25. *See also council docu-
　ments by name*
Vatican II, 24n8, 26, 49, 105, 120, 131n3, 133,
　136–38, 143–55, 158, 165n76, 180n25. *See
　also council documents by name*
Veritatis Splendor (John Paul II), 41n60,
　49, 51, 65–66, 73n145, 84, 151n54,
　221–24
virtue: acquired vs. infused, 42–44, 48,
　55–56, 97, 101, 108–10, 162; cardinal,
　42–45, 48, 57; epistemology, 18;
　nature of, 42–43, 56–57, 108–10, 162;
　theological, 43–44, 97, 101, 108–10,
　112n45, 114, 162. *See also virtues by
　name*
voluntarism, 41n61

will to power, 27n18, 41, 82, 193, 197
wisdom: divine, 25, 37–38; as gift, 44n69,
　53n96; philosophical, 46, 180n25, 201

John Henry Newman on Truth and Its Counterfeits: A Guide for Our Times was designed in Garamond, with Scala Sans and Garda Titling display type, and composed by Kachergis Book Design of Pittsboro, North Carolina. It was printed on 60-pound Natural Eggshell and bound by McNaughton & Gunn of Saline, Michigan.